Sea Fantasy

JoAnn Orr

ISBN-13: 978-0-9885250-3-0
Publisher: Burning River Books

DEDICATION

To my Captain Stan, who led me into an adventurous life, often kicking and screaming. It was enriching, and I thank you! "Whither thou goest, I will go.

CHAPTER ONE

It was a beautiful day in the Bahamas, sunny but with a brisk wind. I saw a boat approaching the dock, and moved forward to catch their lines and help tie up the boat. The first mate told me they were "live-aboards," as were we, and the conversation reached the point it so often did, with my query, "How do you like it, REALLY?"

The first mate laughed and replied, "Well most of the time I like it, but I sold my business in Baltimore, which I loved, because this was my husband's dream and I wanted to do it for him. But there are days where I wonder, what am I doing here, living *his* f-ing fantasy?!"

Almost every first mate I have told this story to howled with laughter, but admitted it was so true with many, if not most of us. I guess that's Lesson One for wives who will become liveaboard boaters. So how did I get here?

We had always been "boaters" since early days of our marriage. Our kids loved it also, and every weekend was spent aboard *the Six Oars*. As do many boaters, we started with a fourteen-foot boat and worked our way up to a twenty-eight-foot Lyman cabin cruiser.

We were active in the Power Squadron, a boat safety education group, and learned many boating skills. We practically lived on the water until the kids were in high school and wanted to be home, where the action was. By then, we had traveled all over Lake Erie, Lake St. Clair, Lake Michigan and Lake Huron. We particularly loved cruising in Canada, with its wonderful islands and beautiful waters.

Stan had worked for U.S. Steel for thirty years and was able to retire at age fifty-four. We were empty nesters, so were able to embark upon the dream. We sold our house in Cincinnati quickly to dear friends, and started searching for THE boat. We knew exactly what we wanted, a forty-two-foot Grand Banks trawler, big and beamy.

We flew to Fort Lauderdale and with the help of a broker, found exactly what we wanted. She was big enough to liveaboard, but could be handled by the two of us. A Grand Banks trawler weighs twenty-one tons. She was forty-two feet over all, and had a fifteen-foot beam (which means she was nice and wide). She drew five and a half feet, which is a big advantage in shallow waters. Sailboats generally draw seven feet or more.

Inside was the main salon with a helm for steering and running the boat, and the galley. Below fore and aft were two staterooms, each with a head (a bathroom, for the uninitiated). The master stateroom was roomy and had two dressers and a large closet. Our head even had a bathtub, a true luxury on boats. Outside, there were steps leading up to the flying bridge. It had a nice roomy area for sitting, as well as a full helm, which was where we generally ran the boat. This rapidly became our outdoor living room. On top of the stern cabin we kept a Dyer dinghy, which had both sails and a one and a half horsepower engine. This was our second form of transportation, and we used it a lot.

She was a second-hand boat bought from a retired General and his wife, and was in good condition, at least cosmetically. We had to do some redecorating, as this was going to be our home for what we hoped would be a long time. I know boats always need something done! It's the nature of the beast. Someone once said the definition of boat was, "a hole in the water down which you pour money." The "innards" of course were very important, as we wanted a safe and well-performing boat. After a pretty frantic period of getting rid of cars, furniture and unnecessary possessions, we drove south to Fort Lauderdale, where the boat was docked to begin our new life.

We were docked in Rogers Marina, where we had some work done and settled in, making the boat our home. We named her *Steelaway* (no, it's not misspelled; Stan worked for U.S. Steel before he retired at age fifty-four.) We chose to have her port be Cleveland, even though we didn't intend to have a base anywhere.

This was in January of 1977. People often ask me how we handled the everyday basics like banking, mail etc. Remember then we didn't have computers, email, ATM machines, cell phones, and many of the things that we take for granted these days. I think with envy of today's live-aboards, and how easy it would be, but then we would have missed many an adventure.

Our daughter Barbara in Cleveland had our power of attorney and handled all our banking, mail, and whatever else came up. Traveler's checks could be difficult to use, particularly in the Bahamas, where we were often really in the boonies. Barbie flew down to the Abacos one time with two small children and $2,000 pined in her bra and other inner parts of her clothing. Was she ever glad to get there!

She would save our mail, which all came to her house, and when we told her where the next fairly reliable general delivery was, she'd send it there. I remember how excited we'd be when we got a big package of letters from family and friends, and often sat on the post office steps happily reading all the mail. This really helped when I was feeling homesick.

So there we were in the Rogers Marina, getting ready to sail off into the dream. I'm quoting from a family letter:

I'm sitting here in the cabin, typing and trying to keep cool. It's about eighty-five today and my frozen northern blood isn't up to it yet. Stan already looks like an Indian, as he never really loses his tan, and he's been working outside more than I have. He is in seventh heaven, even when he's crawling all over the sweltering engine room working on the generator cover and getting scratchy fiberglass all over him. Different strokes for different folks I guess!

We're slowly discovering how to make everything work, which is quite a project. You must turn off the hot water heater when you use the stove (and vice versa), and if you use the oven, only one burner on the stove can be used. I think I'm starting to get the AC and DC systems sorted out more or less. I still have a horrible feeling that if I push the wrong button, the boat will blow up or something! Stan patiently led me through all the systems.

Getting used to the noises at night was interesting too. I love the water lapping noises of course. Then there's the ice maker, which goes chug-a-chuga-thunk. The thunk is the ice maker dumping the cubes into the container, which it does all night. Remember the fairy tale of How the Sea Got Salty? I have this funny feeling that some morning I'm going to get up and find the cabin overflowing with ice! (At this time we had no idea of how popular our ice maker would make us as we hit the road, so to speak!)

Life at this marina is interesting. It's off the beaten path (also cheap), so you don't have any fancy yacht people. Bessie and Harold, our neighbors from West Virginia are very nice. They work on their boat constantly, and their boat has the most gorgeous teak and varnish I've ever seen. Bessie is anxious to get me going stripping teak etc., a project I'm resisting. It's not in my job description!

There's a family from Quebec two slips down and I love to hear them chattering away in French. Their children are educated by correspondence system. Another family is English and very nice also. They have two teenagers, who were quite agog yesterday over one of the free spirits on the dock who was sun bathing topless. However, as Bessie said, she was rather under-endowed, so they didn't see much as they skateboarded past. Then there's the ancient boat next to us, occupied by a bunch of grad students who are doing field work in foreign studies. I can't quite figure out what they're doing here, but they surely are having a good time. Stan thinks they're majoring in orgies and we were born many years too soon!

There's an old codger who looks like Hemingway and just staggers around most of the time. He was sitting in the middle of our rubbish pile yesterday, bottle in hand and looking quite content.

Our electrician lives here too. He's a sabra from Israel, who's lived there all his life, but he couldn't take the killing anymore. He said that of the kids he was raised with on the border kibbutz, there were only two left besides him. This was in the 70's. He's a very nice man, and has helped us a lot with the electrical systems.

We met a really interesting couple yesterday who are about our age and doing the same thing we are. They bought a ten-year-old Chris Craft and are completely gutting it and rebuilding. They've been working on it for eight months and it is gorgeous. Phyllis has done all the decorating and it's a knockout! She's offered to show me how to do some of the things she's done, and I plan on picking her brains. They've done their boating on the west coast and have a home in Hawaii and now want to see the east coast and the Caribbean. He's a retired Navy test pilot and quite a character. They took time off this winter and took their boat down to the Caymans, where they converted all their assets into Swiss francs and deposited it there so the U.S. government couldn't get at it.

Yesterday was a busy day. We went out and shopped for some essentials, boat stuff and practical things like a dish drainer. I'm coming to terms with the single small sink I think. It's either that or losing two cupboards in the galley with a double. Plus, paying those bandits in the boatyard a fortune to install it. We've paid bills in here that would make a strong man cry!

Stan is going to put a new control on the stove as one burner only cooks on high. (We burn stuff a lot!)

The transom man shows up at intervals and puts another coat of varnish on, so we hope MAYBE the name will be painted on one of these days.

It's been very hot and we have the air conditioning on (it works!). We'll be happy to have it at dinner time, which tends to be very hot. It blows a gale on the galley, which is great. Actually, we have two conditioners. One cools the fore bedroom and aft cabin. The other cools the main salon. You can only run one system at a time, which involves some juggling, but basically works out okay.

The upholsterer came this morning and we picked out the material for the salon, which has a huge sofa that curls around the dining room table. Opposite this is a large buffet type piece of furniture, which houses among other things, the ice maker and a second small sink and bar. We found fabric for the sofa and chairs, which we think is pretty and has the sand and water colors which I wanted. We should have it in a week, so I'm keeping my fingers crossed.

Also we went out and stocked up the cupboards and the freezer so we won't be so dependent on Burger Chef! Harold and Bessie are coming over for dinner tonight. They've been so nice and helpful to us. I only hope I get those burners synchronized so the food is all done at the same time!

I plan on getting to work on the stateroom curtains and bedspreads as soon as I finish washing down all the walls, trying to keep ahead of the mildew. I did the guest room and head yesterday and it looks really good. Stan continues to spend hours crawling around the engine room getting everything up to his standards. He was down there hours today cleaning up oil spills and repairing a pump. He tells me it's so clean in there you could eat off the floor. It's the first time he's let me down there. I suspect there's some storage spaces down there he's hiding! In the supermarket yesterday he eyed the boxes of groceries and said, "I don't think they're all going to fit," which has become his mantra! The cashier looked a little startled when I said, "If you say that once more, I'm going to go running out screaming into the night!"

A U.P. photographer from the Fort Lauderdale paper came out yesterday to take pictures of us for the Enquirer, which is doing a story on us. I hope our friends in Cincinnati will clip it out and send it to us via our "agent" Barbie. He was a nice young man, who stayed and had a beer and chatted with us. He told us some interesting things about the area including the fact that this marina used to be part of the Everglades before they started digging all those canals.

Stan just came in with new parts for the stove and said, "How long do I have before you have to start cooking?" which should be great. He is a very talented man and he's surely learning to fix a lot of things. Luckily he can read and understand manuals!

CHAPTER TWO

By now it was the end of March and we were still tied up at the dock waiting for some things to be finished. Most of the work on the boat was finished except for the radios. But our dinghy hadn't arrived yet, nor our documentation papers, so we were stuck. Meanwhile, I had made bed spreads, curtains, and fitted all the sheets to the beds. The main salon was all slipcovered now and looked great in spite of the trauma involved. The material we had picked out was unavailable and we had to start all over again. The decorator had the flu and sent her upholsterer to take me to the fabric shops. Do you remember Luther Billis, Bloody Mary's sidekick from South Pacific? Well, this guy looked and sounded just like him! You haven't lived until you've tried to decorate with Luther Billis! He would keep holding up ghastly swatches of orange, purple, and red fabric and saying "This is nice and cheery," and I'd try not to wince as I agreed that it was cheery alright, but not exactly what I had in mind. So when he said I'd have to go with him to the shops to be sure we could get what I wanted, I panicked and stuck my head down into the engine room and begged Stan to come along. Bless his heart, he did even though he had something all apart on the floor and he was covered with grease.

We did find some material we really liked in spite of Luther's expertise, and he actually had it done in two days! He kept popping in and out, taking two chairs or cushions at a time and giving me advice on the curtains I was making. Every sentence of his was, "Ya know what I mean?" This was going to be our home for an unknown amount of time and I did want it pretty and comfortable. Stan's Mother had given me her old original Singer portable and it did yeoman duty all our years on the boat.

By now you're wondering if we're ever going to get out of this marina and so was I! We finally were all ready to go, but a swing bridge on the canal out of there was stuck, and they said it might be a month before it was open again, so we were temporarily stuck at the dock.

Meanwhile, Stan broke a toe while moving around the deck barefoot. He couldn't believe he did it after all those years of lecturing the rest of us about going barefoot on the boat. I was always barefoot and never wore shoes. So far, I hadn't broken any toes either.

The last week we were there, there was a party on the pier for all the live-aboards, twenty-six of us in all. It was quite an occasion! One of the men blocked off the quay with his van so the "tourists" couldn't drive down. We all put down blankets and chairs and sat down in the street drinking for six hours before we ate dinner. There was quite a mix of people in our little community.

The only other first wife was half of a Canadian couple who were readying their catamaran for an extended cruise in the South Pacific. They had two boys, but only one was going because the older one was in college. Jamie was going to school via the correspondence route. Peter, the father, was an ex-Air Canada pilot and owned a plane, which the whole family could fly. He discussed some piece of machinery with Stan and said his engine was "going tickety boo," so they would be ready to depart when we did, if the bridge ever got fixed.

The other couple that we thought we might have much in common with had turned out to be a little strange. They came to the party with banjos and really could have gone on stage. She knew the words to every song ever written and sang until the party was over, not even pausing to eat! She was an ex-supervisor of stewardesses and was appallingly cheerful.

Getting back to first wives, and in the yachting world we are few, believe me! Harold said that's because too many of the first ladies gave the ultimatum, "It's me or the boat," and he continued, "What woman could win that one!" This was sort of a macho community, the last bastion of something or the other! I hasten to say I have nothing against second wives; it's just that they're all so darn young! Harold, the philosopher, says that's just so the older men can train them. I felt at age fifty-two like everyone's mother!

One group at the party was from the *Pat C.*, an enormous Bertram with a captain and a crew. The "crew" was a nice little Australian guy named Warner, who was quiet as a mouse until he had a few drinks, at which point he started singing "Waltzing Matilda" at the top of his lungs, competing with the banjos. They left for the Caymans the next morning, despite Warner's hangover.

Our son Tom came down just before we left and spent Easter with us. We took him around all the tourist sites, and this was the time when Fort Lauderdale was first choice for spring breakers. We tried the beach once and it was bedlam. Luckily, our friends the Altschullers invited us to use their beach at their place in Pompano, and this was a godsend. Easy to get to and beautiful. Then, our friend Heidi from the *Altare* told us about the beach the natives use to escape the crowds and it was the closest beach yet and great.

Easter was fun. Early in the morning Dale, a bachelor from California, tiptoed around and hid Easter eggs on everyone's boat. We went to our newly discovered church where they had a super Irish tenor who sang all my favorite old hymns, the ones you don't hear any more. Then to the beach and to the Firestones' condo for dinner. They were old boating friends of ours and we promised to give them a ride aboard *Steelaway* before we left.

This was before the bridge shut down and we had a good day so we cast off. The boat handled nicely. She really rode well and didn't roll as much as we had feared. The ride through the canals to the ocean was really interesting, passing gracious homes and gardens. The ocean was pretty calm, with seas about three to five feet. A school of dolphins swam with us. They dove right under the bow like some suicide squad and you'd swear we were going to run them down, but they always timed it perfectly. Then they rolled over on their sides and almost winked at you as if to say, "Fooled you again didn't we?!"

The best thing though was being in our boat at last and actually seeing what she could do! She was so much bigger than any of our former boats that we were a little nervous about just the two of us handling her. We docked back in the marina feeling much more confident about our new life!

I spent quite a lot of time readying our supplies for takeoff. I sat on the stern deck surrounded by canned goods marking each can (in case the labels came off, which could happen if they got wet). We had hundreds of cans, which would be stored in the lazaret beneath the stern deck. I also made master lists of the whereabouts of what was in the lazarets, freezer, and various other lockers. I also planned on making all of our bread. This would enable us to be free of supermarkets and thus we would only need to stop occasionally for fresh stuff. I felt like a bushy tailed squirrel with both cheeks bulging, sitting in a backyard full of buried nuts.

Our forced wait for the bridge did give us a chance to finish a few chores that we had planned on doing en route. We got new mattresses for our beds, which were heavenly. I just couldn't fit my body into the contours of the General (or Mrs. General's) mattresses. We did a lot of fantasizing about what they were like. He has left his imprint all over the place. He had all the drawers in the galley marked "small forks, large forks etc." and I always felt guilty when I put a utensil in the wrong place.

CHAPTER THREE

Hooray! On April 17th they finally opened the bridge and there was a grand exodus from the marina. It was a little scary at first, the largest boat we'd ever had was twenty-eight feet and here we were moving along with forty-two feet under us. It was fun having bridges open for us as we went through and watched the heavy Lauderdale traffic stopped for us. There were so many bridges and we had to circle around after signaling the bridge and wait for them to open. We decided to go out to the ocean and go up to the Fort Worth inlet buoy and then go back to the Intracoastal Waterway there.

This had taken us a lot longer than we thought it would, so we went into the Palm Harbor Marina and docked for the night. The Intracoastal is a canal really, except when it comes to a river, bay, or sound, some of which are really big water. The canal parts were really pretty narrow, and we were pretty big so I was glued to the Waterway Guide, an essential book which told us what to expect at every inch of the way. It rapidly became our bible for the Intracoastal. There were abundant areas where it was easy to go aground and we were running scared! I literally guided Stan inch by inch for several days until we realized we had more room to maneuver than we had thought and one didn't have to be exact, although we surely tried! It was very tiring to say the least. We did go aground once but not much and got off without much trouble.

Whew! We went into the marina and heaved a sigh of relief. We thought we'd run on the ocean the next morning, but it was very rough with a head wind, so after eight or nine miles we turned around and headed back up the Intracoastal.

What a beautiful day we had, just the thing for we wary and nervous boaters. A lot of the scenery was wilderness and so beautiful. We kept our bird books and binoculars beside us and we added many new birds to our list. Most of these were ocean and shore birds, ones that aren't seen so much around the Great Lakes and a source of delight to us. Stan claims he'd hear me muttering, "Come on you dumb bird and lift your feet out of the water so I can see if your feet are yellow or black." The Snowy Egrets have great big funny yellow feet, which they put down gingerly like picky ladies wading through a puddle in big yellow boots. We went by many wild bird preserves and since this was nesting time we saw lots of babies in the rookeries.

Another thing we had to learn was tides. We were pretty experienced with the rest of nautical knowledge, but having never encountered tides in the Great Lakes, we had a lot to learn. Stan studied Chapman's, the old stalwart book from Power Squadron where he had taken many courses and later taught most of them. We discovered that the NOAA weather reports always gave us tide depths as well as times when they were coming in and out. We also purchased the books of tide tables, which we used a lot and they got quite battered!

The Intracoastal was not at all what I thought it would be. I had sort of visualized a canal dug by some Teddy Roosevelt types that ran all the way up the coast. Well, it isn't like that at all, as I suppose many of you know. It is made up of many lakes, rivers, and sounds connected every so often by man-made canals. Some of these bodies of water are enormous. The Indian River in Florida is bigger than Lake St. Clair in Michigan and can kick up in a wind like it too!

We went out in the ocean every so often, but not for very long stretches. Our boat was so heavy that it just plugged along serenely, about the speed of a covered wagon (a little faster), and was not affected by waves unless it was really quite rough. Then, we'd go back into the Intracoastal and would go by a big city like St. Augustine or Jacksonville Beach, and that was interesting too.

It was such an old part of the country and there was such a strong feel of history here. We could see a lot of it from the waterfronts, the old forts and the settlements that are so beautifully preserved and cared for by the National Park Service.

We were anchored one night beside Fort George, Florida, where an old fort and plantation were preserved. We were the only people anchored there and we felt that perhaps the people who had lived there had enjoyed gazing across the river at the same tidal flat and marsh that we were, and had seen the same beautiful sunset while watching the herons catch their evening meal. It was totally quiet and so peaceful, yet a little haunted. We found out later that it was the former home of Don Juan McQueen, whom Eugenia Price had written about in her book of the same name. These totally peaceful moments at anchor were one of my favorite things about living aboard.

The other thing about the waterway that surprised me and was a source of continued delight was the wildlife. For instance, I never thought we'd see porpoises all the time, but we did. They're very sociable creatures and seem to love to play. They would stick around the bow a lot, and cruise quietly around the boat searching for food at feeding time. One night when we were anchored in an extremely quiet cove far from cities or people, we could actually hear them breathing which was wonderful.

One of the funniest things I've ever seen was a dolphin playing with us as a friend, Jack, fished off the stern. The dolphin jumped way up in the air and instead of its usual graceful entry back into the water, did a real belly flop landing, getting Jack soaking wet. We all laughed while the dolphin rolled over on his side and I swear laughed too! Then, he promptly did the same dive again really soaking Jack. No one will ever convince me that that dolphin didn't know exactly what he was doing.

In the marshes we learned the meaning of the food chain when the tide went out. There were millions of little bugs, snails and crabs, each eating whatever was smaller than they were. In turn, they were being eaten by herons, cranes, oyster catchers and bigger birds. The law of the jungle (or marsh) prevailed.

We passed lots of beds of oysters and always put the crab trap out when we anchored. We had many feasts, although crabs are a lot of work from crab to mouth! The crabs we caught were stone crabs. With stone crabs, one is supposed to break off one of their legs and throw the rest back into the water and they'll grow a new leg. As much as I love crabs, I hated to do that. It seemed so cruel, so I'd make Stan do it! How's that for passing the buck?

We had our first "system" problem when we anchored at Vero Beach. The freezer didn't seem to be cold enough and it was packed with meat. Stan dinghied into the marina and found an electrician who agreed to have a look at it. He'd never worked on a boat before and was fascinated by the dinghy ride out and the boat. He worked on the freezer and thought he'd found the problem and left. Unfortunately, it didn't work long and the next day he came out and worked on it again. It was okay, but this was but the first of many tries on the freezer in the next two or three years.

It was the first of many "tech" problems on the boat. I was to learn patience, sort of, on many stops for parts, etc. After a year or so, we realized that the freezer had been installed right over the starboard engine, which generated lots of heat when running. We loved to anchor out, but did spend a night or two at a dock so we could run it on the electric there and really get it cold. This was hard to do at anchor because we'd need to run the generator some of the time to cook, charge the batteries, and cool the freezer but it was noisy and we disliked losing our peace and quiet. The freezer had holding plates, which kept the cold in, but had to have electricity to get properly cold so it could go fairly long without electric.

About this time we began making friends with the many sailboats that would anchor with us most nights. They discovered that we had an ice maker and were willing to share. So when we'd drop the anchor, several dinghies would come over with pails to get ice for happy hour. We got a lot of invitations to said happy hours too, so it was fun. They all called us "Big Mama," as we usually arrived in the anchorage first, being a little faster than the sailboats. We were pleased they liked us, as sailors generally do not like "stink pots" as they call power boats. They tended to be tolerant of trawlers, because we didn't go much faster than they did, didn't pass them with big wakes, and with our strength, we pulled many of them off sand bars, etc. We also frequently towed them to where they were going when their engines stopped. It always interested us that sail owners kept their boats in great shape, but almost took pride in not maintaining their engines. "Those dirty, noisy things," they would say. In fairness this did not apply to all sailors, but an awfully lot of them that we've known.

The days slipped by so quickly! We had trouble remembering what day of the week it was as we traveled up the Intracoastal. Most of our days were delightful, interesting, and/or invigorating. But some days we had a real bummer. We were gaining confidence in our skills and in our good ship. Then, we hit a lulu!

We had reached St. Simon's, Georgia and Stan decided to anchor in their harbor beside the Golden Isles Marina because Stan wanted to do some varnishing and felt there would be less dust blowing around. We had a quiet evening and went to bed early as we were tired after a long day. In the middle of the night, a terrible storm hit. It was the tail end of a tornado that hit Jacksonville and St. Simon's with gusts of wind of seventy-five miles per hour. Like an idiot, I decided this was the night I would be brave and not wake Stan up. He was sleeping soundly right through it. The boat was pitching like mad and finally one wave almost tossed us out of bed. Stan awoke and ran forward and said we were dragging our anchor and fast approaching the shore and other boats. As he tried to start the engines, I peered out the windows through the sheets of rain, seven foot waves and lightning flashing like mad. It showed me in flashes that we were really in trouble! The engines had been behaving beautifully all the way we'd come and wouldn't you know this was the time one of the engines wouldn't start. Stan said he was going to try to come up on the anchor using the remaining engine and I was to try and get the anchor up, then we'd head out to sea, where we wouldn't be in danger of being blown ashore.

The boat didn't handle well on one engine, and where we were anchored there was an open eight-mile stretch to the sea, and the wind and the waves were literally screaming down it. At that point, a wave threw us so high up in the air (all eight tons of us) that the heavy metal anchor chain flew right off the windlass and there went the ball game! We watched helplessly as one hundred feet of heavy chain raced into the sea followed by two hundred and fifty feet of line, which was swept into the water under the boat and cut loose by the props. Then, we had nothing to hold us with no anchor and only one engine and we were tossing around like a bottle cap in a washing machine. Stan wrestled with the helm with one hand while trying to start the other engine with the other hand and trying not to hit other boats.

"You'll have to call the Coast Guard," he yelled. Now, you realize we had only been running the boat for two weeks and here we were operating in the pitch dark and I wasn't sure where anything was either! I tried to operate the radio without my glasses, but couldn't see to put it on the Coast Guard channel. Naturally I had left them back in our stateroom where I'd been reading in bed, so I stumbled back there in the dark. I had always wondered if I'd ever use those ceiling hand holds and had hoped I never would, but I clung to them and thanked God for help that night. As I made my way back quickly to the cabin, I heard the clean supper dishes go crashing into the sink and other unsecured stuff flying around. I looked for the pepper mill the next day and found it in my sewing box!

The Coast Guard didn't answer my first call, so I gave out with a Mayday, Mayday and got them right away. They said they'd be with us in fifteen minutes. Stan said we'd be ashore by then and probably in the marina restaurants kitchen! I told the Coast Guard that we had our searchlight on to help them find us, as well as for Stan to see where we were going. They were asking me more questions, when suddenly the recalcitrant engine started and Stan yelled, "I see some men on the dock over there and they're motioning me in. I'm going to try and get over there and you'll have to go out on deck and throw them some lines."

I stumbled out on deck in my pink shorty nightgown, which immediately was plastered to me in the rain and tried to get ahold of some lines as we wildly pitched in the general direction of the dock. I tossed a stern line to the men and hurried to the bow and threw another, only to discover that neither of them were tied to the cleat and that I'd have to grab two more lines, desperately tie them to a cleat and prayed that my nautical version of a granny knot would hold. The men tied us to a houseboat but not before the wind threw us into it and broke a rail. Stan rushed out and helped the men tie about ten lines to the boat and dock and put out four fenders. He changed quickly into foul weather gear and went to help the men as the marina was in trouble. Boats were tossed all over the place and the waves had washed one part of the dock away, so there was a lot of damage and they needed to retie many boats. I turned on the generator, (and yes, it was music to my ears) as the lights went on and I put the kettle on to make some tea, weeping with relief.

We learned a lot from this experience. I only wished that we had more experience under our belts. I learned that even when I'm in the clutches of stark terror, I can manage to function, and do what I have to. Stan is always calm, at least outwardly, and I do envy him. He is not scared of anything. He thought it was an exhilarating experience and I was ready to jump ship. I was beginning to wonder if I really belonged there!

The next day dawned clear and sunny, and we had visitors. The sister and brother-in-law of our dear friends the Mileses from Cincinnati stopped by to see if we had survived the storm. They took us to lunch and showed us all over St. Simon's and Sea Island, and we had such a good time that the horrible memories of the night before subsided. Truly, they were the good Samaritans we needed.

The next day, Stan and George Baker, who was an underwater diver who usually worked for the police department looking for underwater weapons, started looking for our anchor, chain, and line. It really was looking for a needle in a haystack, but I did have a recollection of seeing it happen when a big bolt of lightning lit up the harbor. I pointed out the spot and the metal detector indicated it was there. Getting it all up was something else. The two of them pulled for hours to get the anchor out of some really hard clay and it finally came loose along with a big piece of the bottom, which they had to hammer to get the caked mud off. This was such a relief as it saved us at least $900, replacing anchor, chain and all that line!

We were very lucky. If we had been blown ashore, we probably would have taken the bottom out, at least all the props, shaft and propellers. We had no other damage and the houseboat rail could be welded back on quite easily and, we hoped, inexpensively!

By this time, it was May 3rd and we were very anxious to get going and to be in Cleveland for the family's annual 4th of July picnic and reunion. Now, I had learned Lesson Two in liveaboard boating – never set a deadline because something ALWAYS goes wrong! Lesson Three is: machines always act up when it's most inconvenient. Lesson Four is: I hate machines! I have never been even faintly mechanical. I always think machines will do what they're supposed to. Not true! Stan has a great relationship with them. He is never happier than when he's down in the engine room where it's about 102 degrees and talking to the machinery. He likes making engines go "tickety boo," as our Canadian friend would say.

We had ordered a new starter to replace the recalcitrant one and installed it and thought we were ready to go. We started out, only to discover that the engines were smoking. There was water in them and a hole in the exhaust. More damage than we thought from the storm. We turned around and docked back at the marina for what would be a long month of frustrations. However, we discovered how wonderful everyone there was and what a beautiful place the Golden Isles were and fell in love with that corner of the world.

One of the things that saved my sanity at this time was the presence of my sister, Barrie and her husband Terry, who were vacationing at the Cloisters on Sea Island. Stan was busy in the engine room and Terry was working on a book, so Barrie and I had a fabulous time shopping, lying by the pool and generally driving everywhere. What fun to have a car again! We had dinner together every night that I could pry Stan away from the engine room, which wasn't always possible. My sister and I have always been very close and it was heavenly to have this time together.

We got to know all the people at the Golden Isles Marina, as well as a lot of people who kept their boats there. They were all so good to us! They loaned us cars for grocery shopping, and church and showed us much of the town of St. Simon's. We still keep in touch with our special friend,

Nancy, whose husband was in charge of the Marina. St. Simon's had lots of good restaurants and friends introduced us to them all. At the end of our dock was Emmeline and Hessie, a popular restaurant that we visited often. We soon discovered that we were part of the atmosphere there and while waiting for a table, the patrons would stroll down to the boats to see all those strange people who lived on their boats. Ours was easy to look into, so they'd peer in the windows if you didn't pull the shades closed and look around as if we weren't there. We sort of felt invisible but definitely part of the scenery.

One day, we had been promised that our parts would be ready, and as usual, had been let down. By now it was Memorial Day weekend and we were terribly depressed because we knew there wasn't a prayer of them working on the boat before Tuesday. We shut ourselves up in the cabin and turned on the air conditioning and sulked. There came a knocking on the hull and Nancy's voice saying, "Come on out and play!" They suggested we join them for a Chinese dinner and a movie in Brunswick, which was a lot of fun and chased the blues away.

Another night Dave and Nancy took us up to Savannah so Dave could check out a huge yacht to see if they could dock it at the Marina the coming summer. We loved the waterfront and Factor's Row and stopped for ice cream as we strolled along.

General and Pat Collins stopped by one day and brought us some of the locally famous Vidalia onions, which the natives claim are so mild you can eat one like an apple. So many people told us this that we have a mental picture of everyone in St. Simon's strolling around with an onion in hand in the spring. Maybe one has to in self-defense! I'd never heard of Vidalias thirty years ago, but of course everyone knows of them now. We joined the Collinses and the Davises for dinner twice, once on Jekyll Island and once at Blanche's Courtyard in St. Simon's.

Our young mechanic and his wife took us to Sara Sara's for an evening of jazz one night, which was great fun, and they stopped by to visit often. They were so thoughtful, trying to make our long wait not so stressful.

One night we had liver and onions (Vidalia naturally) for dinner and the liver was too strong, so we had lots left over. I wondered if a Great Dane we had seen earlier would like the leftovers. Stan went to inquire of his mistress, who was a young girl eating a plate of cold beans. She asked if humans ate it which, Stan thought was a little odd but he said, "Sure, we had just had it for dinner." The dog, who obviously understood people talk, came galloping down the dock scattering people in his wake and screeched to a halt politely waiting for me to put down the plate. He cleaned the plate with one enormous schlump of his tongue, just as his mistress came panting up plate and fork in hand. "Oh," she wailed, "I was going to try it." We were starting to meet quite a few liveaboards who lived off the land, as money was tight. Fish and sea food were easily caught and edible weeds like lambs tongue made up a good deal of their diet.

We also learned that liveaboards were called yachties instead of boaters, sailors or stink potters, and found this to be true almost everywhere except "up north." This was especially true in the islands. Everyone in Georgia called Stan "Cap'n." As we pulled into the dock they would call out, "Right over here, Cap'n." At the Golden Isles we were known as Cap'n and Miz Orr. Fun!

At night as we lay in bed, we would hear the strangest noise. Not everywhere, but definitely in our boat. We went nearly crazy trying to find out what it was. It was a clicking or pecking kind of noise like a seagoing woodpecker tapping on the hull. Stan spent hours crawling around the engine room checking different systems for electrolysis, which was what he expected. Finally, Dave Davis told us it was crabs eating the grass on the bottom of the boat. Stan said they should put up a sign for Yanks who didn't know this! There were lots of new things to learn!

We were known locally as "those poor souls who were trying to get to Cleveland." Everyone stopped to chat and we had several invitations for drinks or dinner. People would ask us how we got to Cleveland and Stan would reply, "slowly!" Then of course, the strollers from Emmeline and Hessie's couldn't resist peering in our windows because it was so easy to see in. They would look to see what we were having for dinner, practically reading the book we were reading over our shoulder, and sometimes would make hilarious comments. One night I was doing the dishes and a couple strolled by. "Oh look," the man said, "She's doing the dishes." "What do you think she'd do with them, stupid, throw them overboard?" his partner replied.

Speaking of dishes, I was doing them one night while it was really windy. The gale blowing in the window shot the suds right off the dishwater. One of the minor hazards of yachting. See, I was getting the nautical lingo down pat!

We met a dentist and his wife who kept their boat in the Marina and who were very friendly. He looked just like Walter Matthau. I could never talk to him without wanting to call him Walter. Anyway, he got quite inebriated one night and while cleaning his bilge put forty gallons of water in it and forgot to drain it out! He was observed the following morning at six a.m. standing on the dock dolefully staring at his boat. "It's sinking," he said. As it did look pretty low in the water, Stan asked him where his wife was. "She's still sleeping," he said, "Don't worry I can watch her from here." His real problem was that he had just sold the boat and didn't know how candid he should be with the new owner. Stan's comment was, "What better time to have sold the boat!"

CHAPTER FOUR

It was June 3rd and time was running out, but it looked like we were finally getting ready to get underway again. Dave, the manager of the Marina, and Tim, the mechanic, suggested we take her out for a test run. We were barely out from the dock when Tim came running up from the engine room crying, "Take her back! The shaft is vibrating like mad!"

We moaned, but dutifully did so and they hauled us out of the water about at 6:30, which is the height of the cocktail hour at Emmeline and Hessie's. The "ways" at the marina are in the middle of the marsh and when this platform that you can't see moves the boat forward and up, it looks for all the world like the docks are moving! Quite a crowd at the restaurant came out to watch and we heard a few swore off the booze when they thought their eyes were playing tricks on them! So there we were for the night, way up in the air, with a very precarious ladder to climb down and a windy thunderstorm headed our way. We stayed put, although I considered abandoning ship. It was an interesting night! They fixed the shaft, but we had to wait for high tide Saturday to float the boat off the ways and it was seven p.m. before we did. We decided to skip the test run till morning and to combine our leave taking with it. All seemed well as we left the beautiful Golden Isles the next morning at 6:30, and went well all day. We had decided to make ten and eleven hour runs in hopes of reaching Cleveland before snowfall.

We were really gun shy the first few days, going through some pretty hairy shoal waters, and falling exhausted into bed at night. On the third day, we had gone ten hours and were coming up on our destination for the day and congratulating ourselves on not going aground, when bump, darn it we were aground! We would have eventually floated off, as it was low tide when this happened, but a passing boat threw us a line and pulled us off. We went into the marina, hearts in our mouths, praying we hadn't hit the shaft again. Luckily, all was well, but we decided we'd better run shorter days as it was too easy to lose that edge of alertness when you're tired. We did take turns at the helm. One ran the boat while the other read the Guide and kept a sharp eye out for shoals, etc.

We were getting quite good at docking and anchoring now. Of course, we'd done lots of this in our boating years but this boat was so much bigger, almost twice the size of our largest Great Lakes boat. Stan handled the boat like a pro and I seemed able to get my lines out and attached and not fall over my feet like I did for a while. Trouble was, in our boating days, I'd always let the kids do all that stuff because I was the chief cook and bottle washer, so did not have the experience Stan did. Now it was learn or die! There are usually people on the dock to catch your lines, but I learned to do it all by myself if I had to. When we anchored, I took the helm and Stan threw (set) the anchor and this worked well, as the anchor weighed a ton, then I put it in reverse or ahead as Stan signaled me. We'd worked out hand signals, as we'd heard too many captains screaming at their first mates and that did not make for a happy crew, believe me!

The next day, we went to the Little Wicomico River and had to set the darn anchor at least five times as the bottom was mud and it was windy with strong currents. We had anchored there the night before and it was fine. We started out at 6:45, but turned around as the wind was twenty-five knots on the Chesapeake Bay and we would have had a miserable nine hours to Annapolis. We hoped for better weather the next day and enjoyed a "lay day" as well.

As we came up the waterway, we saw a lot of interesting things. At Myrtle Beach, we saw the aerial tramway, which went right above us, carrying golfers from the parking lot to the tee. It reminded us of being in Myrtle Beach in our golfing days, although not at this neat place. We did see many golf courses coming up the waterway, many of which we had played, and in those days we had looked out onto the waterway and wondered if we'd ever be on a boat out there. Yay! We'd made it!

We were tempted to go into Hilton Head, one of our favorite pre-boat places, but we kept to our schedule and promised ourselves to stop there in the fall. We stopped one night at a beautiful place called Belhaven, North Carolina, which is a resort. They had a fantastic seafood buffet, which we enjoyed, and met fellow boaters, (oops, yachties!) Mary Kate and John Smith.

They invited us aboard their boat for strawberries and ice cream and boat talk and introduced us to the owner of the *S.S. Dom*. Stan asked the owner, who had a considerably younger wife, if his name was Dominic. "No," he said, "It stands for Dirty Old Man and the S.S. is for her, Sexy Shirley." John Smith said, in a marvelous southern drawl, "I sure hate to see a man take on a full day's work late in the afternoon!"

We left Belhaven the next morning, happy to see a beautiful day because we had to cross the Albemarle Sound and it had the reputation of being nasty water sometimes. The weather continued to be good though, and the crossing was easy. Horror of horrors though, our chart blew overboard about half way across! Stan had really studied the chart that morning, but this was new water for us and we couldn't see all the way across the Sound. We headed in the general direction of where we thought the opening to the waterway left the Sound and hoped to see another boat heading that way, but no luck. Finally, to our great relief, we saw a marker buoy and headed inland to Coinjock. The marina there was run by two Annapolis grads who kindly copied a Coast Guard chart for us, making it easier to run to where the next chart started. We didn't make very good time that day due to having to run slowly when our chart blew over. New lesson---always anchor the chart!

The *Gamecock*, a Grand Banks trawler, whom we'd met several times en route, offered to lead us the next morning as the Coast Guard chart wasn't too great. We followed them to the lock at Great Bridge. The lock wasn't too high and we maneuvered nicely through it and onto Norfolk, Virginia.

But ever onward and upward for *Steelaway*. We enjoyed Norfolk a lot. The marina where we stayed was part of the Holiday Inn and was right downtown. We looked across the river at the Norfolk skyline, which was particularly pretty at night. As we went through the harbor heading north, we saw lots of navy ships, many in dry dock. Two subs passed us and we saw a helicopter towing a boat, which we were told was a nuclear sub. We saw more military activity at Camp Lejeune, where we were stopped in the canal and told to anchor and wait until the marines, who had target practice ahead, were through. We hoped their aim was good! It was about thirty-five minutes until we could proceed.

We headed with great excitement to Annapolis and two months accumulation of mail. We were also making good time and hoping to get to Cleveland by June 28th, barring bad weather. All the mail, which the Post Office general delivery had held for us, was such a treat as we had been pretty much incommunicado for a long time.

We passed loads of shrimp, crab, and oyster boats plying their trade. We bought some every chance we got, thrilled with the treasures of the Chesapeake. In Moorehead City, we bought lots of shrimp and put it in the freezer and hoped to do the same with crab when we got to Annapolis, which had a huge fisherman's market right on the dock.

We pulled into Annapolis around three, and were lucky enough to get a spot at the dock that was right on the town square. Our friends the Donihis from Washington came down for dinner and we had a delightful time enlivened by the hordes of people who were there for the Art Show on the dock. They waved; they stopped to visit, or just plain stared as we had drinks on the flying bridge. This was the first time we heard the oft repeated question, looking at the home port name on the stern, "How do you get here from there?" It was sort of like being on stage. When we went inside to have dinner, we had to close the curtains to have any peace. People still knocked occasionally and said, "We're from Cleveland and just had to say hello and ask how you got here from there?"

I had gone to the post office and only had one letter and was so disappointed, as I knew there had to be more. Stan went the next day and there was a whole bunch. Hooray! We depended on this so much. Today we'd be communicating by email. What a joy that would have been!

The next morning I had my hair cut, shopped for seafood and groceries. We got the stuff stowed and we left Annapolis around 1:45 and had an easy run to Schaeffer's dock on the C and D canal. This was a neat place with a beautiful restaurant, where we had dinner. This was where freighters came in and out from the Delaware Bay and the ocean to change pilots, and it was fun to watch while we ate dinner. We were sort of girding our loins for the run across the Delaware Bay the next morning, as it had a reputation for being a really nasty piece of water a good deal of the time. Unfortunately, it lived up to its reputation almost every time we crossed it!

We left early and found the Bay cold, rainy, foggy and horribly rough. I was seasick most of the way and very glad to arrive at the Cape May Beach Marina. It was lovely, but very expensive and isolated. They did have a courtesy car, which took us into town for church Saturday night. Cape May is a charming little town and on a gorgeous beach. My family had vacationed there before I was married and I loved seeing it again.

We left the next morning running on the ocean. We had a following sea and twelve knot winds, so it was comfortable running and we made Atlantic City by early afternoon. We read the Sunday paper and loafed for a while before taking a cab and exploring the boardwalk and casinos. I had expected something glamorous, but it looked a little seedy and tired. We walked awhile and had dinner at one of the casinos. Didn't try the gambling, as it didn't look fun!

We left at 7:20 on a "flat ass calm" sea and headed for Atlantic Highlands. It was very hazy, so we ran a lot on compass and radar, sharpening our navigation skills. There were some threatening thunderstorms, but we caught just a few showers on the edge. We docked at five o'clock, tired but happy to be getting close to New York City. It was a very nice marina and close to stores, laundry, and a post office, which would be a good future mail drop. We missed anchoring out, but were still trying to make good time to Cleveland. I loved the peace and quiet at anchor. That was real boating. Oops, yachting!

The passage to New York Harbor the next day was a good one. It was awesome to be passing by the Statue of Liberty and other New York landmarks. It was just fun to be there! It was smoggy, but we encountered very little traffic for which we were grateful. We were busy dodging debris, which was horrendous. We heard a thump and thought we had hit something and the engines made a horrible noise. But we decided all was okay after checking, and proceeded with hearts in our mouths. We were trying to find a marina we could get into to get some charts of the Hudson River, but they were all too shallow for a big mama like *Steelaway*, so we gingerly ran onto Tarrytown. We stopped at the Tarrytown Boat Club and just barely got into our slip before we went aground. The tide was really low. After all that I needed the long walk uphill to town. I found a nice Italian delicatessen and splurged a little. I figured we needed a little celebration after our somewhat harrowing day!

We checked the tide tables and left early at high tide and floated nicely out of our slip and the marina. About noon, the starboard engine threw a fit and we pulled out of the channel and anchored so Stan could check it out. Then, we started up the river again heading for Hop-O-Nose at Catskill on one engine, with a thunderstorm following us all the way. We tied up and found the nearest diesel mechanic was thirty miles back the way we'd already come! We were pretty frazzled by then, or I should say I was. Stan never was afraid, scared or seasick, which is a little hard to live with when one is the ship's coward. We decided to stay put and head back to Kingston the next morning at five o'clock. I headed into town, finding a walk was good therapy while Stan started to clean the "mustache' off the hull. The hull was red from the tannic acid in the rivers through Georgia and the Carolinas. Someone tipped us off to using toilet bowl cleaner to take off the stain without hurting the paint. I guess that was good therapy for him.

We left as planned early the next morning and ran on the one good engine at six knots, which was painfully slow. Nice to know we could do that anyway. We pulled into a very pretty marina, but it really was in the back of nowhere. However, as usual the people here were very nice, offering us a car to the store, etc. The mechanic started taking the engine apart and predicted three days there. Oh woe! It was the 22nd of June and we still hoped to make Cleveland by the 4th of July for the family party.

A little later we got the bad news that the head and piston were broken and heaven only knows what else. Apparently when we hit something in New York Harbor, a push rod broke and dropped into the engine, causing chaos. They were trying to figure out if they could get the engine out the front windshield, which luckily was big, otherwise they would have to tear the boat apart to get it out! They've also had to order $1,200 worth of parts already and that wouldn't include labor. They decided to wait till the next morning to start work, which gave us time to absorb the whole ordeal. There was a quaint restaurant at the marina and we went to dinner there, reeling from the shock.

CHAPTER FIVE

The next morning, much to our relief, they discovered that they could pull the engine up and hang it from an A-frame and work on it there instead of hauling it out the window. This, however, entailed taking up most of the floor in the main salon and replacing it with a board. As a result, we had to walk the plank so to speak to get forward to the galley or back to our bedroom looking down on a cavernous engine room with the engine dangling over the space. I could barely cook in the galley and we couldn't get to the dining table, so for the next two weeks we ate on our stateroom floor or up on the flying bridge, depending on the weather.

This became my first real taste of dealing with the frustrations and reality of living aboard. I was determined to be patient and cheerful, but it was a struggle. I was to spend many times in boatyards over the next few years, usually in uncomfortable situations, finding ways to keep busy and calm. I eventually reached a point where I was philosophical and took it in my stride, but I have to admit that this time was tough.

Boredom is a big part of daily living for most first mates living aboard. Sure, you are passing gorgeous scenery many times, but the brain does sometimes feel like it's in a coma. On many long runs on open water, there is nothing to look at except water, and also after a few years, you've seen it all. My main problem was that I got seasick if I tried to read or do needlework, so I'd be just sitting there. I'm an avid reader and had brought along over a hundred paperbacks. One of the fun things though was that I could always find someone wanting to swap books and I surely did a lot of this. It widened my horizon swapping with so many different people from different places. I remember one time I traded several books for a three volume set of the history of Russia! I must have been desperate! Almost all the marinas had a swapping library, which was another good source for me. I did write a lot, and kept extensive journals. Correspondence kept me busy too and I tried my hand at writing articles for magazines. What a thrill when I finally sold one to *Yachting* magazine.

I should explain that Captains don't get bored. They don't have time. On a boat there is always something that requires checking, work, repair, painting and on and on. Plus, there's the responsibility for the ship and the crew. And it's really all his. This is why first mates might joke about how "the Captain's word is Law," but they knew it was the reality and had to be obeyed. There was no time for discussion when fast action was required. There was no women's lib in the yachting world! Even the women I knew who could do everything the Captain did knew the status there.

So here I was, with two weeks to keep myself busy. I walked a lot through the pretty countryside. We made many friends while sitting up on the flying bridge, watching people come in and out of the restaurant. As usual, people tended to walk along the dock after dinner looking at boats and many stopped to talk and often came aboard.

That place on Rondout Creek was beautiful, if isolated, and the people were so nice. John Hoy, our mechanic, and his wife and assistants were so kind and did all they could to help us. One day, we took the dinghy down to Kingston and stopped at the marina there. Someone gave us a ride into town and someone from the laundromat gave us a ride back. In midstream the dinghy engine conked out, which it was prone to do until a year or so later when Stan gave me a new one for my birthday. Trying to get it going didn't work, so Stan started rowing. A passing boat stopped and towed us the long way back, which was a considerable distance. A little later, we took snacks and drinks in the dinghy and had a fun cocktail hour sail even without much wind. We at least got home under our own power!

It was the weekend and no one was working on the boat, so Stan joined me in exploring our environment. We swam off the boat, sailed a little, and took a long walk. We found a little general store which had minimal groceries, a phone (halleluiah, we could call home!), and even a small post office, which cheered me up no end.

As we prepared to go to dinner, a couple stopped by and admired our boat. We started talking and they invited us to have dinner with them at the restaurant. They were Al and Ann Motzkins and they had a daughter living in Cleveland, who was married to a Case Western Reserve medical student. They insisted we go home with them and meet their family and loaned us a car to use all day Sunday.

We drove into Kingston and went to Mass in an old church on the river, which reminded me so much of the churches of my childhood. When we came back, we sailed to the sandy beach, swam, and washed our hair, then went off to the grocery in town where we really stocked up. We had a hasty supper and went to the Showboat and saw a fun play. We felt we'd really made the most of our day's use of the car!

We met Mike and Pat Gropuso on the dock and they took us to see a restored house on the creek that we had admired, then to his golf club for lunch and later to his factory that manufactured raincoats. He even gave me one! Such a nice man!

The two weeks went by faster than we had expected. Stan was hanging out with the mechanics and said he was learning a lot about engines. We even drove down to New Jersey in John Hoy's truck to pick up a part which would speed up the process. I made many treks to the phone booth to call the kids in Cleveland and tell them it would be pretty soon when we'd be heading their way. In a way, I loved spending so much time up on the flying bridge. I loved being outdoors most of the time. It was a great place to read or sew.

It was July 7th, and though we had already missed the family party, at last we were ready to go! On the test run, Stan thought the new shaft we'd gotten from Dominey at the Golden Isles was bad again and there was lots of vibration, smoke and a whining noise. Stan checked the shaft and thought we could make Cleveland before getting it fixed. John Hoy agreed and suggested getting double shafts when we changed this one. We stopped at Al Motzkin's dock on the way out Rondout Creek and took on one hundred and twenty gallons of fuel at his wonderful price of forty cents a gallon!

Then, at last we were headed up the Hudson again. We had gotten a call at the marina that a boat had accidentally taken some of our lines when they had come there for dinner and invited us to stop at their yacht club to retrieve them. So we stopped at the Tri-City Yacht Club and were warmly greeted and invited to stay overnight, which we did. It was lovely to have a floor again in the main salon of our home. It really made one appreciate the little things of life!

We were under way at seven the next morning and ran without any problems to Albany Yacht Club. We even went through the Federal Lock uneventfully into the Erie Canal. We did need to stop at a dock before the Lock, where an enterprising guy who made his living helping people like us, took the mast down and laid it horizontally on top of the cabin so we would be able to get under the many bridges on the canal. We also had to take down the bimini canvas top that shaded the flying bridge. Otto Honniger, our friend from The Tri-City Club, met us at the Club and drove us to the Albany Airport, where we picked up our son Tommy who had flown in to "do" the Erie Canal with us. This was nice as we didn't have the hassle of renting a car and finding the airport. Tom was very excited to be with us on the boat again and he turned out to be a superb crew member.

As soon as we got Tom unpacked in the guest cabin, we took off and headed up the canal to the Van Schaik Marina. I probably should tell you a little bit about the Erie Canal. The three hundred and fifty mile waterway from the Hudson River to the Niagara River traces the earliest passage ways from the East to the Great Lakes and the heartland of the continent. The route is connected intimately with the history of our country, with the development of industry, and the settling of the heartlands.

The waterway itself is the third to follow this route. The first was excavated by manpower, the early settlers came and made this part of the country theirs and many Indian wars were fought.

The Erie Canal opened in 1825, but traffic soon outgrew the limitations of the forty foot width and four foot depth. In 1862, they enlarged the canal to increase its capacity. Construction of the present canal began in 1905 and the entire new system, handling tugs and self-propelled barges, was completed in 1918. This was the waterway we cruised. It takes you through agricultural land, industrial centers, cities, and villages in land cuts, rivers and lakes. It intersects trails used by prehistoric man, hunters and trappers and traders and follows the path of westward bound settlers who found their way eased by the original canal.

We particularly enjoyed stopping and visiting many of the historical sites along the canal. There was usually easy docking there so we could explore. It was also interesting to see the remnants of the old original locks as we went along. The original locks have not been used for a long time; instead there are new locks with lovely little parks beside them.

Also, at many of the small towns on the canal, boats can tie up and be handy to the town. They even had electric and water for free. It gave us a real feeling for what it must have been like in the original canal days, with the canal being the main source of commerce and travel. There was a sense of history all along the canal, dating back to early days when the Iroquois made the area their home.

The up locks were easier than we thought. When the gate opened, Stan drove the boat in and Tom and I tied on fenders and slipped a line over the rungs in the wall. As water came in, we slowly rose up, moving the line up to a new rung. Then we went along. It sounds simple, but the locks are old and have deep craters in the wall. The fenders kept getting caught in the holes and Tom and I tried to fend off, which turned out to be impossible! Steelaway was one heavy boat! We damaged a lot of fenders before we learned to try and anticipate the holes and move before we got stuck. We would tie the line to the top rung until they closed the gate behind us and we glided out. We were pretty scared at first, but the lock tenders helped us and we thought it a piece of cake till we hit a down lock.

On the down locks, as we pulled into the lock, I would jump off the boat and run with a line to the bow bollard and put the line around it, and then Tom would do the same with the stern line. Then back aboard, each holding our line. The lockkeeper would close the gate behind us and let the water out. Again we placed the fenders along the boat. As we went down, we let out the line praying we had enough! We learned fast to use a longer line than we thought we'd need! When we reached the bottom, the lockkeeper would toss the rest of the line down to us and we'd coil it up for the next lock and we'd leave the lock. We had almost all up locks on that trip and Tom and I got pretty good at it.

Our first day we went through nine locks, and Tom and I were proud of ourselves. We were also very tired (make that exhausted) and decided to tie up for the night at the Amsterdam terminal. This was not too smart a choice, as we discovered when we went for a little walk. It was obviously a bad part of town and rather isolated, but we were too tired to move. We were in bed early that night and about midnight I heard people talking near our boat. "Let's go aboard and see what it's like." And then feet hit the deck. Stan can sleep through anything, especially if he's lying on his good ear. His other one is totally deaf.

I leapt out of bed and said to the man standing in front of me, "What do you want?"

"Oh," he said, "I just want to see your boat."

I heard one of the men on the dock wondering if there were any men on board and I called down to Stan and he stumbled up the companionway. I said, "Say something so they'll know there are some men aboard," and having no idea what was going on he said, "Whaaaat?"

He was quick on the uptake though and realized these guys were drunk and reasoned, "Look guys, we're really tired after a long day and this isn't a good time to show anyone the boat. I'd appreciate it if you'd leave." Luckily they did leave, but it took me a long time to get back to sleep. I never did find out if Stan had grabbed his gun coming up the stairs, but I doubt it. Needless to say, we put Amsterdam on our do not stay again list! On the upside, Amsterdam did have a grocery that delivered, which was good to know for future use, because otherwise we couldn't buy more than we could carry!

We cruised through a beautiful area all the next day, but had ten locks to go through. We did learn a lot about locking though. We ruined one fender at the Little Falls lock, which had terribly big holes all over and used one of our teak saddle boards, thinking they wouldn't take such a beating. Wrong!! Tommy rescued the fender and surely was a big help to us. We really needed that third pair of hands. We tied up at the Ilion Marina, which was very handy and within walking distance of a very nice shopping mall and post office. We slept well that night.

The next morning was cold and it stayed that way all day. We had more down locks that day and on Lock 22, I tripped and pulled a muscle. I crawled to the bollard with my line and back to the boat while Tommy did the stern line. We just went to the State Park at Lock 23 and tied up for the night. It was a beautiful spot and so peaceful and quiet. The lock tenders competed with each other for the most beautiful gardens and it was always a treat to see their efforts. However, I had bad muscle spasms all night.

We crossed Lake Oneida the next day. It was a big lake and was rough, but the trip uneventful. We had good charts and the mile markers were easy to spot. We were surely glad to have Tommy along, as my leg was very sore. He was getting very knowledgeable at handling lines. We took down the bimini top that day, as we would be going under some very low bridges the next day.

I woke up the next morning with a terrible muscle spasm, but it was better after Stan kneaded it for me. We had to tie up and wait at the Bennettsville lock because the tender wasn't there yet. Tom and I got off the boat and he mailed his postcards while I limped up to the bridge to see when the lock would open. A nice man gave me a bouquet of flowers. It was a sunny day, but not too warm, which was good as it could get quite hot with the bimini top down.

It was a good thing we did take the top down, as we went under fifteen low bridges. It looked like we weren't going to make it as we approached the bridges and Tom would sing, "Low bridge, everybody down. Low bridge on the Erie Canal." We cleared some of them with only inches to spare. We saw the old tow paths, now people walks, alongside the canal where the mules used to pull the barges. One day when we were coming up the canal with Tommy, we had to tie up at the foot of the lock to wait till it opened and I leapt out with a line and was walking ahead of the boat with it, looking for a place to tie it. Tommy started to laugh and said, "Mother looks just like the old mules."

I felt kind of insulted when a runner came along and was faster than we were! There were very strict speed limits on the canal. It did heat up in the afternoon and we missed the shade of the bimini. We had a difficult time at Lock 29 when a line broke. It was cut in half by the rough wall. We pulled into Lock 30 at six p.m. after a long day and tied up at another state park. Tommy went fishing but didn't catch anything. No fish for dinner!

We left at eight and went past many lock towns, which had state parks where boats could tie up and made a note to try them next time. We encountered our first lift bridges that day one after the other. We got through most of them quickly, but had to wait for one with no bridge tender in sight. We tied up to two telephone poles and chatted with some local kids. Finally one of them said the tender was having his lunch and he would run and tell him a boat was waiting. The guy came out of a restaurant wiping his mouth on a napkin and hurried to the bridge. Later in the afternoon we saw a charming looking clothing store with its own little dock. As we slowed down, one of the owners came out and invited us to stay overnight at their dock. We happily accepted and thus met Sam and Ruth Hall who were delightful people and became good friends down through the years.

We had another long day the next day, tying up at Middlesport. We had water and electric and there was a laundromat and grocery there, as well as a nearby church where we could go to Sunday Mass. This was to be the place where we would stop many times on frequent trips to do laundry. We could stop right in front of the laundry and run in and out between loads. It was a fabulous place.

We were almost to Lake Erie after all this time, and it was very exciting to be at our old favorite stomping grounds. We stopped in Buffalo and found it difficult to find a marina, but went a little below town and found Smith's Marina. It was to become the favorite jumping off place for us down through the years. We found the usual friendly help there—offer of a loan of a car, etc. and several interesting new friends. But we were anxious to get on, and said, "See you in the fall" and headed out.

We got as far as Dunkirk, New York that night and stayed at the yacht club there. It was very nice, but the harbor was quite shallow for Big Mama and we were a little concerned, but it worked out very well for that night. As we were heading for Cleveland, Lake Erie lived up to its reputation and became very rough, a quick storm coming up. Tom and I finally went below because it was so terribly rough and we were sitting in the salon. The TV set was secured with a bungee cord but we had a feeling it might come towards us any minute as the boat violently rocked. The cord held, however, a plant that was in a pot that was tied down was thrown right out of the pot towards us and gave us a scare. Stan decided to go into the River at Ashtabula to get out of the storm and we were lucky to find a nice quiet marina there where we were certainly happy to start putting things back in place. It was calm next morning and we set out for Cleveland at last!

CHAPTER SIX

When we got to Cleveland, we headed for the 55th Street Marina and anchored in there as all the docks were occupied. We took the dinghy ashore and quickly called the kids to let them know we were in town at last. They all came down soon, Barbie and family from Shaker Heights and Chip and Cindy from Lakewood, and we had a very happy evening and the first of many cook outs on *Steelaway*. They were so happy to see the boat at last. We certainly had a lot to catch up on and talked till a quite late hour.

The next day we met a very nice man who told us he was going to be gone from his slip all summer and asked if we would like to use it. Of course, we were delighted and settled in for what was going to be pretty much our home all summer, thanks to Dick Greiner. We met many of our neighbors who were down at the dock that night and found that we were considered quite exotic as we were an oceangoing boat, which was something you didn't see every day on Lake Erie.

We had a wonderful summer and the days flew by only too fast. We loved our location at the 55th Street Marina, and found this a great place to see all our friends and family. We took everyone out for rides on the boat and had several old friends come and spend a weekend with us. We also had several delightful trips to Put-In-Bay, Kelley's Island, and Gem Beach. At Gem Beach, we saw many of the old gang from our Great Lakes boating days, and took twenty-seven people for a ride to Put-In-Bay and back. On the way home, we answered a distress call and towed a disabled boat back to Gem Beach. Big Mama handled the big load beautifully. We loved having the grandchildren come and stay overnight. It was a big adventure for them and a joy to us. It was especially fun to go to so many of our old haunts on Lake Erie.

We were at Cedar Point with Barbara, her children, and a friend of our granddaughter Chrissy's, and were getting ready to go to the amusement park the next day. That night I bent over to pick up a sheet when I was making beds and somehow hurt my back. I was in terrible pain and the next morning we called our doctor and he told Stan to bring me back to Cleveland. Barbie and Stan put me in my bunk with pillows and blankets packed around me for the trip and we headed for Cleveland. Chip had arranged to have an ambulance waiting for us at our dock and Stan kept in touch over the marine radio with him charting our progress.

We were in an area where our phone didn't work so the Coast Guard called Chip at the office and told him when we would be there. The ambulance was there and the paramedics strapped me to a back board, carried me out the rear companionway, and quickly took me to the hospital, where they diagnosed my back as sprained. All I could think of while this was going on was how interested Tommy would have been, as he loved disaster movies! The doctor told me to go back to the boat and stay flat on my back for two weeks. They gave me pain killers, so I was fairly comfortable and if you have to stay in bed this was a pretty nice place to be.

A neighbor who had a telephone on his boat came over and plugged it into the outlet near me and this was wonderful, as I could communicate with the kids freely. I could lie in my bunk and see the blue sky and seagulls and clouds go by. Our boating neighbors came calling with pies and tomatoes and the kids were in and out all the time helping Stan take care of me, doing laundry and cooking, and so it really was a blessing to have such wonderful kids as well as such a nice husband. One tends to count one's blessings while flat on the back and helpless.

Two weeks later, I was gingerly moving around and started an exercise program trying to strengthen my back so we could leave for the south. The boat is no place to have a bad back. It took us until almost October before it was okay to leave. Just before we left, we celebrated Labor Day with the family. We had a cookout and since the Air Show was on, we had "box seats" for watching as the Blue Angels flew right over our heads. In fact, for a while I kind of worried they were going to come right through the boat! We had a wonderful afternoon and finally sadly said goodbye to them all.

The morning we left it was sunny and cool. We hated to be leaving so late in the summer, but really didn't have a choice because of my back. We were just hoping October would be beautiful. However, that morning it became quite rough and we decided to go into the harbor at Erie, Pennsylvania. We found a nice marina and enjoyed a lay day. The next morning was calmer and we went on as far as Dunkirk, New York. We had quite a following sea as we were going in, which was a little difficult, but they had a breakwall in that harbor and we thought it would be a good place to stop.

We found a dock on the outside of the Dunkirk Yacht Club and tied up. We decided to walk down the road a little way and try out the nice-looking restaurant there. We had a very good and leisurely dinner, but were increasingly worried as we looked out the window and saw a Nor'easter coming in. We thought, however, that the breakwall would give us a safe berth. We retied some lines when we got back to the boat and were very tired, so we started to go to bed, but changed our minds quickly. The waves got bigger out away from the dock. At Stan's command, I let go the after spring line and we powered forward at full speed. What a relief to be away from the dock! We slowly headed out to a point just in front of an electric plant, which was fairly sheltered and in deep enough water to anchor safely—we hoped! I took the helm while Stan set the anchor and we both watched anxiously to be sure it wasn't dragging. It was still blowing like crazy and we sat and watched for a while and it seemed to be okay, so Stan went to bed. I was too scared and shaken, so I sat up and watched till about 2 a.m., when I couldn't keep my eyes open. Years later, I still contemplate how nice it is to wake up and know my bed is still exactly in the same place it was when I went to sleep!

We developed more confidence in anchoring as time went on, which was great. I got so I could tell from my bed what the anchor was doing by watching the swing of light as it swept across the front of the room as the boat swung at anchor. Even on the calmest nights there was a little motion of the swing. I knew exactly where it should begin and end and felt secure.

The next morning, we sort of heaved a sigh of relief as we exited the harbor. The trip to Buffalo was uneventful and we soon tied up in the Smith Boys Marina. It was fun to see the Ernsts again. They were local Buffalo people who kept their boat at the Smith Boys Marina. They invited us over for dinner and we had a lovely evening. They introduced us to quite a few people and their son David, who became a good friend of ours and a correspondent down through the years.

The following morning I put my laundry in my little cart and headed for the laundromat, where I washed the curtains and slipcovers. Stan was busy with a lot of last minute things getting ready to go down the canal again.

We were really looking forward to it this time, having had a little experience with it and we had finally reached the stage in our lives where we had no deadlines, no pressure and could go at a pace we enjoyed. From now on, we would stop were we wanted, stay as long as we wanted to, and leave when we wanted to.

Autumn has always been my favorite season and I was glad we were not missing it. The air was nippy, but the sun was warm. We departed the Smith Boys Marina a few days later and did very well going through the locks. We were wondering how we would do with just the two of us and without Tommy's third hand, but all went well and we were able to manage nicely. A good deal of the trip down the canal was quite rural and very pretty.

We soon got to Middlesport and tied up there. I explored the city a little and went to the grocery store and the post office. It was fun to be able to do this by walking from the boat and I took full advantage of it. We tied up at Albion and tied up to two trees for lunch and enjoyed our picnic ashore. That is, until we noticed the boat wasn't still tied up! My not-so-great knot around a tree trunk had let go. We ran for the boat and Stan was luckily able to jump aboard while I retrieved the line and tied us up again. We finished lunch and climbed back aboard and went to Brockport. It was a nice easy day except for my little escapade with the knot, and we went out to dinner at Brockport. I decided I really needed to work on my knots.

The next day, we went as far as the Halls' dock and tied up there. I went into their shop and browsed through their beautiful sweaters and other lovely merchandise and did quite a bit of my Christmas shopping for the girls. The Halls invited us out to dinner at their country club and we had a lovely evening. We discovered that evening that Ruth Hall had a roommate and old friend for many years who was the General's wife from whom we bought the boat. He and his wife both grew up in Rochester and lived there until he was in the military. Such a small world! The General was now retired and they were living in Florida, so we hoped that possibly we could meet them one day.

We continued through the locks and down the river. In a rather deserted area, we hit something again that we couldn't see, but the boat was not running well. The next town was Baldwinsville and we stopped at the marina there, but they were unable to haul the boat as big as ours, so we went on to Brewerton, New York and they said they would get us up on their ways.

They had had a bad fire though and they had to find a different way to haul us up. They fastened chain to us someplace and a tractor pulled us up to the ways. Then, they were able to get us up in the air. We discovered we'd bent a prop or shaft, but the boatyard seemed to be really good. I really didn't like being up in the air very much, it seemed so high, but they put a ladder up so we could get up and down.

The boatyard sent our shafts to Rochester to be straightened and there was a fairly good chance that they'd be back the next day or the day after. Meanwhile, we had some of the peripheral damage to the boat from the Dunkirk storm repaired.

Of course, up in the ways we couldn't use the plumbing or the heat and it was pretty cold at night. In the daytime, the solar heat warmed the boat up pretty well. I climbed down the ladder to check out the bathroom, which was pretty grungy, I guess because of the fire, but the guys were so nice and a man gave us a key to use at night when they were gone.

The next day the shafts came back and with Stan's supervision, they put them back on the boat. During the day, I did some sewing, as I was making a lot of presents for Christmas, but it was cold and drafty and I sewed with my golf gloves on. They finished up and came back the next morning to get us off the ways and back in the water.

We were very fortunate to have this repaired so quickly. The bill wasn't so great though, but as Stan says, we must be philosophical about these things. He pointed out that we had traveled over three thousand miles so far and that in our last boat we didn't put on that many miles in five years and we'd only been hauled twice, so it all averaged out. I just worried about my "facelift fund" all going into shaft and prop repair! The Intracoastal and canal were really bad as far as debris. The bad stuff was waterlogged and not floating where you could avoid it, but just under the surface, not sunk yet. The big water didn't have this problem.

CHAPTER SEVEN

So, we headed back down the Erie Canal. The up locks are harder on the boat and the down locks harder on the crew. Going up, the water is very turbulent and pushes the boat against the wall really hard. However, the line handler just keeps moving the line up the rungs of a ladder in the lock wall. Going down, I leaped off the boat as Stan maneuvered it close to the wall and put a line around the forward bollard as he jumped off and put one on the stern. Then, we both got back aboard and paid out the line as the boat went down with very little motion. At the bottom, we pulled the line back aboard which was a little hard for me as it was very heavy. Stan pulled both our lines back aboard when we went through the forty-foot down, as were still being careful of my back.

We saw lots of joggers and walkers on the tow paths and we'd always wave madly. It was fun when we'd go under a bridge and people standing there would call out, "Where are you headed?" and we'd reply, "The Bahamas." They'd groan, "Take us along!" Sometimes the canal was higher than the surrounding countryside and we looked down on homes and farms. We also went right over a highway, which was sort of a funny feeling. Then there are the guard gates, which can be lowered when the water level is too high, and they look just like guillotines. I always sort of cringe when we went under one as we just barely cleared them.

Anyway, to get back to the next day, it was really cold. To use Stan's words, it was as "cold as a well digger's ass." Luckily Stan was a Spartan type who leapt out of bed and into his clothes, and then turned on the heat and the kettle while I burrowed down into my warm cocoon, trying to steel myself to get up. I would get into my long underwear, jeans, wool turtleneck, Irish fisherman's sweater, Stan's wool socks, and was ready for the day.

We left the dock and were underway. We thought we'd probably have to run from below all that day because of the cold. Being up on the bridge was like being dunked in ice water. The only thing that looked more uncomfortable was being out in a duck blind, although why anyone would want to shoot a poor duck is beyond me! Undoubtedly, the duck hunters would say the same thing about us. The cabin was pretty comfy now. We were rigged for rough seas, as it was very windy and we had a twenty-two mile run across Lake Oneida, which the book said could be pretty rough. Luckily, it was a following sea. The lake was beautiful and ringed with a kaleidoscope of fall colors.

It was a funny sort of day, almost foreboding. It was raining on one side of the lake and on the other side; the sun was spotlighting the trees. The sky was leaden and looked like snow, God forbid, and the sea was steel gray and lumpy. We had just passed a fisherman, now he was crazy! I could see though, that I was going to have to learn how to fish. When we see a big fat fish leap out of the water, Stan sees a lovely flash of silver, while I see a couple of nice filets poached in white wine and butter! And there were so many of them out there—a giant fish market of the sea.

We could see the hills rising above the far side of the lake. It looked like someone took a giant paint brush and tipped the trees with scarlet and orange. We would be going through them, as we had two up locks when we left the lake. I was frustrated to not be able to get any good pictures of the foliage because the darn sun went down every time I got a particularly good scene set up. I didn't see much of Lake Oneida when we came up the canal because I had pulled the muscles in my leg the day before leaping off a lock, so I was below and asleep when we crossed at that time. So I was enjoying the return trip across.

Stan and I took turns at the helm and when we were above it was pretty miserable, and it turned into a really rotten day. Murphy's Law was operating full force. First, it started to rain, so we lost our "solar" heating as the temperature dropped rapidly. Then, the generator quit so we had no heat, electricity, or hot coffee, and the nearest place we could stop that had electricity available was five hours away. Stan tried to fix it underway while I took the helm, but had problems.

Then, we hit the lock, where the lock master let us into the lock and then disappeared, leaving us struggling with a terrible wind that just about tore our arms out of the sockets while holding our lines. He came back in twenty minutes and we got through the lock only to find that the same moron was operating the next lock too. Another boat came in behind us. Then, the lock master let the water out too fast and both boats were torn from the wall and loose in the lock. We were blown into the opposite wall, but not too hard because Stan was able to control the boat somewhat with the power.

It got colder and rainier, and at every darned lock it just poured. I added foul weather gear and boots to my several layers and looked like a nice fat teddy bear—a cold bear! As I was standing on the deck in a really hard icy rain, holding my line in sodden discomfort, I thought of the cows I had seen in a field a little way back that were just standing there motionless, enduring, and I felt a kinship.

We finally got to Illion and plugged in the electric and luxuriated in the heat, blessed heat. We had a couple of hot toddies and a warm dinner and felt restored. Stan got the generator fixed so that day didn't seem so bad, despite the fact that we'd had rain at almost every lock. Going through one of them, it hailed for heaven's sake! But at least we came into a warm cabin and a hot cup of coffee, so it wasn't too bad. Stan said, "If you don't have snow, you'll never have that Indian summer."

We saw lots of wedges of geese and ducks flying south. The ducks often landed in the water near us. Stan quacked at one and I don't know what he said in duck talk, but the duck sounded mad when he squawked back! We also saw lots of giant blue herons. They were funny birds. They flew into the air in alarm as the boat approached, flew ahead, and landed again, only to fly away as we neared them. One bird did this for miles and we named him Harry the Heron. There were lots of pretty birds, especially in the bird refuges, so I had my bird book and the binoculars ready.

We were going through beautiful mountains and the color was spectacular! The New York Throughway ran parallel to us every so often. In July, when we ran from the bridge, we used to talk to the truck drivers on the CB radio and they would spot us and honk and wave as they barreled by.

We knew we would be in Kingston in another day or so, and planned on staying there for a few days and having John Hoy give the generator of good checkup, as we would be totally dependent on it in the Bahamas. We filled the freezer with meat and planned to replace it with the lobsters that Stan would catch for us. Then, we put about two hundred cans of stuff in the food lockers so it was Bahamas or bust!

CHAPTER EIGHT

We had been aboard *Steelaway* for eight months now and I could hardly believe it. The time had passed so quickly. We felt saturated with scenery and new experiences. It had been a tremendous learning experience for us. Not always an easy one, but rewarding.

I feel as if I've written fifteen years on the Erie Canal! It had been quite an experience! We wondered what future experiences lay in wait for Captain Bligh (he wasn't really, he was very patient—most of the time!) and Wonder Woman (the kids called me that after watching me try and pull twenty-five tons of boat into the dock).

We soon got to Kingston and the weather had warmed up! It was in the seventies and we had the windows open and had actually discarded our long underwear, thank God. I had about felt like the good old days when one was sewn into long johns for the winter!

The generator had started leaking oil after Stan had fixed the impellor. He could have fixed this too but it would've meant four hours or so of work, and since John was going to be tearing it down anyhow, it seemed silly to do it. So we suffered along without it during the day and sought an electric source at night. Unfortunately, it had been mostly cold and rainy in the daytime. I don't know what possessed me to bring along a hot water bottle that we hadn't used for years but I did and it was the greatest invention since fire! Rondout Creek, where we were, was in a basin surrounded by mountains, and the flaming foliage was reflected in the still water and was absolutely glorious.

The ducks that I had trained in the summer when we were here came quacking over to greet us, looking for a handout. I was sure they remembered me. It was so much nicer than in July, when they had the whole salon floor up for ten days, and just 2 two-by-fours for us to walk across, and the huge greasy engine hanging on a saw horse. It was a tremendous improvement!

We quickly settled in at the marina and Stan got busy working with John Hoy on the generator and a few other things he wanted checked out. We saw our friends the Motzkins again and had a fun reunion. We called Nancy Grimshaw, who had lived with us for a while after her mother died, and who was living in New York now and studying fashion at the Institute there. Nancy was able to get a bus that brought her to Kingston. We picked her up and brought her to the boat and had a great time. The Motzkins had loaned us a car again and we took advantage of a beautiful fall day to take Nancy and drive down the Hudson. We went to see the Vanderbilt home and Hyde Park, which was President Roosevelt's home and now a museum, which we enjoyed a lot. It was such fun to see Nancy and catch up on all the things that had happened since we last saw her and we hated to put her back on the bus.

The rest of the time we were there we spent getting the boat ready for the trip down the Intracoastal. Al Motzkin again offered to sell us diesel from his facility right on the river at the wonderful price of forty cents a gallon. This was really super, as we had to take on three hundred and sixty-four gallons of fuel and you can imagine what that cost! Of course today with the diesel at something like three or four dollars or more a gallon, it would've been impossible for us to afford the boat. At any rate, we saved quite a bit and were very grateful to Al.

After John finished working on the boat, we were feeling very good about the condition of the ship and anxious to get on. We said goodbye and thanks and headed back down the river. It was a sunny day but cold, darn it, and we got the heavy clothes out again. The next night we were right across from West Point, which was fun to see up above us on the cliffs. That night it actually snowed, and up on the bow we had quite a bit of it. Of course, we didn't have a snow shovel aboard! Thankfully, it quickly melted and we went down through New York Harbor again kind of holding our breaths and hoping we wouldn't hit anything. The debris included things like telephone poles. However, it was always a thrill to go through the Harbor and see all of New York in front of us.

We headed back down the Intracoastal and now began one of the things that I liked best about living aboard. Every day we would meet more boats that we had met coming up the Intracoastal. As they were all liveaboards too, it was like old home week when we'd drop anchor for the night and enjoy seeing friends we had made. We'd all go from boat to boat in the dinghies to say hi and in many cases were invited aboard for a drink and discussion of the day's run. Since we all went about the same speed, we found ourselves in the same places almost every night. Sometimes we'd take an extra day or two to do some exploring, but as everyone else was doing this too, we kept running into each other. We also made new friends from the boats, excuse me, "yachts' that were making the trek south. We were to see the same friends over and over again down through the years in the Bahamas, around Florida, and back up the Intracoastal again and it was always the same thrill of seeing good friends.

We stopped at pretty much the same places going down as we had coming up. We had a couple of days of pretty rough seas, as we had to run outside to Cape May. The Intracoastal is pretty shallow between Atlantic Highlands and Cape May, and we didn't want to risk it. We were delighted to pull into the marina at Cape May and went out to dinner at a very nice restaurant to celebrate. By now, I knew that I really didn't like rough seas. I always felt kind of seasick and couldn't read or sew because it would make it worse. I discovered my best bet was taking a Bonine and stretching out flat on the deck or in my bunk. It made me very sleepy and when I slept the time went by faster, but Stan said he felt as if he were soloing when he was all alone on the bridge. However, of necessity this became what I did. Fortunately, as time went on my stomach got a little more accustomed to the motion of the ship and it really had to be pretty bad for me to get seasick.

I lay in bed that night and prayed that the Delaware Bay would not be rough; however that was practically never the case. That darn body of water was my nemesis! So I was very happy when we pulled into Schaeffer's Marina on the far side of the bay at the entrance to the C and D Canal. This was always a fascinating place. They had a wonderful restaurant and we went there for dinner and enjoyed watching the big freighters going by as much as the food.

The next day, we went to Annapolis and anchored there. It was kind of rough and there was a lot of traffic, but our anchor held well and we relaxed. We called our friends, Rosie and Bob Donihi, who lived in Washington and arranged to see them that night. They came down and we dinghied into the dock to meet them. Rosie worked for the *Washington Post*, so they took us to the Press Club for dinner and pointed out many columnists and reporters who were well known.

Bob was teaching a class on the Middle East at one of the universities and we sat in on the class and enjoyed it very much. However, near the end of the class we could hear it was storming pretty hard outside and we worried about the boat. They took us back down to Annapolis and we stood on the dock looking for our boat. It was raining and blowing like crazy and it was hard to see across the bay. Finally, we thought we saw it on the opposite side from us against a dock near the shore. We jumped into the dinghy and hurried over to it. Later, people told us that during the storm, a sailboat dragged anchor and hit us, pulling loose our own anchor. Their big prow took a chunk out of our teak rail, which actually was a good thing, as it saved our windshield, which they would have hit otherwise. Stan and I went aboard, motored out and re-anchored. The sailboat that had hit us was a hit and run and long gone. We felt very fortunate not to have suffered any more damage than we had, and that our boat had not been hurt from being blown ashore.

We didn't sleep too well that night and woke to a quiet sunny morning. We did sleep late, and got up and did a once over of the boat to see if we had any more damage. There wasn't much more than we had found the night before. We talked to some of the other boats that had been there during the storm the night before and got more details about the boat that had dragged into us. They were a bunch of young kids who were living aboard and pretty much living off the land. They obviously had no insurance and couldn't afford to pay the damage they'd done to our boat. Luckily, we did have insurance and planned to have the teak rail and some other things repaired farther down the Intracoastal. There was nothing that needed to be done for safety's sake at that time.

It was a beautiful sunny day, the calm after the storm so to speak. We had a lazy day to sort of calm our nerves and get ready to leave the next morning. This was one of those days that I especially loved, because we were living outdoors most of the time and basking in the sun. I loved to sit up on the bridge and read or embroider or write letters and wait for the sunset. They were really spectacular as seen from the boat. I took so many pictures of beautiful sunsets that Stan had sort of despaired of my ever getting enough. We surely used a lot of film. One of the things I miss the most since we no longer live on the boat is the feeling of always being outdoors, even when you were inside the boat. We were so close to nature with all its facets!

We departed at 8:30 the next morning and had a very long day. There were head seas of two and three feet, which made for slow going and we were a little concerned because the starboard engine would lose rpms intermittently. Stan went below and changed the filters on both engines and this seemed to help some.

It was a good day even though we were a little uneasy that we may have had damage that we didn't know about. Around five o'clock, we pulled in and anchored at Mill Creek, which was at Solomon's Island. We got in the dinghy and explored a little bit and had dessert later with Gerry Barnes and his crew, who were also anchored there. We took a lay day the next day to enjoy that lovely place. The following day, we went to Dividing Creek in Prentice Cove and anchored there off the Wolf Trap light. It started out as a nice day but got worse. Stan blamed bad weather reporting! We were happy to get the shelter in the creek.

CHAPTER NINE

The next day, we ran to Norfolk. It was cloudy, and we had rain part of the way and six-foot following seas. To top it all off, we had trouble with the starboard engine again. We had an airlock, lost the rpms, and it shut down. Stan got it started again, but we had trouble with it while docking at the Holiday Marina.

We definitely needed a lay day! It was Sunday and we were able to go to church nearby. Then, Stan worked on the darn old engines while I did some laundry. You can see what I mean when I say you're always fixing something on a boat! We laid over another day because it was very windy, ten to thirty knots out of the Northeast. The wind was a side effect of Hurricane Kendra, which was four hundred miles offshore at that time. Stan worked on rebuilding the spare generator fresh water pump. We knew we'd probably need it at some future time!

We were strolling down the dock the first night and noticed a yacht with the home port of Cleveland on the stern. The owners were sitting out on the stern and we stopped and were delighted to meet Gail and Jack Shannon. They invited us aboard and we had a great time exchanging stories about living aboard. They were still not full time, as Jack was close to retirement, but not quite there yet. So they were bringing their boat south in segments. They would take it a certain distance, leave it there, and then drive back home. Fortunately, Jack owned the company, so he could take pretty long chunks of time on the boat. We were to see them many times up and down the Intracoastal, in Florida, and in the Bahamas. We were so happy to have such nice new friends from Cleveland. They were going back from Norfolk after the hurricane threat was over, so we said goodbye and we'd see them farther south. These were very special friends and we still see each other a lot thirty years later.

It was calm the next morning, so we headed for Coinjock. There were strong tidal currents, but the engine ran all right and we had a half-hour delay at the North Landing Bridge and another half-hour delay at the lock at Great Bridge. We were happy to arrive at Coinjock, where we had stopped on the way up and they had helped us with the charts. We left Coinjock in heavy fog, but it soon lifted and we anchored south of Buck Island. We had noticed that there was a bad vibration on the starboard shaft. Stan got out his mask and snorkel and dove under the boat. He found a piece of line on the shaft and took it off, and we had no more trouble the rest of the day. The Captain noted in the log that "Jo is good." I think he meant that I wasn't too hysterical about the whole thing! A lot of adventure there!

Incidentally, the Shannons had changed their minds about going home and were running with us, which was great fun. We ran to Belhaven the next day and anchored in the harbor. It was a pretty and sheltered place. We launched the dinghy and went into the marina with the Shannons for lunch. We were finding it pretty easy to get the dinghy up and down and into the water from its place on top of the rear cabin, using the mast to swing it out. The next day was a lay day because we wanted to do lots of exploring there. It looked like a charming little town.

I baked a loaf of bread and some cinnamon buns for the next day, while Stan was busy rebuilding the foreward head. We had had some trouble with it, and felt this was a good time to be sure it was working well, as this is something you do not want trouble with, especially when you have guests. Stan had a special kit to do this.

We explored the town with the Shannons and found it was a great place to buy cigarettes, liquor, and other things such as a heavenly canned soup called lobster bisque. There was no sales tax on cigarettes and since it was a tobacco state, their prices were less than half the cost elsewhere. Stan was still smoking at that time, two packs a day, and he bought quite a few cartons that he would not be able to get in the Bahamas. He didn't like British cigarettes either, so this was great for stocking up.

The next morning we left Belhaven and ran to Adams Creek, where we anchored. It was a warm day and a nice anchorage. We had a long run that day, as we had to cross Pamlico Sound, which thankfully was calm, as well as the Neuse River, which had been quite rough our first crossing. It surely was easier to cross because this time we had our charts.

We kept in touch by radio with the Shannons, who were doing the Intracoastal for the first time. Their boat was called the *Odyssey*, and when we used the radio we always called with the boat's name. For example: I would say, "*Odyssey, Odyssey*, this is *Steelaway, Steelaway* Yankee Whiskey 8386." Yankee Whiskey was radio code for the letters Y and W. Gail would answer saying, "*Steelaway, Steelaway*, this is *Odyssey*. Switch to Channel 8." I would answer, "Switching," and turn to Channel 8. We always had to use our number after our name. We always called on Channel 16, which was the main channel. You could not carry on a conversation there as that was for calling purposes only and the FCC was very strict about this.

We headed for Beaufort, North Carolina and anchored there off the town dock. It was a quiet anchorage where many boats that were crossing the Atlantic left from or returned to, which made it all a very interesting place. We faced the town and looked over the stern at a big island where there were many wild ponies to be seen. They went back to colonial days, when they were brought over to this country. They escaped from their owners and ran in wild herds and these are their descendants. We planned to spend several days there, as there was lots to see and do. There was a strong current at anchor and we took a little extra time anchoring there, but the holding was good.

Gail and Jack came over for drinks and we celebrated our good day. The sunset was beautiful that day and we were excited about our time ahead. Sharing our good times and new places was especially fun with good friends.

The next morning, Gail, Stan and I dinghied over to Horse Island and went clamming. We were lucky and dug up quite a few. Jack, the ardent fisherman, was fishing off the back of *Odyssey* while we went exploring and clamming. We were able to get fairly close to the wild horses and it was fun to see them.

Then, we decided to go to the shore and explore Beaufort a little bit. We walked down the street the docks were on, and explored the shops and checked out the restaurants. Stan went back to the boat while Gail and I went shopping. It was fun to have a companion to do this with. I missed having "girl time."

Later, we called Harold and Bessie, our friends from West Virginia whom we had met in Fort Lauderdale at the beginning of our adventure. Bessie had changed her name to Linda! They were currently living on their boat near Beaufort, docked at a friend's house, which was right on the water. It was fun to see them after six months and hear all their news. They had decided to stay put in Moorehead City for quite a while. I suspect they had pretty much run out of money. Linda was working as a waitress at a restaurant in town and they seemed quite content.

We left the next morning and went forty miles, where we anchored in Mile Hammock Bay. We had noticed a bad vibration in both shafts or props and anchored so that Stan could go overboard and check them. The props and shafts seem to be clean, so we started up again and it seemed to run okay, so we decided to go on to the Southport Marina. We thought it might have been some kelp on the props, which eventually washed off. Stan had noticed that the vibration was intermittent and seem to be mostly in narrow cuts with a lot of current. We decided to check the next day when Stan could go overboard with the air tanks.

He got up the next morning and put on the air tanks and scuba gear and went overboard. When he came back up he said everything looked okay and decided to do some basic maintenance. He changed the transmission oil and he bled both the engines to get rid of any air. Then, we went to Mass in Southport, which we enjoyed and relaxed the rest of the day.

We left the next morning and the engines seemed to be working well. There was one rumble when we got Pine Cut, where two trawlers were passing one another in different directions in that narrow cut. But that was it, and we went onto the anchorage south of Enterprise Landing. We were anchored in twenty-two feet of water behind the island and had a comfortable night.

The next day, we cruised to the anchorage at Harbor River, which was south of McClellandville. We heard only one engine rumble all day, which was reassuring as we had gone through some strong currents.

We headed for Charleston the next day, where we anchored. The day after, we waited for the slack tide that came after lunch, as we wanted to go through Elliot Cut when the water was quiet and the usual fast currents were slack. We went on to Beaufort, South Carolina and docked there. It's confusing having two Beauforts in the Carolinas, but one is in North Carolina and the other in South Carolina and one is pronounced Bo-fort and the other Bew-fort.

When we were anchored in all these coves, we would find many of the same boats each evening. It was fun to see *Tug II*, *Cerulean*, *Honey Do*, or

Blue Velvet, all of whom would usually come in a little after we did. As usual, most would come over for ice and we'd often have happy hour on one of the boats. We'd also check on each other via radio during the day.

Beaufort was a lovely small-town. Beautiful Civil War era mansions dominated the waterfront. We had dinner on *Odyssey* and lunch the next day at a restaurant in the Marina and thoroughly enjoyed our time there.

CHAPTER TEN

The next day, we were in Harbor Town at Hilton Head Island. This was a beautiful place, with many lovely stores and restaurants right at the Marina. We were docked stern in, and many people stopped to say hi while we were working on the boat. Stan decided it was a good time to completely hose down the boat and shine everything up. Soon after, we heard a knocking on the stern and discovered our old friends, the Adairs standing there. They were vacationing at Hilton Head and when walking along the docks, spotted our name on the stern! It was such a wonderful surprise and we had a great visit, including dinner with them. More of the small world mystique.

We headed for Skidaway Island the next day and pulled into the Landings Marina. Our dear friends Bob and Margaret Miles from Cincinnati were now living there and we were eager to see them. We called and they came right down to pick us up. Their daughter Beth and her husband Bobby were visiting, so we got to see them too, which was a nice bonus. They took us to their home, which was lovely, and we had a wonderful visit catching up on all the news. After dinner, we returned to the boat and planned to get together the next day.

They all came down to the boat early and we departed for the Isle of Hope so they could have an idea of what our living quarters and new life were like. It was a very pleasant day. Then, the next day we left Skidaway with Beth and Bob aboard and cruised to our very most favorite anchorage, Queen Bess Cove. It is a beautiful sheltered little cove just off the Intracoastal and many miles from any kind of a town or city. The quiet is intense and the cove is surrounded by a wooded shore where we often saw deer. With no city lights, the darkness was total black velvet. As we were having a drink before dinner up on the bridge, the dolphins came in, fishing for their dinner. We enjoyed watching their graceful antics and it was so quiet we could hear them breathing. Watching this made us hungry, so we grilled some steaks and shortly fell into bed.

We were up early at the Captain's behest and explored a little bit of nearby Bear Island. It was very pretty and looked like people had lived there at one time. We took off and wended our way into St. Simon's Golden Isles Marina around 4:30. We were delighted to see we had mail there, including a package from Barrie that contained a pair of flannel pajamas with feet. God bless Barrie, was that ever going to be nice for the cold nights! We went to the Sea Palms Club for dinner with the Bakers, Mileses, and Stowalls. It was shrimp night and all we could eat, which was a treat.

Thanksgiving Day was fun. We joined the others at the Bakers' for a scrumptious Thanksgiving dinner. We were so lucky to be there on that holiday and to share it with good friends.

Jean and Frank Baker came over the next day and we took them for a short boat ride down to Fort Frederica. It was a lovely anchorage there and we explored the Fort. The Bakers loaned us their car for a few days, as they were going to be out of town. We hurried to the grocery store to stock up, but unfortunately a tummy bug hit me and I hurried home to my bunk. We had to cancel our dinner plans with Nancy and Dave Davis, darn it.

We took a layover day to pamper my tummy. We were able to have dinner with Dave and Nancy Davis that night. That was fun, and we made plans to meet them in the Bahamas that winter. They were anxious to sail their boat *D'Artagnan* somewhere on a cruise.

We were up early, as Stan wanted Dave to help trouble shoot the engines. All seemed to be okay, so we left and cruised to Fernandina. We took the dinghy from the anchorage and saw *Cirrus Two* and visited with them and then explored the old town, which was quite historical. We had a windy, but warm night.

We fueled up at Fernandina, hating to pass up the cheaper dock, but it wouldn't open until two o'clock and we wanted to get on. The cheap dock was where the shrimp boats fueled up and had very low prices. This became a regular stop for us up and down the Intracoastal. We dropped our hook at Spanish Landings that afternoon. It was surrounded by a pretty wooded island and was full of the ever present "no-see-ums." Thank goodness for the Avon Skin-So-Soft stuff, which worked so well keeping those tiny pests from biting! It was a really quiet, calm night with no sounds at all and no signs of civilization.

We left Spanish Landings early and got to St. Augustine by ten o'clock or so and discovered they were working on the Lions Bridge. This meant we would have to wait till low tide at 1 p.m. to get under it, as well as take down our aerials and even then, we would just barely squeak through. We were lucky though, as the sailboats with their tall masts had to wait three days to get under the bridge.

We decided to lower the dinghy and go ashore exploring this fascinating city. We just had a taste of it, and it was time to go back aboard, pull up the anchor, and hurry under the bridge. We just barely made it. We pulled in to a Marineland dock around 3:30. We walked to the beach and through some shops, looking around. It was very warm out that day. I'd been wearing summer clothes for almost two weeks now and it felt really good.

We had a long day's run next day to Titusville. We saw *Cerulean* and *Misty* anchored there, but the harbor was so crowded that we decided to dock at the Titusville Marina. It was only nine dollars a night and there was a shopping center right across the road. We had hoped to see manatees in the Indian River in the passage but didn't, much to our disappointment. I baked bread, vacuumed, sewed, read, wrote letters and did exercises on the long trip.

We saw that the boat, excuse me yacht, *Third Fling* was in there and we decided that we must duck the old geezer and his poor wife. She got crushed between the cabin of her boat and the bowsprit of a sailboat that he ran into. She broke almost all her ribs and squeezed her jaw so hard that her false teeth popped out. She was such a nice person, but everybody tried to avoid docking or anchoring near them as he was a real menace. They had a forty-two-foot Grand Banks also, so we did feel some kinship there. This was his third boat, hence the name *Third Fling*.

We did visit her the next morning and she was still hurting. We had to give her credit though for not abandoning ship! Though, I'll bet that she was wondering what she was doing there "living his effing fantasy."

It was a long hot day to Vero Beach, where we anchored about four o'clock. Such a beautiful anchorage, with a lot of birds. Then, the next morning we went onto a lovely anchorage right in the middle of Palm Beach. It was a nice spot and very peaceful. *Third Fling* followed us in, but left when they saw we were anchored. Phew!

The next morning, I watched as a woman from one of the beautiful homes around the cove came out into her yard with her children and picked grapefruit, for their breakfast I imagine. It felt sort of strange to watch this domesticity on land while I was drinking my coffee on the boat. Our lives were somehow so very much apart. We ran outside that beautiful day and I even wore my bikini. I couldn't believe we were already in December!

We tried to dock at the Lauderdale public docks, but had no luck, so decided for old time's sake to go to the Archimedes Marina. It felt very strange to be back there after our first long journey. We had the boat hauled and painted and she looked beautiful. While all this was going on, I got all my Christmas shopping, decorating, Christmas cards and mailing done.

We picked up Tommy on December 15th and he was very excited to be back on the boat. We saw our friends the Altschullers several times and enjoyed swimming on their beach, as well as renewing old friendships. It was very windy and we had to wait until December 18th to leave the Marina.

We cruised to the Bahia Mar Marina and what a plush place that was! They even placed a telephone on your boat, and what a treat that was, not having to find the public pay phones! They also had a very nice beach and Tom and I enjoyed that. We ran from there the next day down to the Miamarina, another very nice spot. However, it took us all day to get there, as there were tons of bridges, and we had to wait a long time at most of them. The Marina had a beautiful view of Miami all dressed up for Christmas. It seemed really strange to see Christmas trees, wreaths and all kinds of Christmas decorations in a sunny warm climate.

CHAPTER ELEVEN

Miamarina was a very popular jumping off spot for the Bahamas and we were to use it several times during our boating years. We left at 6:45 in the morning for Cat Cay. We discovered we could get under the bridge near the Marina at low tide with our antenna down. It was a flat ass calm day! Somebody up there really liked me, as we had that gorgeous day for the crossing.

We could see our wake miles behind us as we headed across the Gulf Stream. There is an awfully lot of ocean out there and we were heading for a small island. Stan's navigation as always was great, and just about when we thought we should, we could see Cat Cay. We pulled in there around two o'clock and went through customs.

There was a gorgeous private club covering the whole island. We decided to stay overnight, despite the $26 dock fee in order to celebrate our reaching the Bahamas. The island was all private except for a small public dock for customs. We were not allowed to walk around the island, but we had our own private little beach, which was a lovely half moon of white sand and the beautiful colors of blue, aqua, and green that you see all the time in the Bahamas.

They also had very nice restroom and shower facility, and a little lounge and restaurant for us. We definitely had the feeling of riding in the back of the bus, but they were very pleasant to us. We were delighted to hear that a priest from Bimini was coming over to say Mass and that they would let us walk to the chapel. The members all had their own fancy golf carts to zip around in. We met another Grand Banks, a thirty-two-foot boat owned by Lloyd and Pat Pelley and their son, Skipper. Their boat, the *Nonesuch*, had followed us across the Gulf Stream into Cat Cay. We had been talking to them by radio as we were crossing and they turned out to be fun new friends that we traveled with quite a lot.

The two boats left Cat Cay and anchored at Gun Cay. It was a very pretty anchorage and we took our dinghy into a nice sand beach and swam and explored. We also snorkeled a little and had a lovely lazy day. We invited the *Nonesuch* crew over for drinks that evening.

The next morning, we left Gun Cay and ran to Bimini with the *Nonesuch*. There was a beautiful harbor there, and we had a hard time anchoring, but we finally succeeded. It was hot and the water looked so beautiful that we went snorkeling. There was not much to see there, except some fish, but hey, we were finally in the Bahamas and it was great!

We put the dinghy down and went ashore to explore. It was kind of a honky tonk place, but fun. We saw Hemingway's home, which looked like one would sort of expect it to. We checked out the Catholic Church, which was beautiful.

As we strolled along, we saw the usual blend of beauty and squalor along the beach shore. It seemed as if the people in the houses with the beautiful background of beach and water would just throw the garbage and rubbish out the front door! In fairness though, we had to realize that they probably had no rubbish pickup, and not too many options to get rid of it.

We went to the Anchorage Inn with the Pelleys for drinks, but didn't stay too long as Tommy wasn't feeling well.

We went ashore again the next day to do some errands. We bought bread at $1.30, which was expensive for those days, but not in the Bahamas. It really was great and a treat.

We upped anchor in the late afternoon and returned to Gun Cay, planning to jump off to Chubb Cay the next morning. It became very rough that night and we were pitching all over in the surge. We decided it was too rough to cross the Banks to get to Chubb Cay, so we decided to go back to the Cat Cay Club. It was the 24th of December, and we thought it would be a fun place to celebrate Christmas Eve and Day.

We upped anchor and thought we might as well tow the dinghy over, as we would probably want it while there. We learned a good lesson that day about pulling dinghies. We started the engines, and as it was very rough, the dinghy line was swept under the boat by a big wave and became tangled in the prop.

Stan decided to dive under the boat to check things out and see if he needed to use the scuba gear, which we always had on board. He was a certified deep water diver and had been scuba diving for quite a few years. I was concerned because it was so rough and we were so close to shore, but Stan said not to worry because the wind was blowing us off shore. My other worry was that he would be under the boat and the waves would whack the boat down on his head, but he was too smart for that. He jumped off the back platform and dove under the boat. Before he went under, he grabbed hold of the platform and then quickly transferred his hold to the shaft of the boat underwater. This way when the boat went up he went up and when the boat went down he went down and it didn't hit him in the process.

He discovered that the line had only wrapped around the prop twice. He came up for air and then dove down again and freed it. I was really relieved to see him come back up and aboard. Then, we quickly pulled the dinghy in and cranked it up into its place on top of the aft cabin. From there on in, we were very wary of towing the dinghy until we learned what kind of line to use (nylon which floats) and how much to use. I have to admit that I was very frightened, alone in the boat while he was underneath in rough water. No one was in the vicinity and if Stan hadn't come up, I would have had a lot of quick decisions to make!

We soon pulled into Cat Cay, docked, and had a wonderful day. We were permitted to walk around the island to go to church. We enjoyed the walk, as we got to see some of the exclusive colony. They even had a nine-hole golf course! We were intrigued by the way they used conch shells as markers on the tee boxes.

The chapel was a lovely small building about the size of a nine by twelve room. It was beautifully decorated for Christmas with poinsettias and greens. The crèche looked like it was Belleek, undoubtedly from someone's home, as was the small organ. The altar boys were in scarlet vestments and the whole effect was gorgeous. I figured it would be hot so we sat next to one of the deeply shuttered windows. As I sat there, I spotted a lizard right next to my elbow! I gave him my best gimlet eyed "you stay in your territory and I'll stay in mine" look and he ducked back into the shadows. While we waited for the priest, who was coming by boat to say Mass and was delayed by the bad weather, we listened to the black choir leader play cocktail lounge-type music which the priest later complained about. He had a great voice. He also passed out song sheets and we sang Christmas carols—every verse! Father finally got there, but was kind of cranky as he was seasick from the very rough ride. Some of the Keatings from Cincinnati, who had a home on the Cay, did readings and it was fun to chat with them for a minute after Mass. It was a great experience and we were grateful to the Cat Cay Club for permitting us to come onto the forbidden ground to go to church.

We put the Christmas turkey into the oven to bake while we swam at the beautiful white beach and in that gorgeous Bahamian water. Tommy practiced his long jump for the Special Olympics on the beach while we swam. He figured he'd have a good head start for the state finals in May.

We spent the rest of the afternoon decorating the boat for Christmas. We put up our little tree with the tiny ornaments that I had been collecting as we traveled. Our daughter-in-law Cindy had crocheted red and green wreaths and we put them on the port and starboard doors—red for port, and green for starboard, as every boater knows—and we felt quite elegant, and certainly ready for the holidays. We were having our Christmas dinner that evening because we thought we would be heading for Chubb Cay the next morning.

I had bought a turkey in Lauderdale and put it in the freezer. We had the works—cranberry sauce, dressing, and all. I'm happy to say the oven worked and did a great job cooking the turkey and we all enjoyed our special Christmas Eve dinner. Our table looked so pretty with Barrie and Terry's Christmas arrangement, which was a fat red candle surrounded by holly. It had come just before we left the States.

We thought of the family so far away in Cleveland's ice and snow as we sat there in swimsuits to eat our dinner. We opened our presents that night while playing the Christmas tapes that Chip and Cindy had sent. We discovered that the tiny candy canes I had bought for the tree were a big mistake in the tropics. They looked great until they started to melt and dripped sticky goo all over. We had the candy-stuffed stockings that Barbie had sent on the doors until they too started to melt. A new lesson we were learning about the climate there.

We were amazed at the creativity and thoughtfulness of the family in their choice of gifts. All were things we really needed/wanted for our adventure. It meant a lot to us when we were so far away and we felt their warm and loving presence!

The next morning, it was still too rough to cross the Banks (but eighty degrees!), so we had Christmas Day on Cat Cay. We radioed the *Nonesuch* at Gun Cay, who, after having a miserable night, were only too happy to come join us for Mass and brunch. Some other Catholics who heard our radio transmission came over too and were delighted to be able to go to Mass on Christmas Day. We all trekked over to the chapel and again waited for Father's boat. His ride was better that morning, so he was in a very good mood. We sang Christmas carols led by the man with the gorgeous voice and again we sang every verse there was. We enjoyed it to the fullest!

Our Christmas brunch was very festive and we all enjoyed it. All of us were spending our first Christmas on board our boats and I think it helped us to be with friends. We discussed plans about leaving together in the morning and then everyone dinghied back to their boats.

Tommy and I spent the afternoon on the beach, while Stan worked on something or the other in the engine room. We discovered that the huge Burger next to us was owned by the people who had given the island the chapel. Later in the day, the power on the island went on the fritz, probably from too many people trying to cook turkeys at once, and we felt very fortunate to be able to switch on the generator and have power. The shore people were all in the dark. Of course, this meant we couldn't make our phone calls from the office either, so we were not too happy about that aspect of it. However, we did have a very nice day and we went to bed happy.

The next morning we joined *Nonesuch* and made the run to Chubb Cay. It was their first time too, and they were a little nervous, as were we, because the markers were as far as thirty-five miles apart and easy to miss because of the tidal drift. On top of that, those tiny little Cays were mere specks in the ocean and easy to lose! The sky looked really ominous, but nothing developed, thank goodness and we hit all the markers right on the button!

Stan really was a super navigator and had good backup with radar and LORAN. The water was flat calm and looked shallow all across the Banks, which made us nervous at first, until we realized that the water was deeper than it looked.

The water looked like aqua Jell-O and we could see lots of starfish on the white sand bottom. We also saw lots of flying fish, which I loved. They looked like blue oversized sparrows and we couldn't believe they were fish as we watched them skim the waters like birds.

We came into the anchorage at Chubb Key about 4:30 in the afternoon. It was fairly calm there and we thought the island looked pretty. The next day, we laid at anchor and saw many of our friends come in there. *Fayaway*, *Bounty*, *Tioga*, *Harmony in Four*, and *Cicada* were some of those boats. It was the usual old home week greeting friends. We dinghied into the Chubb Cay Club and bought butter at their commissary for $2.50 a half pound. Wow! We had dinner there, which was a treat. I had cracked conch and Tommy had the grouper. I can't remember Stan's choice. It was probably beef!

That night, bad winds and a storm came up and Stan was up all night on watch. I bounced up and down out of bed as I decided it was less scary to get up and see what was going on than to lie in bed and worry. All told it was a miserable night. It was still blowing the next morning, and everyone was tossing around. There was a bad surge in the anchorage.

Stan and Tommy took the dinghy into the Club to buy some flour for me. By the time they got back, a bad storm in was coming and I got panicky because the guide said this anchorage was untenable in south to southwest winds and it had definitely changed to that. We decided to go into the Chubb Cay Marina and get a dock. We had quite a time getting the anchors up in a rough sea. As we were entering the harbor, we noticed the harbor master up on the cliffs above us counting the number of boats in the anchorage to see how many slips he would need.

We just made it into the dock when the storm hit and as we tied up all hell broke loose. The other boats from the anchorage all came barreling in except the blue catamaran from Canada. They had an awful time because of the wind, which was gusting up to fifty-five knots. Pat Pelley was in hysterics by the time *Nonesuch* had tied up!

"See," said Stan, "You're not the most nervous one around. Pat started crying a lot sooner than you would have." After she had time to calm down, we went over there for our delayed cocktail party, which had been planned in the anchorage. What heaven it was to be tied up in a nice place in that awful weather!

It blew horribly all that night, but we were well tendered up and we slept well. It was a lovely place, with a pool for the yachties, plus a gorgeous two mile stretch of almost deserted white beach. There had a pretty decent commissary, but there was no lettuce to be had. I had my alfalfa sprouts jar going full force. They also had a nice, but expensive restaurant. Tommy and I swam and walked the beach while Stan varnished teak. I baked hamburger buns, as I still had some ground beef in the freezer. One of our neighbors brought over some whelk chowder that they had made from some whelks they had collected on the point, and it was great with hot fresh bread from our oven. Skip Pelley, the fifteen-year-old boy from the *Nonesuch*, was going conch hunting that day and I traded him some hamburger for some conch. I planned to make some conch burgers for dinner that night.

CHAPTER TWELVE

Little did we know that it was going to be almost two weeks before the weather would be decent enough to run to Nassau! We had gale force winds for almost the whole time and no one could safely get out of there.

The Bahamians were a riot. They tell you what they think you want to hear, regardless of whether it is accurate or not. They would say things like "We will have bread tomorrow," or "The weather will be nice tomorrow." Tomorrow never seemed to come or maybe it did eventually, but no matter.

Meanwhile, I was beginning to feel like a pioneer as I made do. It really was kind of fun once we resigned ourselves to the fact that we were stuck. I felt really sorry for Tommy though, as he had really wanted to see Nassau and go island hopping.

The place was full of other stranded boats, and they had us docked kind of Mediterranean style, which means stern to the dock instead of alongside the dock, so we were all only about a foot apart and there was not much privacy, but great camaraderie. We supplied everyone with ice for the cocktail hour, and they showed us how to get and clean conch (yuck!), and someone else brought us fresh coconut.

A bartering system was going full force, especially as the days went by and everybody was running out of things. I traded two pieces of chocolate marble cheesecake for a package of dried milk, which I had run out of. The commissary had mostly cocktail things and a few of the basic necessities. I imagine that under normal circumstances, they didn't sell much because their prices were so high. Butter was $2.50 for a half pound, eggs were $2 a dozen, flour was $1 a pound, bread $1.30. They never had lettuce and Crisco was $5 a can.

We found the best beaches and some gorgeous shells, and the manager's wife told Stan where to go for some really rare ones, so we did that at low tide. Tommy and I spent a lot of time on the beach, as we both loved to look for shells and most afternoons found us doing this.

One afternoon, one of the women told me that she liked to collect tiny shells because the rare ones were very hard to find full size and the little ones were perfect, not having been battered around so much. It made sense and I did discover that I could find lots of shells I hadn't been able to find in the regular size. I could keep those in an empty spice bottle and they didn't take up any room at all, whereas regular shells had a way of accumulating quickly and took up a lot of room.

There was an enormous ninety-seven-foot yacht on our right called the *Misty Blue*, with a crew of a captain and a cook. Stan talked to them, and they invited us over for a drink and it turned out that the captain's wife was from Lakewood, a suburb of Cleveland! They gave us a tour and if you can imagine a boat decorated to the nth degree, you've got the *Misty Blue*. This was the kind of boat you read about, an ocean going boat that was plush. This was a YACHT! The master bedroom was huge and even had two bathrooms, his and hers!

We sort of got the needle from the other boats, who were all very curious to hear what the yacht was like. Stan and I thought they were lonesome because no one was talking to them, figuring that they were snobbish. They weren't at all, and we enjoyed visiting with them. We saw them looking out their windows wistfully at the rest of us visiting back and forth and having fun, so we invited them over for a drink aboard *Steelaway* and they seemed to have a good time. You could have put our whole boat in their main salon, but they raved about ours. Nice people.

Our days began to be routine. Every morning, we got up, looked at the weather and listened to the weather report on the radio and groaned, "Oh Lord, another day in this wind." About day seven, some of the sailors felt really desperate and decided to try and make a run for it. They soon came limping back in, with damage to sails and various other parts of their boats, because it was still vicious out there. We may have been stranded in paradise, but the boredom was getting to us. Most people would probably have loved to have spent two weeks in that gorgeous place on vacation, but we were all into cruising!

At any rate each day I did boat chores, baked bread, beached it with Tommy, and tried to think of something creative for dinner. I also did laundry with a lot of the other boat wives and that was an experience! Only one of the two washers worked and the working one didn't fill, so you filled it with your pail. Then, the dryers only worked for about ten minutes so we hung our laundry over the nearby trees and bushes. We tried hanging it on the boat but the captains objected to looking like a "Chinese laundry." Quickly, the laundry became like the village well. All the boat wives would gather there and talk about our adventures, what we were going to do, and wonder if we were ever going to get out of there. The story of "what am I doing here, living his effing fantasy" had all the women laughing hysterically. The first mate from the *Myann* impressed us all, as she and her husband were going to sail around the world. I imagine that they probably did so, as we would frequently see little stories about them in the *Cruising* magazine. I always felt happy to read about them.

The time was getting close to when Tommy needed to fly out of Nassau. There was a flight once a week out of Chubb Cay to Nassau. We were able to book two seats on that flight and Stan was planning to go with him to put him on the plane for Miami, where our friend Virginia Altshuller was to meet him and transfer him to the plane back to school. She was such a dear friend and we appreciated her doing this several times for Tom.

Meanwhile, before he left we celebrated New Year's Eve. Tom had decorated the boat with things at hand. He used pretty shells and plants to make all kinds of decorations for our party. The Pelleys came over for a pot luck supper and we had a very pleasant evening. I attempted to stay awake with Tommy until midnight. We made it, but I dozed off several times before the witching hour. Boaters seem to turn in pretty early normally, so Tommy appreciated my efforts. Tommy had spent quite a bit of time putting paper into confetti and at midnight we had a glass of ginger ale and tossed paper all over the place. I kept finding little bits of Tommy's confetti for a long time afterwards.

The next day it was still blowing to beat the band. A new nor'easter had blown in and we were still stuck there. New boats came in all over the place, fleeing the storm and the place was really jumping then. A very nice couple in the sailboat *Zorka* squeezed in next to us.

Dave and Zora Akins, who were both working artists, were living aboard and painting as they went. Their work was displayed in galleries in both Annapolis and Hilton Head. Many of the boats around us seemed to have no visible means of support, and even though they lived on conch, I wondered sometimes how they managed. There were quite a few children living on the boats, all going to school via correspondence course.

Tommy's last day, we woke up to a chill sixty-nine degrees and the wind was howling as usual. We called Barbie and it was so good to talk to her. We socialized a good deal that day. Tom and I discovered the beach was warm and placid, so we spent several hours there that afternoon. We went aboard the *Misty Blue* for cocktails with Sam and Margot Finney. What a huge luxurious yacht that was!

It was still blowing the next morning, in fact gale force winds, what else! Stan and Tom left on the plane at 8:30 for Nassau. I did some laundry and hung it on the trees and tried to clean house, but had visitors all day! Tommy got on his plane to Miami okay, but Stan had to charter a plane with three others to get back. Bahamas Air had sold him a return ticket, but didn't reserve him a seat, not an uncommon thing we heard! Luckily, the wife of the manager of the club was also supposed to be on that flight and she knew that this frequently happened and what to do. The next scheduled flight back to Chubb was Tuesday of the next week! She, Stan, and two other people chartered a plane to fly them home. It turned out to be cheaper to do that than pay the Bahamas Air ticket!

Stan had called to let me know what was going on and since there was a time gap, offered to bring home some groceries. Boy was he popular when he got off that plane with two heads of lettuce and assorted goodies! The Finneys from *Misty Blue* came over for cocktails and the other people from the plane came over around eight. Lots of activity that day and I had trouble keeping my eyes open that evening.

Since the next day it was still blowing gale force winds, Stan and I spent some time on the gorgeous beach, which was sheltered and found a lot of pretty shells. I particularly liked the sunrise tellins, which were a form of clams and came in many beautiful pastel colors. It was getting very chummy in there with all the stranded boats. Visiting was about the only thing to do and we did have a lot in common, if only because we all wanted to get the heck out of there!

It was still blowing the next day, what else? As usual, I beached it while Stan varnished. Skip Pelley gave us some conch and Stan cleaned it and we had Cracked Conch for dinner, which was great. Skip also got four huge lobsters and Stan is determined to get a spear and go lobster hunting. I certainly encouraged that!

As usual, it was blowing hard the next morning and everyone's spirits were very low. This was a beautiful place, but we wanted to get out of there. We were all running out of food and the commissary was terribly expensive and we were tired of trying to live off the land and sea. Most of us didn't have anything much left to barter with, so we decided to have a "weathered in" party.

Midnight Special, Myann, Nonesuch, and *Windsmith* all came on our boat for drinks and a pot luck supper. Everyone brought some kind of dish that they could make with what little stuff they had left. It was lots of fun and we hoped it would change our luck. There were some interesting dishes!

The wind actually died down the next morning and everyone dashed around like mad, getting ready for a grand exodus to Nassau. *Myann, Nonesuch, Midnight Express, Windsmith, Great Dane, Chelique,* and *Cicada* all exited the harbor in parade. The seas were not too bad, but there was that awful rolling motion and I got seasick. So did everyone on *Nonesuch.* As we came into the Nassau harbor, I got on the radio to call the harbor master, as we were supposed to do to get permission to enter the harbor. His answer was somewhat garbled. The dark radio was on the fritz again, but I could make out that it was okay to come in. As we came down the harbor, we passed a sailboat with a first mate naked from the waist up at the helm of the boat. "Wow," said Stan, "we are in the tropics!"

CHAPTER THIRTEEN

We planned on staying at a dock in the Nassau Harbor Yacht Club and pulled in there around 12:30. It was a very nice marina with a very friendly dock master. We had lunch and went out to explore a little. We found a fabulous supermarket, hallelujah, and wonderful fruit stands everywhere. We ordered a lot of liquor as we surely had gone through it fast at Chubb Cay. As I imagine you might surmise, the liveaboards are mostly a pretty hard drinking crew. Every so often some of us decided to "rest our liver," as Alice Farinacci from *Andiama* said and skipped the happy hours for a few days.

The next day dawned sunny but windy. Again. I baked while Stan varnished. People on land cut grass, people on boats varnish! I decided to explore this neat place and walked into the center of town. I checked out the old cemetery and old church and felt the history there.

Nassau is an old town and capital of the Bahamas. Many of the white families came over after the revolutionary war and brought their black slaves with them. For the most part, they were Tories, thus loyal British subjects who were more comfortable there. All along the waterfront they built lovely homes in a tropical style. The British were a strong presence there until after World War II and the Governor's home is very imposing. People there still talk about the Duchess of Windsor's lavish decorating while they were there during the war and the Duke was the Governor. Now the Bahamas are no longer a British Crown colony and have their own government. As a member of the Commonwealth, they elect their Prime Minister but still have a Governor. There is a very British feel in Nassau.

We really liked Nassau. Everyone had said we'd hate it because it was too touristy, but we found it to be very picturesque and pretty and the people friendly. It still looked very British in spite of its Commonwealth status. We had a cab driver take us on a tour around the island, which was fascinating. They had a bunch of old forts and an awfully interesting old monastery, which had sort of primitive paintings all over the walls. It was a missionary base to most of the out islands and there was a seminary there.

The driver also took us on a drive through the different residential districts from the enormous old estates to the middle class attractive homes, which had the loveliest yards with huge flowering shrubs, to the awful Foxhill district, which used to be the old slave quarters where people were still living in the remnants of the old buildings. It was a truly dreadful slum and the center of the crime rate, which was certainly understandable.

The Supreme Court session was opening that day and the town was full of colorfully uniformed policemen who had British Guardsmen-like uniforms in bright colors that must have been dreadfully hot! I loved the policewomen who were directing traffic. They must have picked them for their looks, as they were all so pretty. They were all tiny, with teeny little waists and they stood in the middle of the street in their spiffy uniforms and white helmets and gloves directing traffic (there were very few traffic lights in Nassau). They would smile and gently wave their hands and never say a word.

The straw market was very colorful and lots of fun. I found out later that you're really supposed to bargain there, which is something I don't much like to do. The waterfront also had fruit vendors and you could buy what looked like a whole tree full of bananas for a dollar. I found it hard to resist such a bargain, but I had visions of one hundred bananas ripening at once and no one but me to eat them! Also, they were so heavy that I would have had to take a cab back to the marina for two dollars, which sort of negated the bargain. I loved to walk along the market place and try some new fruits and vegetables that I had never heard of before. I did buy an enormous avocado, which was divine. I kept meeting many of our buddies from Chubb and it was fun trading our experiences with Nassau with theirs. Crew from the *Fayaway* and *Cicada* came along, each carrying a huge hand of bananas. We also would meet many of our friends for drinks or dinner and there was a pretty lively social life.

One night I heard sirens and got up and discovered there was a bad fire at one of the beautiful old homes on the waterfront that was awfully close to our dock. There weren't any fire hydrants in Nassau, so the firemen were fighting the fire with water tank trucks. They finally got it under control, but then ran out of the water and it took over a half-hour for another truck to come, by which time the wind was blowing hard enough that the fire really got going again. It was kind of scary, but they finally put it out. The next morning we noticed the house had burned to the ground.

The same wind was keeping us all in Nassau. I decided the time had come to catch up on the laundry, so I checked out the facility in the marina. The only problem was that there was a garbage dump right in front of the laundry room door! I realized that the waiters we had seen in the dining room who were throwing garbage right out of one window were throwing it right in front of the laundry room! Stan came to my rescue and shoveled a path right through the garbage to the door. It looked pretty bad, but at least I didn't have to walk through the garbage. However, a big rat suddenly ran out, almost over my foot! I did do my laundry, but the rest of the time when I went there, I was very careful to look up before I ventured in so I wouldn't have garbage land on my head! I tell you, when you live on a boat, laundry is an adventure.

By January 12th, we were pretty organized and just waiting for the wind to die down enough to go. I had stocked up the larder and done all the laundry. Since it was Sunday, we went into the cathedral downtown and that was a wonderful experience. The music was lilting in a very Bahamian calypso way. We came home and I swam in the pool and wrote letters and chatted with Betty and Larry Smith from *Windsmith* and George Tout from *Midnight Express*. That night, the whole gang met at our favorite restaurant in town to celebrate our being able to go the next morning.

CHAPTER FOURTEEN

We left early the next morning for Spanish Wells. There was a mass exodus of the gang when the wind finally died. Most of our friends were going to the Exumas and we all planned to meet somewhere later. It was a nice crossing and not too rough. We passed *Midnight Special* en route. As we passed the Royal Island anchorage, it looked very nice and we thought we should stop there one day. We had out the book and were reading the directions as we came into Spanish Wells, but it was a very tricky entrance and we went aground once. We finally gave up on the directions of the book and navigated by the water color, which we should have done in the first place.

We went down what looked like a river, with the Cay going up one side and down the other, but it was an anchorage. Spanish Wells was a darling little village with rainbow bright houses. And clean! We didn't often see that kind of clean in the Bahamas. We anchored opposite the village and walked ashore a little and it was so pretty. There was a great beach on the north side that we were looking forward to exploring. We wanted to go and explore Russell, which was on the other side, across from the village. It was uninhabited except for a lot of goats and the meanest old boar I had ever seen. I was going to go ashore and explore till he came charging down, making angry pig noises, not at me, but at a goat. Three black goats came along that looked just like the three billy goats gruff even to the funny little beards and horns. I kept expecting them to go "trip trop, trip trop!"

In Spanish Wells, men all wore the famous wide brimmed hats, which looked great, but I didn't quite know how they kept them on their heads as they came zooming by in their boats! The town is a fishing village and also raises fruits and vegetables for the Nassau markets. It was obviously prosperous and clean, which was rare in the Bahamas in those days where everyone seemed to just throw garbage and rubbish everywhere. Their grocery store was well stocked and the prices the lowest we'd encountered anywhere, which was surprising as they were surely much farther out than Bimini, Cat or Chubb Cay. The homegrown tomatoes were so good and we bought a lot of those, as well as other fresh veggies that we hadn't been able to get in other places. I loved to watch the farmers zooming by in their boats with fresh produce and their boats piled high with green bananas.

We walked around Spanish Wells a lot, and had fun exploring it. It was a great place to get mail and to use the telephone as we could do both at the post office. One day, we took a picnic in the dinghy and went around to the other side of the Cay where there was a beautiful beach. We walked to the beach, swam and shelled and didn't see another soul! It was a wonderful.

They had grass there, which if they could have exported and grown in other climes, would have made them a fortune! We admired the lawns, which looked like golf greens and the people told us they just planted it and it grew to the perfect length and stopped. One man told us he hadn't cut grass in ten years!

Stan did some varnishing while we were there and I walked around and talked to people and explored. *Midnight Special* came in and we visited with George for a while. Now there was an odd situation. We met his wife while at Chubb Cay. She had come down for two weeks and then flew back to her job in Canada. They were a young couple in their early thirties and he had a bad case of wanderlust. He bought the boat and was cruising around the Caribbean while she stayed home and worked (and supported him?). She flew down when she could get some vacation every three months or so. She seemed content with the arrangement, so I guess it was the old "different strokes for different folks!" Or maybe she just didn't want to live his fantasy.

We had beautiful weather while in Spanish Wells and I enjoyed our time there. I sewed two pairs of shorts while Stan varnished. I made most of my clothes while on the boat and it was something I enjoyed doing. We lived in bathing suits and casual clothes, so it wasn't too hard to keep my wardrobe up in style. Stan did some varnishing and I did a lot of walking, and I swam and went snorkeling, but the water was icy! I also practiced running the dinghy by myself, which was a good idea as its balky engine was pretty temperamental and I have to admit I swore at it a lot. We even had hamburgers one night by candlelight, very romantic. I loved Spanish Wells!

The last two days had been pretty windy, but it finally stopped blowing enough for us to head to Hatchet Bay on Eleuthera Island. We had the Bahamas Cruising Guide out as we approached the Cay looking for the entrance to the anchorage. The guide described almost every anchorage the same way, "surrounded by casuarinas on the hills around the harbor." Casuarinas are a type of shrub or tree. Well every darned harbor looked like that! But we found the entrance and made our way in. It was a hurricane hole and the entrance had been blasted out. It was very narrow, but deep and this was why it was so hard to see from out on the ocean. The book also compared it to the Scottish Highlands, which I had never seen, so that wasn't much help. I can only say I suppose it did, but does Scotland have tropical vegetation and fruit? It was an enormous bay, a lake really I guess. There was no civilization that could be seen except on one end where we could catch glimpses of Alice Town.

We saw the native settlement and the government docks, where the little inter-island freighters came in and out, loading the fruits, veggies and dairy products that they raised there. Their little pineapples were heavenly, tree ripened like those in Hawaii and so sweet. And they were just the right size for the two of us, or really just me, as Stan could take it or leave it, mostly the latter. We picked up a mooring for two dollars a night and tied up. This was really nice, as our anchor never slipped because it was a hurricane hole. It offered good hurricane protection because of the tiny entrance and the hills surrounding the bay. We also could get water there for two cents a gallon at the marina run by the genial Harold Albury, who was mentioned in the cruising guide as being an extremely helpful person, which we found to be true.

I walked about three quarters of a mile to the government produce exchange and could buy whatever they had that day. Then I usually walked through Alice Town to the post office or to the baking lady's house for bread. It was a little break from baking it myself. Lettuce was hard to come by, and I missed it. Spanish Wells had it, but here where they grew it, I couldn't find it! It's the one thing I really craved, so I needed to get my alfalfa sprout jar going again.

They also raised chickens there in a big way, as we discovered when we tried to find the beach on the other side of the island one day. We walked and walked and kept walking in the direction we had been told to go, and kept passing huge smelly chicken barns and some goats. One of the goats had its head stuck in the fence, so Stan did his good deed for the day and helped him get loose.

Finally, we came to a path that seemed to be in the right direction and found that it did lead to the beach, but also to the shark pit where they dump all the chicken guts. They spilled a lot en route, and we almost turned back several times as we walked through tons of chicken feathers, innards and enough feet to support a large voodoo ritual! There were also clouds of flies and a horrible smell, but by that time we had walked about two miles and hated for it to be in vain, especially as Stan hated to walk and I could seldom get him to go very far with me. Finally, we found the beach and it was very impressive with huge ten foot tall breakers pounding on the beach.

We walked to the shark pit, which was really a blow hole in the very rocky cliffs. Anything they threw in there was quickly washed out to sea and it was an awesome sight to see the huge waves pile in there and throw spray hundreds of feet into the air. However, I decided I really didn't want to swim there, as there were a lot of sharks, although they were certainly well fed with the chicken guts!

By this time, we had walked about another mile down the beach and were getting tired, so we tried to find a shortcut through the bush back to the road. It looked like we were in the middle of an impenetrable wilderness but old Boy Scout Stan said, "Never fear, just follow me." I was just about to rebel, as it looked like we were really lost, and I had visions of wandering in the wilderness for days, when he gave a triumphant shout and we were on a path that eventually led to back to that terrible chicken road. Eventually, we hitched a ride on a truck and got back home.

There were seven boats anchored in the bay and again it was blowing like crazy. The *Capricio* next to us had a young couple from Switzerland with a two-year-old aboard. They were very nice and such interesting people. Roger had a ham radio aboard and tried to get through to Cleveland for us to wish Chip and Cindy a happy anniversary. We didn't have any luck, but he said he would try later.

When they were anchored at Current Cut, a bad storm came up and Roger lost the tip of one of his fingers when he got it caught between a cleat and the anchor line. His wife Dita tried to stop the bleeding and went through two dozen diapers with no success. She put a tourniquet on it and went for help. Luckily, they were near the Current Club and the manager called for a plane, which flew him into Nassau. They were very lucky, as he almost bled to death. Meanwhile, Dita who had stayed behind with the boat and the baby, brought the boat to Hatchet Bay by herself with a boy from Current Cut to help her with the sails. She was a very gutsy lady!

Roger was in the hospital for a week and she was unable to get any news of him, which was pretty scary. Then he was able to call her, tell her he was all right, and fly back to Hatchet Bay. They had to stay in Hatchet Bay for a whole month so the local nurse could change the dressing on his hand every day.

Roger had taken two or three years out of his career to cruise as far south from Switzerland as they could get in that time. They had hoped to be in Haiti by this time. Dita had to fly to Nassau to get funds released from their Florida bank, as they had spent days of expensive phone calls and cables and got nowhere. They finally decided that it was simpler to simply go to Nassau.

I offered to help baby sit their daughter Monique while she was gone. They only spoke German to her, as they wanted that to be her first language, but her English was a little better than my German, which is practically nil. She'd look up at me with those big brown eyes and rattle off a request in German and I'd think, "Oh Lord, does she want a drink? A cookie? To go to the bathroom?" Not getting the response that she wanted from me, she would pleadingly say, "bitte, bitte!" Which I knew meant please in German. So I winged it and we got along quite well, although I'm sure she thought I was a pretty weird lady, taking her to the bathroom when she wanted a cookie.

Roger told me he had bought Dita a three dollar washing machine, and I told him I didn't think I even wanted to know what it was. He told me anyway, and said it was a plumber's helper that she plunged up and down in her tin tub on the deck. I decided I was going to get one too, as I'd been doing my laundry in the bathtub. I hadn't seen a laundromat since Nassau and that one was a joke!

One day when I was walking to the produce exchange, I saw a little old lady walking along with a crate of tomatoes on her head over a floppy white lace hat. I stopped to talk to her, and she told me that she walked two miles to the exchange with her stuff on her head all the time. She also said she felt rather poorly, and that the nurse had said she had tired blood. I forbore saying that if I were seventy and had to walk two miles with a crate of tomatoes on my head, I'd feel poorly too! When we went to church one Sunday, there we saw a woman all dressed up in her Sunday best carrying a big box of hymnals or something on her head. I wondered if your head would get flat after a while.

We were pleased to find that there was a little mission church there at

Alice Town, as we had never been in a native church before. They just had one Mass, when the priest could get there and a catechist conducted services when Father couldn't be there. We dinghied into the dock in the rain Sunday in our foul weather gear and walked into Alice Town, which had maybe fifty houses in it.

The church was small compared to the Baptist one. They welcomed us warmly and invited us to "rest our wraps." The altar was a table heaped high with scarlet hibiscus, which matched the six altar boys in red robes. The singing was fantastic! The idea was to sing as loudly as you could, never mind what key it was. At the Amen, they swung into the good old Sydney Poitier Baptist version, with a lot of hallelujahs and hand clapping. It was great! We didn't know all the tunes, but you could just sing along anyway and it didn't make any difference in the general effect. When Father gave the homily, the old man across the aisle, who was so crippled with arthritis that he could hardly move, kept saying, "Yes, yes!" with great fervor. Others were nodding their heads in agreement too, which I thought was quite polite, as the subject was the Church Unity Octave, which has to be one of the duller topics around. All told, it was a lovely experience and their faith was a wonderful thing to see.

We had quite nice weather while we were in Hatchet Bay and Stan got quite a bit of varnishing done. He liked to do it in places like Hatchet Bay, where we could be anchored away from the dust you find on land or in the marinas. *Steelaway* had a lot of teak everywhere, even the decks were teak. If Stan always seems to be varnishing in my stories, it is because we never seemed to be able to keep ahead of it. The teak was beautiful and I guess it was a good thing that he liked to varnish.

I got quite a lot of writing done in Hatchet Bay and trekked my letters to the post office, but often felt as if I were casting them off in a bottle because the mail there only went out when the inter-island ferries came in. They were supposed to pick up once a week, but if it was a holiday or bad weather or engine problems, it could be a whole month. They still hadn't processed all their Christmas mail at the post office. We hadn't had any mail for six weeks, and I was really anxious to have a mail pick up somewhere soon. We planned to go back to Spanish Wells around January 31st to pick up our friends from Cincinnati, the Crossetts and the Temples, and were looking forward to our mail that Barbie had sent to them, which they were going to bring down. When we were cruising, as we were doing that winter in the Bahamas, our mail drops were few and far between and I missed contact with the family.

We were there for about two weeks in all and we got into kind of a routine. Stan had finished the varnishing and was working on painting the rest of the boat. I decided to do a lot of practicing runs in the dinghy to shore, as I was pretty intimidated by it. Our engine was cranky and very hard to start, but I really needed to get to shore and do my daily chores. I actually got pretty good at running that darn engine and safely got to shore and back. The dinghy was heavy and I didn't want to have to row back. I was so afraid that I would miss the dock that I would head for it full speed and sort of crash. But that worked!

I tied up the boat and grabbed my canvas bags and started out on my daily shopping. Tommy's correspondent at Stewart Home School, Shirley, said we reminded her of the hobbits. I did feel like one when I took my walk into Alice Town and a huge sow would leap out of the bushes at me. I debated whether or not to scream if she attacked me, or run, or hit her over the head with my canvas bag, which usually had at least two pineapples and a sack of flour in it. We'd just eye each other and warily go our respective ways, but I did wish I had Bilbo Baggins' sword Sting! Everyone let their animals roam there and I suppose you could recognize your own pig or goat maybe, but the chickens? Maybe they had more personality than I thought!

When I made my daily trek for lettuce one day, they finally had some at the produce exchange and I asked for two heads. The man emerged from the back room with what can only be described as two enormous shrubs! You could landscape your yard with them! I gulped and said, "I guess I'd better just take one, that's all that will fit in my refrigerator." So I walked back with this big tree sticking up above my head out of my canvas bag like a pharaoh's fan, wondering what on earth I was going to do with all that lettuce! The whole darn fridge was full of that lettuce, which tasted like turnips and Stan wouldn't touch it. I thought I might have to contribute it to the sharks, but one of the boats anchored nearby was thrilled to have it.

Stan and I would take the dinghy and go ashore to the restaurant bar in the marina and have drinks with friends from the other boats. We picked up a lot of information on other good beaches, places to see and so on, and watched the beautiful sunsets. The night before we were to leave for Spanish Wells again, we filled up with water. It was very good water there, so much better than that at Nassau or Chubb Cay. Most of the water was pretty brackish and tasted terrible. We had a few hot showers while we were there, but we mostly conserved water and jumped off the swim platform with soap and shampoo and then took a quick fresh water rinse with a hose when we came back aboard. I had a salt water pump in the kitchen and used that to wash dishes, and then gave them a quick rinse with freshwater. We saved quite a bit of water with these two systems. You did want to rinse salt water off your body, because if you didn't, you felt very sticky.

On January 31st, we left at 7:30 a.m. It looked like a beautiful day, and the weather report sounded great, but unfortunately that wasn't so. We had big swells, waves and a beam sea. A beam sea is when the waves are perpendicular to the boat, and hit you from the side. I was scared and sea sick. I lay down in my bunk till Current Cut, and boy was that wild! The wind, which was fierce, and the current were both against us trying to get through the cut. We didn't think we were going to make it, but we did, very slowly, and it felt like the boat was standing still a lot of the time. We happily pulled into Sawyers Marina at Spanish Wells about 1:30.

CHAPTER FIFTEEN

We enjoyed staying at the dock for a change and got some errands done in town. We also used their phone to call home and check-in with the kids. I did some laundry in their laundromat, which was a joy because it was the first one I had encountered in the Bahamas that actually worked!

We anchored out again the next day and I changed all the beds, putting on my nice clean sheets to get ready for our guests. We put the Temples in the forward cabin and the Crossets in our cabin. Stan and I slept on the dining room table, which made up into a pretty good-sized bed. It went down on a level with the sofa and all the cushions made up a bed. It was kind of a nuisance to make it up every night and take it down in the morning, but we were so happy to have guests that we would have done anything.

While we were anchored there, we also saw Pam and Ray from the *Pursuit*, who had been looking all over Spanish Wells for a hot shower. Pam was a hairdresser, so we traded two hot showers for a haircut for Stan, and all parties were most happy with the swap!

Dick and Jodelle Crosset and Dave and Joyce Temple arrived by water taxi the next afternoon. They had flown into Eleuthera and had taken Ivan "Churchill" Curry's water taxi, which brought them right to our boat. They were laughing about the trip, as the water had been pretty rough and they were really tossed around. Joyce said the cocktail crackers that they had brought down so carefully on the plane were probably crumbs by the time they got there. We got everyone settled and went up on the bridge with drinks and laughed and caught up with all the news. It was so great to see these good friends again and we had a wonderful time.

We couldn't believe our good luck with the weather. It had to have been the best weather we had all winter. Our friends wanted to fish and snorkel the most, so we set out the next morning for Egg Island and the guys started fishing right away. They didn't have any luck and I said there'd be hamburger for dinner that night.

We snorkeled over a good reef, swam, and explored a little. We took Bloody Marys and a picnic lunch ashore and had a lovely day before we headed for Royal Island and the anchorage there. They were impressed with my home-baked hamburger buns and we had a fun cookout on the stern of the boat. The week flew by so quickly. We cruised down to Hatchet Bay and picked up the same mooring that we'd had before. We had several meals at the Hatchet Bay Club and we showed them all around Hatchet Bay.

One day Harold Albury took us in his truck to his very special beach that he had made. He had dynamited some of the rock to make an entrance to the water and the water had brought in sand to make a very nice beach. He had planted grass and trees to make a pretty picnic area and it was a little piece of paradise, even if we had to drive over the chicken road to get there! He told us that there was a very good reef for snorkeling out there. Stan and Dave tried it and said it was good, but it was very rough that day and the rest of us were little too timid to try to swim that far out from shore. The guys had brought some golf clubs along and were having a contest hitting some sand practice shots. We picnicked on the beach and had a fun afternoon. That night we decided to go into the Hatchet Bay Club for dinner. They were having a John Wayne movie afterwards, but we'd seen it so we decided to go back to the boat. As Jodelle was getting into the dinghy, it slipped away from the dock and she fell right on top of Dick, sending them both into the water. We were all laughing so hard that we attracted a lot of attention. All the little boys who had been watching the movie were now down watching us.

We did a fair amount of cruising to show them the beautiful bluffs of Eleuthera. They especially liked the glass window, which was a rock formation up on the cliff. We never did have any luck fishing, but we did find quite a few good spots to snorkel and at least the guys could look at some pretty fish!

We took a taxi one day to go Governor's Harbor, where we bought some liquor, explored their historical sections, and went to Ciga for drinks and dinner. When we got back to the dock where we had left the dinghy, we were serenaded by the little black boys who sang some great Calypso music. We had been asked not to tip them because the people did not want their children to become beggars, which was a bit of a dilemma, but Dick and Dave gave them two golf clubs and we gave them some cookies and candy to thank them. We also bought some coconuts from them for ten cents apiece, a great bargain except that we needed a hatchet to open them and *Steelaway* didn't run to that. By sheer force, with knives and hammers, we finally got one open and it was very good.

We had a miserable trip back to Nassau. It was very rough and we went through a line squall, which drove us all down from the bridge except for Stan, who stayed on the helm. Everyone but Joyce and I were getting sea sick, so I passed out the Bonine and suggested everybody lie down. We were awfully glad to get into Nassau and the Harbor Club. They took us out to dinner that night at the Pilot House and we had fabulous lobsters, but had trouble staying awake to finish dinner. I think it was the Bonine that got to us! The next day, they caught their plane home to Cincinnati and I felt very sad. It had been so wonderful to have these old friends with us.

CHAPTER SIXTEEN

In Nassau, I went into our old garbage laundromat and caught up on the sheets and towels, remade the beds, and replenished our grocery supplies. The next morning, we went to a two-hundred-year-old cathedral for the Calypso Mass, which we enjoyed so much. After Mass, we went to McDonald's for lunch. I'm ashamed to admit that some good old USA junk food tasted so good! Those Big Macs and french fries were fabulous. Then we went to the airport to pick up my sister, Barrie. It was so good to see her. It was also awfully nice to get back into our own bunks that night.

Barrie loved Nassau and we spent a lot of time exploring the shops, eating lunch at different restaurants, and shopping. We used the jitneys a lot, which intrigued Barrie. We found a darling outdoor restaurant called the Green Shutters, which we loved and visited several times. They had the best rum punches! We spent a lot of time swimming and sunning around the pool at the marina, which Barrie particularly enjoyed, having just come from winter in Indiana. We took Barrie on a short cruise to Sandy Cay, which was a beautiful little island used by the cruise ships to give their clients a taste of island beach and beauty. It looked completely untouched except for a lot of beach umbrellas.

We also went over to Paradise Cay, which was a big resort linked by a bridge to Nassau. It used to be called Hog Cay, but I have a feeling that name wasn't very appealing when trying to attract tourists. We had a very nice dinner over there and enjoyed walking around looking at all the fancy hotels.

On Barrie's last night, we decided to have dinner at the Pilot House at the marina. It was good, but we were slightly turned off by the loads of garbage being carried through the dining room and dumped out the window into the alley above the laundry. Nassau really was kind of dirty and I was feeling hesitant about eating out there.

I hated to see Barrie go the next day when we put her on her plane. However, I had a couple of busy days doing laundry, changing sheets, and replenishing the larder. We spent quite a bit of time with Paul and Laura Welter, and their son Luke, from the yacht *Sundowner*. They were doing the same as we were, living aboard. Paul was a retired Coast Guard officer and Laura was a former PR person. Luke was sixteen and they were doing correspondence school, and he was really enjoying the cruising life.

One big fly in the ointment was when we discovered that we had a bad heat exchanger on the starboard engine. We took it to a mechanic, who had been recommended to us. However, we didn't have any confidence in him, so we called Joe Altshuller in Florida and asked him to get the new part for us. He had a new heat exchanger put on Chalk Airlines for us. This whole procedure turned out to be very complicated, as well as expensive. The duty we had to pay was ridiculous. First of all, we had to get a customs broker to expedite the process, and Stan had to take a very expensive cab ride with the broker to pick up a part. At any rate, Stan got it hooked up just before our daughter Althea arrived.

We went to the airport to meet Althea at 1:15 and found the plane was running very late. I stayed at the airport while Stan left at four o'clock to meet the customs broker and get the new part. Finally, at six o'clock they told me the flight was stuck in Chicago! I had an awful time getting a cab back and finally shared one with a bunch of Germans, who found their motel reservation was non-existent. We got word later that the plane might come in around 4:30 in the morning. Stan went out again at that time and Althea finally arrived. She was exhausted and frustrated naturally, as she had been trying to get to us since very early morning. Among other things, they lost her luggage!

The next day we stayed in Nassau trying to find her luggage. We rode the jitneys and explored the town and bought her some clothes and a bathing suit. She was fascinated with the jitney. It was crowded when we boarded, but a very nice heavy lady said, "Here darlin' sit next to us" and scooted her two hundred and fifty pounds over so fast that I had visions of the people next to her being flattened like those characters in the cartoons! The main thing about the jitneys was that they never seemed to take the same route twice. I would tell the driver that I wanted to get off at the marina and I always did eventually, but I surely saw a lot of the island in the process. We took Thea to the cathedral where they had a Calypso Mass again, which she really enjoyed. We had lunch at the Parliament outdoor café and drinks at Dirty Dudley's. We ran into two of her friends from the long plane ride and took them for a short boat ride. Althea loved Nassau and especially the straw market.

They never did find her luggage and since we had bought her some new clothes and a bathing suit, we decided the next day to take off and do some serious cruising. We left for Allen Cay and had a pretty uneventful ride until we got there, where it was a little nerve wracking, as we had an awful time knowing which cay was which. There were a bunch of them together and they all looked alike, but we finally found the entrance and went in and it was gorgeous!

It was the prettiest place we had seen yet in the Bahamas. It really looked like some of those gorgeous pictures of the South Pacific. The harbor was formed by about six different cays in a circle. They all had lush vegetation with a fruit that looked like oranges, but wasn't. There were about six gorgeous white sand beaches fringing the harbor. There were a lot of boats in there that night, about seventeen in all. *Swedlady* was there and we hadn't seen them since Northern Florida. It was a very windy night and there was much activity around us setting anchors, but our two held us fast. The Canadians on the *Morgan* ahead of us had a terrible time. They probably anchored in a shallow spot and they had to re-anchor after going aground.

The next morning we went ashore and explored. The ocean beach was pretty, but not spectacular. We saw Janet and Mike on the beach from *Swedlady* and we chatted with them. We walked around the island and saw the giant iguanas! They were supposed to be extinct, because they had been a favorite food of the Bahamians, but we saw lots of them and apparently they had made a big comeback. They looked like miniature dinosaurs and some of them were three feet long. They obviously had been fed before, because they would come right up to you. We went back to the boat and got some lettuce and salt pork to feed them, which they liked very much. We spent quite a bit of time with these fascinating creatures.

We snorkeled on a gorgeous protected reef close to shore. It was as good as any we had seen and it was delightfully warm while we snorkeled. The coral and the unbelievably colorful fish were a sight to see. We saw some fishermen hauling in conchs that were tied together. We thought this was odd, but someone told us that this was how they kept their catch for the day until they had time to pick it all up.

The next day we explored some of the other cays around Allan Cay and found another colony of iguanas. These were even bolder than the first ones we had seen. One of them even charged me and I made a quick retreat much to Althea and Stan's amusement. We enjoyed that place so much that we stayed four days and snorkeled and swam and lazed about.

Then, we headed out for Norman Cay. It was another beautiful place and we went ashore to explore. There was an abandoned clubhouse on top of the hill and there was a wonderful view from there. Supposedly, it had been a big drug hangout and the gangs sent out a lot of drugs from there. The anchorage was quite sheltered and there were a lot of other boats there so we really weren't nervous. *Swedlady* came in with guests aboard, and we had a good time with them. We spent several days there also, but all too soon it was time to head back to Nassau so Althea could get her flight home.

Unfortunately it was a horrible trip! We had enormous beam seas all the way back. It was so rough that Stan considered it dangerous for Althea and me to go down from the bridge to the cabin, so we were stuck up on the bridge. We were being thrown around so much that we were getting quite bruised. Then when we begged to go down from the bridge because we needed to go to the bathroom Stan said no, and he told us to "Just pee up here on the bridge and the water will wash it all away!" Horrors! By the time we got into Nassau, I was really a wreck and had gone on a horrible crying jag and couldn't stop for a long time. Poor Stan and Althea tried to calm me down and finally I stopped. We went to the Pilot House for a farewell dinner for Althea and sat with our backs to the garbage window.

We checked again on Althea's luggage and it was still missing and never was found. We took her to her plane and sadly said goodbye, and I'm afraid I cried again because I hated to see her go. We got back to the boat and found that the other heat exchanger had stopped working, which was almost too much! We called Joe Altshuller again and he said he had a better way to send the heat exchanger to us and we got a much better price and didn't have to go through so much of the customs routine. That did cheer me up no end.

CHAPTER SEVENTEEN

The next day we went back to Royal Cay and anchored. It was a very lovely calm quiet day, but we were both gun shy and Stan laughed when I came up on to the bridge with my emergency kit. It consisted of a pail for you know what, Bonine, crackers, Kleenex, cover-ups and lunch for Stan. Of course, when you're all prepared you never need it. Royal was very pretty and serene, but it was starting to blow. We were delighted to see *Cicada* in there and Marty and I immediately started swapping books while Steve, Stan and Stephen were catching up on everyone's activities.

The next day, we were weathered in because of the wind. We had discovered that winter was the windy season over there and was something you just had to cope with. Marty, Steve, and Stephen came over for the afternoon and we had a great time visiting.

By March 8th, the winds had died down a little and we headed for the Abacos. It was still pretty windy and the seas were big. We turned back twice, and then finally decided to head on. I lay down and tried not to look out at the water. It was scary going in the channel entrance to Little Harbor because there was a giant surge in from the ocean. A giant wave billowed behind you and gave you a big shove into the harbor entrance! There was also a big reef that we had to avoid and it was best to go in at high tide.

This anchorage turned out to be probably our most favorite place in the Bahamas. Little Harbor was a very isolated, small, and almost landlocked harbor surrounded by rugged rocky cliffs on one side and high sand dunes on the other. All of this was covered with lush vegetation and palm trees. Ashore was a tiny artist colony founded many years ago by Randall Johnston, a sculptor, and his wife Margot, who was also an artist. There were no roads, phones, electricity or running water except what they generated themselves. When they first arrived there, they lived for a year or so in a cave, and then on a boat for many years until Ran could make enough on his work to build their first primitive home, which he made out of the cabin of the boat. It was now known as Pete's Pub, a little bar that opened for a couple of hours when son Pete was in the mood and there were enough visiting yachts at anchor.

They were doing this in the years when Margot was recovering from polio and still not walking too well and caring for two children. Ran's sculpture was well-known as was Margot's enameled work and ceramics. They were prosperous and had built a beautiful home high on the hill. Ran had apprentices and he used the "lost wax" method of casting his bronze sculptures and had a tiny foundry on the island. One of these apprentices was Debbie Henry, who married their son Pete, and we met her parents who now lived there six months of the year.

We just stayed one night and got an early start the next morning and ran outside again. It was an okay trip this time. We saw lots of dolphins— about thirty of them—and flying fish. We pulled into Marsh Harbor around two o'clock and anchored. It was a very quiet night and we slept well.

The next morning, we went into the Conch Inn Marina and docked. It was a really lovely place and run by some super people. Wally Smith and his daughters Barbara and Maureen ran the Marina as well as a restaurant and the Inn. Stan washed down the boat and I went for groceries. I checked out the town laundromat, the Rub-a-Dub-Dub, and it looked pretty bad, so I had it done at the Marina for $3.50 a bundle. It surely was worth it! We went into the Conch Crawl and had a conch burger and it was fabulous. The next day, I did errands and shopped. I was really happy because I found my "old lady" cart, which I thought I had lost. It was a pretty good walk to the grocery store and the other stores there and it was great to have it to carry my groceries.

The next morning, Barbara and the kids came down. Chrissy was six years old and Stephen was four. We were so excited to see them! Stan had asked Barbara to bring down a lot of money and she had it pinned all over her body in her underwear and was most happy to get there. The kids were thrilled to be on the boat again. We stayed at the dock that day and the next, because it was windy and I thought it would be fun for the kids to explore Marsh Harbor anyway. We went all around and we started a shell collection, which provided many happy hours for the children on the boat. Poor Barbie had a terrible cold, which she probably caught on the plane down, but we hoped that the sunshine would clear that up rapidly.

The next morning, we went over to Hope Town. We went to the lee side beach, which would be most out of the wind, and the children had a great time playing in the sand, swimming, and gathering shells. The kids got quite sunburned so we went into town and bought them each a straw hat. It took time to get used to the tropical sun. The anchorage there was great as it was a hurricane hole. It was dominated by a large lighthouse.

We got an early start the next morning to Little Harbor because we wanted to arrive at high tide. It was a calm trip because we took the sheltered inner passage instead of the ocean. We picked up a mooring and took down the dinghy and were settled for several days.

It proved to be the perfect place for vacationing with the children. We took the dinghy into shore where there was a lovely little half moon beach. We had brought beach toys with us and the kids immediately started digging in the sand. While they were playing, we chatted with Libby Henry who came along.

She was happy to see the kids because they were about the same age as Debbie and Pete Johnson's children. Libby, who was a teacher, had organized a little school for her grandchildren and she was thrilled to have more children keeping them company. Chrissy's teacher had sent along two weeks of homework for her to do so she wouldn't fall behind in her class.

Libby's grandsons came along then, and the children had a lot of fun playing together on the beach. We were able to take the dinghy back to *Steelaway* and keep an eye on the children while they were playing. When they were ready to come back aboard, they would stand up and yell, "Ahoy, *Steelaway!*" Then we would dinghy in and get them. They loved this, and so did we, as they spent a good deal of time playing on the beach.

The rest of the time that we were there, they went to Libby's school in the morning for a few hours. Libby made it fun for them and Chris got her homework done, so everybody was happy. Then, I would make lunch for them all and we'd have a picnic on the beach. The kids spent a lot of time looking for shells and they loved coming back on the boat, sitting on the stern with a pail of water, cleaning their shells, and had a pretty active system of trading. They spent many hours doing this. They also loved hiking around the Cay with us. Chrissy, who knew how to swim, loved jumping off the swim platform and swimming around the boat. We put a life jacket on Stevie so he could be in the water having fun too. After long naps, the kids tried fishing. Steven got bored and Barbie picked up his pole and suddenly got a fish. Stevie was so excited he ran across the stern and fell into the rail cutting his lip. Luckily, he was so thrilled about the fish that he stopped crying pretty quickly.

In the mornings, when the kids were at Libby's school, Barbara and I had a great time exploring all over Little Harbor. We enjoyed seeing the Johnson studio and their work. We bought some belts and some fun ceramics of Margot's. Then we hiked out to the head of the harbor to the lighthouse and explored that. Some of the following days, we hiked along the ocean side for many miles. It was very isolated and we never saw another soul. Libby and Debbie had told us of several interesting things to look at, including a piece of a space capsule that had dropped when the parts separated after the launch. The path of the space capsule was often right over the Abacos. I'll never forget one night about twilight when a capsule passed over us. All you could see was the trail blazing across the sky in a bright pink. The trail hung there in the sky until total darkness.

Libby and her husband Roger had invited us to come and see their house, which they had built mostly themselves. It was fascinating that they had been able to use almost all local things in their building. They used old hatch covers which had blown ashore as tables and glass fishing net balls as decorations. It was amazing how much stuff they found that had washed onto the beach. We invited the Henrys and Debbie and Pete out for drinks several evenings and we felt we had made some wonderful new friends.

We reluctantly left Little Harbor for Guana Cay. We left early so that the kids would sleep a good part of the way. When we got there, we docked at the Guana Cay Club because the anchorage was not very well protected. We had a wonderful afternoon on the beach. It was on the ocean side and was a long beautiful white stretch. We hiked, shelled, jumped over waves, and dug holes in the sand.

We were surprised to see Marty, Steve, and Stephen from *Cicada* on the beach. The children had a good time playing with Stephen. We went back to the boat and cleaned up and went to the club for a wonderful dinner. We grown-ups all had the lobster! The children met the son of the owner of the club, who was our Stephen's age, and we were able to have a very leisurely dinner because the children were all playing out in the lobby while we finished. The little boy's sister, who was the restaurant hostess, tried to get them to move the fleet of toy cars they were playing with outside, but they refused and the people coming in for dinner managed to good naturedly walk around them. They finally went out and discovered that they could somersault the huge hooded wicker rockers over completely while curled inside. Great fun!

After dinner, the club had a band come to play and the kids joined us. The band persuaded everyone to join in the music. Stan played a washtub fiddle, Stevie a tambourine, and Chrissy rattled a stone filled can and we all had so much fun! The next morning while we were still sleeping, we heard a knock and a soft voice saying, "Good morning, good morning!" We found it was one of the women from the restaurant bringing us a pot of coffee. It seemed they were hoping we'd stay over another day so that the children could play. We did so, and the kids all had a great time.

That day, Stevie was leaning over the rail and watching the multicolored fish that were swimming beside the boat. The stones under the dock served as a kind of reef and there were many beautiful ones of all colors circling around in there. A small shark came in and chased them away and Stevie said, "That's Jaws and he's so big because he eats lots, especially people!" Steve's observations were all a lot of fun. He went up to a palm tree and sniffed it and remarked that it smelled really fresh.

We left to go back to Marsh Harbor because Barbara and the kids had to leave that day. We got them some more souvenir shells and very sadly put them on the plane at four o'clock to go home. It had been so great having them there.

Stan had a toothache the next day and Wally recommended a dentist in town, although he commented that the dentist was pretty old. Stan took a taxi to the dentist's house and the dentist pulled two teeth in fifteen minutes and sent him back in the cab! The teeth had been bothering him for a while, but dental care as we knew it was just really not available out there. Luckily, he did fine and was relieved not to have the toothache anymore. I spent the day doing household chores, laundry, and grocery shopping getting ready for the next guests.

The next day, we went over to explore Man-O-War Cay a little bit. They had an excellent harbor, again almost a hurricane hole. Supposedly, this was the best place in the Abacos to have any boat work done. We also found it to be a great source for ice cream, baked goods, and groceries. I wasn't feeling too well and hope that I wasn't getting the bug that Stan had had for about a week.

We left the Man-O-War around nine o'clock the next morning and got to Treasure Cay around noon. It was a very pretty, very plush resort, and had a very quiet sheltered harbor. We anchored, as a mooring was not available, and then dinghied to shore and had lunch. I wished that I had felt better. I was still achy and queasy. We did a little more exploring and then we discovered that our anchor fee included fresh water, so we decided to fill up the next day. We had heard their water was really good.

We had kind of a wild night, what with the wind blowing like crazy, the anchor making weird noises, and my jumping up and down with "la tourista." The next day, I was feeling better but "Montezuma's Revenge" was still going strong.

One sailboat in the harbor had dragged their mooring loose and was aground, so I guess we really were lucky that we couldn't get a mooring. We went into the dock to get water and were pleased to run into Paul Welter, the retired Coast Guard officer from the *Sundowner*. He came aboard and we had a nice visit. He was there because he was thinking of taking a job managing that marina.

CHAPTER EIGHTEEN

We returned to Marsh Harbor. It was blowing, but the seas weren't too bad. We had to anchor out in the harbor until our dock was ready. I took the boat cart and made two trips to the market for food and liquor. It was hot and muggy that day and the barometer was falling rapidly, which meant there was supposed to be a bad blow that night. I took some Lomotil, had a coke, and swam in the pool. I found out that Barbara Smith had the same bug that Stan and I had. It was really going around.

We went to 9:30 Mass at St. Francis De Sales the next morning. We really enjoyed this little parish, which had been set up for the Haitian refugees. The Mass was bilingual again in Haitian, which I could sort of understand because a lot of it was French. It was said by a priest from the Nassau Cathedral. Later, we went to the airport to meet Joe and Pat Altshuller. Their plane was two hours late, which was pretty much par for the course in the Bahamas. It was so good to see them! We got them settled on the boat and then went to the Conch Crawl for dinner. We had a great dinner, as their food was really good there. I felt a lot better that day, thank heavens, and could eat dinner. We had some wonderful grouper.

We left early the next morning for Man-O-War and anchored there with some difficulty. We explored the town and the beach, but mostly loafed all day. It was a pretty day, but cool.

Joe and Pat surprised me the next morning with a lovely birthday present—some beautiful cologne. We left early again for Little Harbor. It was a beautiful day and I think our guests enjoyed the trip through Lubbers Quarters. We pulled into Little Harbor around 10:00 or so. We went through the Johnston Studios and bought his book, which was about the first years they lived in Little Harbor. We walked to the lighthouse and later went to Pete's Pub for a drink. We explored the Johnston's cave, where they had lived when they came to Little Harbor. It was big and they had built a little stove into the wall, but it was hard to imagine how Margot, just recovering from polio was able to get around. Also, there were lots of bats! We grilled steaks on the back of the boat and enjoyed our dinner while we watched the sunset.

We decided to leave for Hope Town the next morning, which was not a very long trip but it was blowing hard and it was rough. Poor Joe got seasick. We came into the harbor, got a mooring, and took the dinghy into the town dock. We took a short stroll around the town until Joe felt better. After lunch, we went back to town and tried to find some grocery stores open. We ran into our first "open at two or so" sign, which meant any time they were ready. We went to the Hope Town Lodge for dinner and it wasn't a very good one. We felt badly about that. It was a matter of lots of atmosphere and poor food.

We explored the lighthouse the next day. We were allowed to walk up to the top and the view was wonderful! We picked some wild dill growing beside the path leading to it. We decided to leave for Guana Cay. The trip wasn't too bad, but Joe did feel seasick.

Guana was really rough in the harbor and we banged up against the dock like crazy, and so, we reluctantly decided we'd have to leave. It was quite a rough ride to Marsh Harbor, which was hard on Joe and Pat. Stan and I got soaked up on the bridge. We were able to get into the Conch Inn Marina and gratefully pulled into the dock. We had lunch, loafed around, swam in the pool, and played bridge. We went to dinner again at the Conch Inn and had an especially good dinner. I loved grouper the way they fixed it.

The next day was a lazy one. It was still blowing like crazy and it was obvious that we couldn't do any cruising because of Joe's tender stomach. So we walked around Marsh Harbor to the stores and explored the new Abaco Club. We swam, played bridge, and went to dinner at the Conch Crawl again and had another really good dinner. This time it was Lobster Thermidor and it was divine! Joe and Pat were so nice to take us out to dinner so often. They were wonderful friends!

Sunday, it was still blowing, but maybe a little less. We went to Mass at St. Francis de Sales, which was such a nice parish. They had great singing led by a jolly plump nun. It was very bouncy music and the locals sang loudly and with much enthusiasm. After lunch, Joe and Pat left early for the airport. I felt guilty letting them do it, as I knew they did it so that we could leave on the high tide, but I hated the thought of the long wait for them at the airport. It was so good spending that time with them and we looked forward to seeing them when we got back to Miami.

We departed shortly after the Altshullers left, and almost hit the bottom. My, but we were having low tide! It was as if someone had pulled the plug out of the ocean! I guessed that these were the famed spring tides that we'd read about so much. The tides were much higher and lower than normal in the spring and in the fall. It was first of April, and we were heading back to the States. And we were really ready.

All of a sudden, the wind was really getting on our nerves. The constant blowing, where we didn't dare lay anything down on the seat beside us, because it would blow away, was driving us nuts. So that day, we were heading for Little Harbor, where we would jump off for Chubb Cay, going outside on the ocean. However, we found the tide was so very low and it was still blowing awfully hard. We realized it would be too shallow to get through Lubbers Quarters and into Little Harbor, so we went and anchored in Hope Town for the night. There was really no pressure to get back to the States, but we were both ready and I was looking forward to not being so isolated again.

The next morning looked a little bit better, although it was still blowing and the weather report didn't sound too great. We took off anyway, at about eleven o'clock, to catch the high tide. It was a pretty rough ride, but I didn't mind as I was below in my bunk. Stan said there were some pretty big rollers near the north cut. We had a lazy day at Little Harbor. We walked the beach and I went shelling while Stan worked on his income taxes.

The next day found Stan still working all day on the taxes, which was a miserable job. I made bread and hamburger buns, typed letters and walked to Bookie's beach, a favorite walk of mine. The Crawfises from Mansfield, where we had lived quite a few years ago, had built a house there high on the hill overlooking the ocean. The Johnstons owned all the land in Little Harbor, but had sold three lots to people they thought they would enjoy having as neighbors. It was interesting that two of the couples were from Mansfield and we had known them both, and a third lot was owned by the Henrys.

Pat Crawfis had been one of Tommy's teachers in the special ed school when we were living in Mansfield. It was fun to renew our acquaintanceship. They invited us up to see their house and to have a drink. Pat's husband Jim was an architect and had designed their house and once again, most of the materials to build it were scavenged from the sea and the beach. The trim all around the windows and doors was driftwood. They had a fantastic view of the ocean and we really enjoyed our afternoon.

The next day was still blowing very hard, so we had to postpone our leave taking for another day. I went for a long walk on the beach and noticed, as I had for a week now, that spring must be coming to the islands. They always looked green, a kind of dark green against the brilliant blue of the sky, and contrasted to the gamut of blues, greens, aquas, and emeralds of the water. But the last week or so, I'd noticed a spring green creeping over the cays.

It seemed like eternal summer down there, but they do have seasons. Winter was warm, as it rarely went below seventy degrees in the daytime, but the wind blew like crazy all the time. The natives considered the winter to be cold. This was evidenced in church when it was eighty degrees outside and I wore my coolest dress and hunted for a seat by the window. I'd inevitably sit beside a little kid in a stocking cap and leather jacket "Because it's winter, mon." The new green on the bushes that I saw that day was accompanied by tiny yellow and white flowers—very spring-like for sure.

It'd been fun running into many of our buddies from Chubb Key and the waterway. We'd seen *Cicada* a lot. Marty and I had a very active paperback swap going and greeted each other with delight each time we met. She did tend to run to the more lurid books, but always gave me a few goodies too. When they were with us, Christine and Stephen were fascinated by the cover of one that was a lulu. It had a naked girl being seduced by a warlock. Barbie and I kept hiding the book and they kept searching for it. We finally discovered that they were fascinated because they wanted to know what Darth Vader was doing with the naked lady. Barbie replied that her parents hadn't brought her up very well, or she would have had her clothes on!

We'd also run into *Midnight Special* a lot. George's wife had finally decided to give up her job in Kinkardine and join him. We saw *Pursuit* several places, but we were just letting our hair grow, so we didn't get haircuts.

On April 4th, still in Little Harbor, we had a really, really scary experience. It was still blowing and we couldn't leave yet. Stan went ashore to talk to Roger Henry, while I did some long overdue cleaning chores.

The generator was running to charge up the freezer etc. It made a funny noise and as I was moving forward to shut it off, clouds of black smoke were coming out at the side of the boat. I was able to take the load off the generator, but I couldn't get it to shut down and the smoke was getting worse! As you can imagine, one of the worst nightmares on a boat is fire.

We had a very loud horn and I blew five blasts, which is the nautical danger signal. I then stood there trying to figure out what else I should do! I could see Stan and the other men ashore running for their dinghies, and all the boats around us did the same, the men all with fire extinguishers in their hands. About seven arrived at once and headed for the engine room. They were able to shut the generator down and luckily nothing was on fire.

We had an automatic C.O. system down there, which didn't go off so, we figured the fire was just in the generator and not hot enough to trigger it. Boy, was that scary! My knees shook for quite a while. Jim Crawfis saw the smoke from his house and he too came rowing out fire extinguisher in hand to see if he could help. It was a very self-contained community, as there were no firemen, ambulances, or doctors, so when anything happened, everyone came running, which was pretty nice!

Stan went down to the engine room to try and diagnose the problem, and I feared that it would be a part that we didn't have. If that were the case, we'd have to go back to Marsh Harbor or more likely Man-O-War Cay, as that was where most of the boat repair took place. We didn't have a lot in the freezer except for some meat that we hated to lose, so we'd need to head for a dock and electricity to hold us until the generator was repaired. This would delay our departure for the States for heaven only knew how long. I was not a happy camper! We pulled up the anchor and headed back to Marsh Harbor and a dock with electricity at the Conch Inn Marina. We called Bill Johnson and he said he would be out the next morning.

Wouldn't you know, the next day the weather was finally good and there we were stuck! Stan talked to Wally and he said the best way to go home was via West End, as there would be no long open ocean passages that way. It was just a fifty-one mile run to West Palm Beach from there.

I trekked to the Golden Harvest laundromat. It was a little better than the Rub-A-Dub-Dub Laundromat because it had warm water and the girl next door gave you your money back if the machines didn't work. The temperature controls and so on were meaningless, but it did wash and dry. It was a long hot trip down the road back and I found Bill Johnson still hadn't come. He felt our problem was in the injection system and if so, nothing could be done for us on Abaco. So we guessed we'd better load up on ice, get a propane hot plate, and run for it, praying we didn't get held up by weather at Great Sale Cay.

That evening, as we sat up on the bridge, we saw a Polaris missile from Cape Kennedy go up. We could see the pink trail even after dark, and there was a rainbow colored puff where the first and second stage separated. We hoped that might be a good omen!

The next day, April 6th, Stan decided to try some more to get some parts. He called Edwin's boatyard on Man-O-War Cay and they did have a pump! Stan decided to take the ferry over there and pick it up and we hoped that the problem was the pump and not the injector system.

While Stan was taking the ferry, I got up early to go to seven o'clock Mass. I got to the church and the sign on the door said Mass was in the convent, so I rang the bell and woke up a nice nun who said Mass was six o'clock that night. I found that very few signs in the Bahamas meant what they said!

While Stan was gone, I went to the post office, the grocery, and liquor store. It was really hot that day and I thought summer was really there. I came back and swam in the pool and saw a darling little redheaded woodpecker and lots of gorgeous white orchids. The night before, the air was scented with jasmine. It definitely was summer.

Stan returned from Man-O-War with the new pump and installed it. It seemed to be working okay! Hallelujah! So if the weather was okay the next morning, we'd head for Green Turtle Cay. While we were rejoicing, a boat came in next to us and docked. They'd been fishing and gave us a good-sized wahoo, which we grilled for supper and it was delicious.

The next morning, we checked out the generator some more, then we left for Guana at high tide and anchored. The anchorage was serene this time. We left there the next morning before seven o'clock and cruised to Great Sale Cay. It was a long day—nine hours—and kind of nerve-wracking, going through very shallow waters and out of sight of land a lot on not the calmest seas. It was also tricky getting around the reef into Great Sale. However, at least we were moving and so far the generator was working. As you can guess, I was having a love-hate relationship with the generator by that time.

Five or so other boats were anchored in Great Sale and we saw *Fantasy* again. *Northern Moon*, *Windseye*, and *Glenda Lee* were also within there. That part of the Abacos was really isolated and we felt very far away from civilization. I suddenly felt a terrible need to get back to the States and things familiar. Even the Waterway would be a piece of cake after the Bahamas and the infernal damn wind!

We left Great Sale at eight a.m. It seemed to be blowing harder and out of the southwest. The anchorage would be open to wind and seas that day. *Fantasy* left and *Northern Loon* and *Windseye* were debating what to do. Our radio was acting up again. What a nuisance! We encountered very rough seas and I went down to my bunk for two and a half hours until we got to the Mangrove Cay and anchored for a cup of coffee, somewhat in the lee. *Fantasy* said they were going on and we did too, but the seas were really getting worse and we both turned back. We decided to anchor in the lee of Mangrove again and *Fantasy* decided to go on to Grand Cay.

It was lonely and spooky there and we were uneasy about the holding and a front coming in sooner than predicted. It was a very wide open anchorage. I decided to wash my hair to try and stay calm, which I certainly didn't feel. Around 5:30 we saw the front approaching and decided to head back to Great Sale. We also were a little nervous about a couple of cigarette boats that had come into the anchorage near us. There was still a fair amount of boat hijacking by the drug people. We headed out and one of the cigarette boats started following us closely. Stan told me to take the helm and he went below and got some empty aluminum cans and his 30-30 rifle and had some target practice, shooting at the cans in the water. It didn't take long before the cigarette boat turned around and sped away. They didn't like to try and hijack boats that had guns.

We had a two and a half hour ride in the dark through fairly big seas. We came into the anchorage in the dark on radar. There was almost a full moon, which helped. There were seven other boats in there and we used our searchlight to find a good spot to anchor. We anchored with no problems and I collapsed. I reneged on my resolution to not drink during holy week and had a very stiff rum and water! A few days later, Walter Stratton told me that when we came into the anchorage that night with our light, we looked as big as the Queen Mary! I was flattered, I guess!

The wind dropped considerably the next day and we took off around eight o'clock again following *Glenda Lee*, *Northern Loon*, *Windseye* and *Tug II* (a thirty-six-foot Grand Banks). We had a comfortable ride to West End and chatted by radio with the others, that is when the radio worked, which was not very often.

The generator was being temperamental again and switched itself off. Good grief! It was quite tricky coming off the Banks into West End, especially as so many of the markers were missing! We made it okay though and came into the gorgeous Grand Bahama Hotel and Country Club Marina. We docked next to *Tug II*, with *Tuktu* on the other side. It was a sailboat with an organ aboard!

We got acquainted with Colleen and Walt Stratton from *Tug II*, who were to become our closest friends during these boating years and also with Bill and Dianne from *Tuktu*. Stan took me out to dinner at the hotel, which was nice and raised my morale. Then we partied aboard *Tug II* with them and Frank and Tommy from *Northern Loon*. They were all Canadians and our conversation was most interesting. Bill played the organ while everyone yelled above it! We planned to meet *Northern Loon* and *Tug II* in the North Channel of the Georgian Bay that summer, where *Northern Loon* had a home in Little Current. The next day, we met Glenda and Jack from the *Glenda Lee*. He was a United Airlines pilot and she was a flight attendant. They were a very interesting couple and we laughed when they told us that they had met those nuts from the *Third Fling*, who had run into their boat!

I went to the *Northern Loon* for Bloody Marys with Barney and Mary Gillespie from *Windseye*, while Stan worked all day on the generator. I went swimming and later Bill and Dianne came over for drinks. There was much socializing in that Marina!

The day after that, Stan worked on a leak in the engine cooling system. Later, we had *Glenda Lee*, *Northern Loon*, *Windseye* and *Tuktu* over for a cocktail party. Jerry and Rea Hart from *Yellow Bird* were also there and they were so interesting. He'd written a book and many articles for *Yachting* magazine. It was a nice party.

Stan and I met the bus from the local church at the hotel gate and went with a lot of children to the Holy Thursday services at the Catholic Church. We were the only white and almost only adults there. There was much giggling by the kids and so on. We did the readings and brought up the offerings.

We had also gone on a fun horticulture tour with Tommy, Bill, Dianne and Colleen. We had a fascinating tour guide and learned a lot.

We really wanted to get back to the states for Easter, so we left early in the morning with *Yellow Bird* and *Tug II* for West Palm Beach. We ran for an hour in terrible seas and then we turned around and came back. *Tug II* was kidding us on the radio about turning back. Stan said, "Well, I may be the Captain, but my wife is the owner and she said go back!"

We had a fun potluck supper that night that we were glad we hadn't missed. It was aboard *Windseye*, and *Northern Loon* and *Tuktu* were there also. We used a picnic table on the dock and even had a floral centerpiece. It was an early evening because we wanted to try to head out again early the next morning.

We were up at five o'clock! Once again Dianne and Bill saw us off. It was rough for the first hour or so, but I stayed below, so I didn't mind so much. Then, it started calming down and eventually became flat calm and was a very pleasant trip. We came into Spencer's Marina and *Tug II* was waiting. *Northern Loon* and *Windseye* followed us. I couldn't believe we were finally back in the States! Hooray!

CHAPTER NINETEEN

Our first day back in the States, we went to Mass at St. Ann's Church and afterwards went over to *Tug II* for an Easter Brunch. We had played Easter Bunny and had hidden Easter eggs on the different boats. We slept half of the afternoon, and then made more phone calls to everybody back home.

The next day, we did a lot of boat chores. I imagine we were a sight to behold in the supermarket, where the first mates couldn't believe how wonderful the shopping was! All that lettuce and the wonderful fresh foods and the variety of meats and so on. We were ecstatic! Then we went onto the post office, where tons of mail was waiting for us. There was a beautiful journal from Cindy for my birthday, which I looked forward to using. We hurried back to the boat to sit and enjoy hearing from everyone. All that mail—sigh! We said goodbye to *Tug II*, who was proceeding up the waterway.

While I was doing all of this, Stan went to the boat stores and bought two new radios and antennas! What a treat! Now we would really be able to communicate. Stan fixed the air conditioning also, which was not working, but he was able to get and install a new motor for it. We were glad to have it because it was hot and humid in Florida.

Our old Ohio boating friends, the Firestones, came over to see us next day and we had a super visit! John took Stan to Sears and he got a new garbage disposal, hooray! As you can see, we were fixing a lot of things and it was heavenly to have these things available in the good old USA. We went with the Firestones to the This Is It Pub for dinner, which was really good. It was so great to see Jessie and have a good chat.

The next day, Stan installed the new disposal and it worked beautifully!

We'd been busy doing all the little things that we couldn't do in the Bahamas and much "fixing" on Stan's part, getting ready to head north. After working all day, we went over to *Fantasy* for happy hour.

The next two days were also busy ones. The new antennas and radios were installed and in my journal I wrote, "Beautiful!" I took the bus downtown to the post office and retrieved more mail and mailed all the stuff I had sewn for the kids and grandkids that winter. I had wrecked the head curtains in Marsh Harbor (I melted them in the laundromat dryer!), so I made some new ones. I did some laundry in the marina laundromat and it was lovely! Everything worked, and it was scrupulously clean. Sheer heaven! We said goodbye to *Fantasy*, who left for home that morning.

We left on the 21st of April and cruised to Port St. Lucie, Florida. It was kind of tricky navigating down the river because they had had a drought and the water was quite shallow. We found a handy marina, docked, and called our old friends the Ongs, who were retired and living there. They came aboard for drinks and then took us out to dinner at Sir Chumley's, a fun waterfront restaurant. It was delightful to reconnect with these old friends, but kind of sad to see them both in poor health.

It was stormy the next day and we couldn't leave, so we had a very nice lazy day reading the Sunday paper. We couldn't get to church, as it was way out someplace. As it rained again the next day, we stayed at the dock at the Sandpiper Resort, which was a lovely place. We met several of our dock mates the next day, Ed and Lillian Rogers aboard the yacht *Lillian*, and Ralph and Millie Rozumalski aboard *Sundowner*. The Rozumalskis had a car and took us all to a shopping center, where we got groceries, and then to a neat restaurant called The Deck where everyone made their own hamburgers. You could go by boat also and dock there.

Everyone came aboard *Steelaway* for drinks, and after dinner we went aboard *Lillian* for pie and coffee. It was raining in torrents the next day and the wind gusting to thirty-two knots, so we stayed put once again. We had cocktails aboard *Sundowner* and then everyone braved the elements to come aboard *Steelaway* for cake and coffee. It was kind of a wild and windy night. Would you believe the weather was still terrible the next day?! We had several leaks in the stern cabin. *Steelaway* did not like her stern pointing into the wind! We heard that they had flooding in Miami and West Palm. I caught up on a lot of correspondence while Stan tackled the leaks. It cleared in the afternoon a little and I walked to the hotel to mail my letters. We had drinks on *Sandpiper's* deck.

We had called General and Mrs. (Katie) Pratt and they came over, very curious about the people who had bought their boat and what they had done to it. The General and Katie were delightful people and we had a great visit. They had sold the boat because he had serious heart trouble, but he was doing well then and they had bought *Compromise 3*, which was a thirty-six-foot Bertram. They said the Grand Banks was their dream boat, but Katie wanted a fast boat should he have problems and need to get to shore in a hurry for medical help. They said they were going to the Bahamas the next week. We hoped to see them again in the fall.

April 26th was a beautiful day and we left at 7:45 a.m., and planned on a long day to catch up. However, we ran into a terrible line squall near Vero Beach and we couldn't see the channel markers, so we decided to call it a day and headed into the anchorage at Vero Beach. As we came into the Bay, we saw a black sailboat, which had dragged anchor in the storm, up against the far shore. We decided it had been a good idea to seek shelter.

When we left the next morning, it was a pretty day, but awfully windy. We ran as far as Cocoa Beach and stayed at Whitley Marina. It was a very nice place in a small town and was picturesque. We discovered that we had ripped the bimini top en route in the bad wind and as this is something that we'd really needed badly, we were anxious to have it repaired. The manager of the marina told us that there was a woman nearby who stitched torn sails up for the sailboats and he thought she would be able to help us. We took it over to her and she said she could do it and would have it for us in a day or so.

The next day, we enjoyed walking around Cocoa Village. This was where many of the astronauts and their families lived while they were working in the space program and it was fun to imagine them there. There was a very pretty little shopping center nearby and it was nice to look around and see the shops. There was also a post office and a quick print shop, which we thought we might use. I kept a special little notebook with information about the different places we had stopped, which came in very handy when I particularly wanted a post office or grocery, etc. There was also grocery store and drugstores nearby, so this was a real bonanza.

Since it was Sunday, we took a cab to church, and it was nice to be able to do so. Stan also got a great haircut in the unisex beauty shop. We stopped at the sail shop and picked up the bimini and she had done a beautiful job.

We left Cocoa early the next morning at about 7:15, and while en route, we met *Sea Lark*, a Grand Banks thirty-six who chartered in the Chesapeake, and we enjoyed chatting with them on our wonderful new radio. There was a certain camaraderie among Grand Banks people, which was always fun.

We tried to anchor at New Smyrna for lunch, but tide, wind and the crowded anchorage made it difficult, so we gave up and ate lunch en route. We saw *Taormina* anchored in there and we had last seen them years ago in the Virgin Islands.

I'd caught a cold and felt kind of rotten. We pulled into Daytona Beach around four o'clock. There was a lovely marina from which we could walk to the stores and the post office. They even had department stores. It was rainy and miserable, so I spent the rest of the afternoon working on a pillow that I was making for Chrissy's bed.

The weather was looking bad the next morning, so we decided to stay there. I did some shopping and found lots of neat stuff I needed, and also found a fabulous discount fabric shop where I bought lots of material! I did some laundry at the marina and met *Resolution* and *Trypanic*, whom we had seen in Marsh Harbor and Man-O-War. Chatting always made the laundry go faster! It rained the whole rest of the afternoon.

We left Daytona around ten o'clock after a pleasant breakfast. It was a terrible-looking day again, windy and a few light showers. The Coast Guard had broadcasted a waterspout warning, but we never saw one and it was an uneventful trip. We pulled into the St. Augustine municipal marina around 4:15. We had some difficulty docking in the wind, with no one on the dock to help us. Someone finally did come along and we got in. I realized I really needed to work on putting the spring line through the hawser port, as I had a lot of difficulty with that. Colleen and Walter Stratton from *Tug II* were there and I couldn't wait to see them.

We went sightseeing in St. Augustine and really enjoyed the old city. We walked miles all over the old city. The Fort there was really super and very interesting! It had been so beautifully restored and the guides were so very well informed that we walked around it for hours. Our feet wore out around four o'clock or so and we came back to the boat and collapsed. Colleen and Walter came over for drinks, and since they had wheels, we went to Anastasia Island to a fun place called Cowboys for dinner. It was an extra nice day.

We left St. Augustine at 7:30 the next morning and came to Fernandina.

We took on five hundred gallons of fuel and anchored nearby about four o'clock. We planned to meet *Tug II* in St. Simon's. We called our friends Jean and Frank Baker while fueling and were disappointed to find that they'd be away till Monday, so we would miss them. Darn!

We were up early the next morning and discovered the black flies were back! We pulled into the Golden Isles Marina at noon and were greeted by Alan, Dave and Tim. It was so good to be back! Jean Baker had left a car key for us at the marina. What a thrill! So far there wasn't any new mail, but I was sure it was around somewhere. Dave and Nancy Davis met us for dinner at Gant's after showing us their new condo, which was very nice. I was so happy for Nancy finally getting to go ashore. It was overdue! We had a great dinner and lingered long catching up on each other's news.

We used the Bakers' car and went to the shopping center, post office, and beauty shop. We stopped at the post office and got our mail, much to our delight. *Tug II* came in shortly after and we invited them for dinner, along with Nancy and Dave. We had spaghetti, salad and fresh strawberry pie. Tim, the marina mechanic, and his wife Cindy stopped by too. It was so much fun seeing everyone again and was a delightful evening. It rained like crazy most of that day.

We went to St. William's Church for 10:30 Mass. Then to an oyster roast with Tim and Cindy, which was such a treat! The oysters as always were fabulous and you could have all you wanted. My dream! It did rain, but not on the party.

We were going to leave the next day, which was the 7th of May, but the rain was coming down in torrents. We returned the car to the Bakers and had a nice visit with them. We loafed away the afternoon—well, I did do some laundry, a joy in that nice laundromat! We went to Dave and Nancy's for dinner, where we met some other cruising couples, and Ann and Jerry, Marine friends of the Davises' who were en route to the Bahamas. The Collinses were also there and it was fun to see the General and Pat again. It was another delightful evening.

The next day was horrid looking, but we started out anyway after saying goodbye to Dave. The Golden Isles didn't charge us anything. They wanted Stan to work there so badly and replace Dave as the Marina manager. Dave wanted to get on to other pursuits. We were tempted because we liked the Golden Isles so much, but we had other things we wanted to do.

It was miserable cruising in pouring rain, but I stayed below and sewed, which was always enjoyable. We pulled into Queen Bess Creek around six o'clock. It still was one of the most super places ever. It was so far from any lights or cities, the quiet was intense, and the stars so bright, when it wasn't raining. We saw dolphins in there again and we had a quiet and peaceful, if rainy night.

We left Queen Bess Creek around eight o'clock in the morning. It was cloudy and rained off and on all day. I stayed below again and sewed. I enjoyed using some of my new material. We were having trouble with the starboard engine again and it kept stalling. Stan had bled the system the night before, but it was still acting up. We had some quite rough crossings on several sounds. We couldn't get into Harbor Town, so we stopped at the new Skull Creek Marina. It was pretty, but unprotected. The laundromat was good, as was the marina store and restaurant. There was no courtesy car though, as per their advertisement. It finally cleared up a little by evening.

We left the Skull Creek Marina at eight o'clock and we talked to *El Mareen* on the radio and they persuaded us to stop at Beaufort Marina in Factory Creek. First, we docked at the downtown marina and mailed some letters and shopped at the great health foods store there and got some things we needed. Their waterfront had been developed and it was gorgeous. We got a case of she-crab soup, a real treat. We pulled into the marina around eleven o'clock and a storm came up shortly after.

Helen and Austin Winter invited us for drinks and dinner aboard the *El Mareen*, a fifty-five-foot trawler. We had a nice time and met the Hewlitts from Lucy Island. They grew orchids. We also heard from *Circe* on their radio. Helen was a writer and had just had articles published in *Boating* Magazine and had a book going the rounds then. It was fun talking to her, as I had been trying to do this also. I finished sewing two halters for Althea and then started the third and it rained again.

At Rogers Marina – No name for the boat yet.

The main salon.

The aft cabin (our cabin).

Tommy in the main salon.

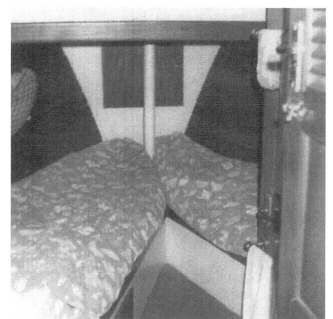

The fore cabin.

Tom at the helm in the main salon.

The *Steelaway* at sea.

Jo with the ship's flag.

At the dock – note the door to the rear cabin.

Stocking the lazaret.

The First Mate takes the helm.

The bridge unoccupied.

Approaching a lock on the Erie Canal.

A deep lock.

Coming into an up lock on the Erie Canal.

One of the lock parks on the Erie Canal.

Tom and Stan in one of the up locks. Note the bad wall conditions.

Tom and Jo handle the lines on an up lock.

Captain Stan handles the lines in a lock.

Ready to leave a lock. Note that the mast is down to account for low bridges.

Top of a lock.

Sleepover aboard *Steelaway* at the E. 55th Street Marina in Cleveland.

Living up on the ways at Brewerton, New York.

On the beach at Eleuthera.

Althea feeds an iguana at Allen Cay.

Anchorage at Norman Cay.

View of Hope Town from the lighthouse – a long climb up!

Hope Town Harbor and Light.

One of our favorite anchorages on the Waccamaw River.

Heading into the anchorage on the Waccamaw.

The Captain relaxes.

Serene anchorage on the Intracoastal.

Jo tends her tomato plant.

Captain Stan fixes the mast light.

Tug I, Colleen and Walt aboard *Tug II*.

The Captain and First Mate in the galley.

Biking in Beaufort, North Carolina.

Althea and Stan on the bridge.

Getting ready to go up onto the ways at Camachee Cove in St. Augustine.

Living up in the air rather than on the sea! Camachee Cove ways for week.

Thus begins Tom's search for alligators. Crossing Lake Okeechobee, Florida.

Christmas tree on the *Steelaway*.

Tom catches some fish at Sanibel, Florida.

First Mate's quarters on the bridge during a rough crossing.

A super sunset at Man-O-War Cay.

Shelling at Pelican Cay.

The Crossets and Temples at the Deck House in Green Turtle Cay.

Althea and Dorie in Ran Johnston's studio in Little Harbor.

The girls at Libby Henry's school.

Jo's water taxi in Guana Cay.

Dorie suits up.

Scuba diving on the Sandy Cay Reef.

The gang at the Green Turtle.

Little Harbor, as seen from "No See-ums Bight."

Preparing for a storm at Hope Town Harbor.

"Father done reach!" Mass at Hope Town.

Treasure Cay Beach with Parker and Joan.

Bill Steelher gives a hand letting down the dinghy at Treasure Cay.

Champagne brunch with the Steelhers at the Hope Town Harbor Lodge.

Jo's Mutton Snapper.

Stan cuts some palm fronds for "Bring your own Palm Sunday."

Outdoor benediction at Marsh Harbor.

Corpus Christie Sunday procession.

Gail and Jo go "junking" at Bookie's Beach in Little Harbor.

Bud Rue finds a piece of a space capsule on the ocean beach at Little Harbor.

The view from the lot in Little Harbor that we wanted to buy.

Chip and Cindy at Baker's Beach.

Chip and Cindy sailing in the dinghy, *The Bop*.

Stan and Stevie check the crab trap in Beaufort, North Carolina.

Checking out the wild horses on the Shackleford Banks.

Cape Lookout Beach.

The Pirate Ship *Meka*.

The pirate ships sail by, ready for battle. Barbie stands guard.

CHAPTER TWENTY

By now, it was the 11th of May and we left Beaufort at 7:30 in the morning. *El Mareen* followed shortly. When we started out, it looked like a beautiful day, but then it started to cloud up again. But my tomato plant had a tomato! That was one persistent plant, it never quit, just rested once in a while.

I must explain that my tomato plant was a real conversation piece. We had bought it somewhere on the way down the Intracoastal, and I potted it in a big container and put it on the roof over our stateroom on the stern. It was a patio-type tomato and believe it or not it regularly produced tomatoes. I had been afraid that the salt water would be bad for it, and even though it got sprayed in very heavy weather, the darn thing flourished and produced the tomatoes off and on the whole time that we were on the boat. I wish I could've had an herb garden!

It was very nice cruising till we got to the Wappoo Creek Bridge just below Charleston. Actually, we were held up at the Lymehouse Bridge. A whole bunch of us anchored there, because it was closed to hold back traffic until the Wappoo Creek Bridge up ahead was fixed. Anchored around us were the *El Mareen*, *Trident*, *Wild Hunter*, and *Dry Martini*. We were there from about one o'clock until 4:30.

At that time, a line squall came through churning us all around and at the same time a barge pushing a tow came down river and they opened the bridge! It was some kind of a Chinese fire drill with us all trying to get the anchors up and get through under the bridge and avoid the tow in the process! Naturally, it was raining so we all got wet. However, we all got through okay and we conferred via radio with *El Mareen*, *Wild Hunter*, *Trident*, *Resolute* and *Dry Martini*. They reported that we could get under the Wappoo Creek Bridge, which was stuck closed, but had thirty-foot clearance which was enough for all of us.

We came into Charleston around 6:15 and tried to anchor. The anchorage was empty, fortunately, but the skies looked ominous and we couldn't get the anchor to hold, so we gave up and went into Ashley Marina, which was very nice. They had new floating docks, which were especially good for Charleston's high and low tide system and only cost $10 a night. We were exhausted, so chatted with *Wild Hunter* and *Trident*, ate a sketchy dinner, and watched a Dean Martin special on TV and then collapsed into bed.

We got an early start the next day because we had a long run ahead of us. We had fun chatting with our friends as we went up the Intracoastal. It was a beautiful part of the waterway. Many bird preserves and so on. We saw about thirty white egrets lining the banks, single file, doing heaven only knows what, guarding their territory maybe? We also saw an eagle's nest in an old tall tree with the mama eagle sitting on the eggs. I went below and worked on an article on gifts for Christmas and I needed to write a query letter too. Then, I also cleaned house.

The tomato plant had two tomatoes that day and it was growing like crazy! I thought maybe I should put more soil in the pot, as it looked kind of like it was sinking from all the rain, but it looked very healthy. We loved seeing the Waccamaw River section again. It was so pretty. The old abandoned rice fields were kind of spooky. Were there bad vibes from the history of the slaves who worked and died there?

We arrived in Bucksport around six o'clock. The docks were very high above us because of the tide and we had trouble docking. Austin from the *El Mareen* was trying to help us, but he had trouble hearing us because he was pretty deaf. Stan really yelled at the poor man, trying to get him to take up on the bow line, and he finally figured out what we wanted. He and Helen were supposed to board our boat for drinks, but couldn't make it— we were so far below the dock. So we managed to climb up and carried the snacks to their boat and had drinks there. Later, we went to the marina restaurant, which was inexpensive and I thought unusually good, but it was mobbed with an excursion boat crowd. Our food was good when we finally got it, but the service was terribly slow.

After dinner, we said goodbye and headed for our favorite anchorage, which was quite close by. It was a gorgeous night with the sky full of stars, but pitch black because the full moon wasn't up yet. We anchored without too much difficulty and the holding was good. It was such a beautiful night. The water was still, an absolute mirror. The moon came up and it was even more beautiful. A crazy loon or something was really screaming when we came in, maybe he thought the Indians were attacking. We sat up on the bridge for a while to enjoy the lovely night and scenery. We saw the *Ebisu* there for the first time that trip. We scared them when we came in, as they thought we were a barge because of the reflection our lights made in the mirror-like water. I guess we looked pretty big on a dark night with our lights on!

We didn't wake up until 7:30, after a rain at 4:30 had awakened us. We had a leisurely breakfast, again enjoying our beautiful spot. That one rated second in our favorites to Queen Bess Cove. We enjoyed the walk, and the Myrtle Beach stretch. We had to pass several tows in a really narrow stretch near Myrtle Beach, which was scary. I had luck communicating on Channel 13 with the tugboat captains and they were all very nice. We really lucked out with the pontoon bridge that day, as they were having a record low tide and just after we got through, the bridge went aground and the bridge tender was unable to open the bridge for several hours, stranding the *Elixer* and several other boats behind.

Anyhow, we pulled in to the Southport Marina about 4:30 joining *Elixer*, *El Mareen*, *Trident*, *Layover*, and *Norjan*. I had a terrible time again with those darn whisker poles, since the dock was so high again because of the tide, and I had to pull the boat hook all the way out and balance myself, teetering on the bowsprit, kind of like Leo DiCaprio in Titanic, until I tossed the darn loop and got it on the pole, or the cleat on the pole. I finally did it after much moaning and complaining! I think I was finally improving my skills in this regard! *Norjan* had been following us all the way that day because they had engine trouble. They were one of the big Hatteras yachts that had rocked everyone so badly the day before as they went by. They turned out to be really nice though and I think maybe they didn't know any better. After having to travel slowly all day and be rocked by other boats' wakes maybe they understood now how we slow boats felt!

Dave and Pat Steel from *Trident* came over for drinks as did Helen and Austin from the *El Mareen* and we had a nice time. We made our calls to Cleveland, had a late dinner and collapsed into bed. It rained hard (what else) during the night.

We slept till 7:30 with the rain pattering on the roof. It was a yucky-looking day, so we loafed over breakfast and watched *Good Morning America*. Then, we went to the store and bought shrimp for $4.50 a pound and some nice bluefish for $.50 a pound.

146

We started off in the rain and it drizzled all day long. I worked below, sewing most of the day. We heard *Tug II* was just ten miles ahead of us and hoped we would catch them the next day. We saw a darling little deer standing on the shore in the rain. Finally, we pulled into Mile Hammock Bay, which is inside of Marine Camp Lejeune at about four o'clock and called *Tug II* and arranged to meet them in Beaufort the next day.

Their dog, who was named Tug One, was sick. I think they were having a hard time with him. He was a Newfoundland, a very big dog, and it was hard to get him ashore often enough for his comfort stops. If they weren't docked, they had to row him ashore in the dinghy. Tug One was funny. When we were swimming in the Chesapeake, Tuggie dove in and was determined to get us back aboard because Newfies were bred to be rescue dogs!

It looked like a whole Marine division was in the anchorage! There were landing craft, tons of trucks, and men swarming all over. We rafted to *Trident* in the pouring rain, and realized we were face to face on the generator side of both boats so we switched to the other side. We figured we'd probably both be using our generators and we didn't want all those exhaust fumes coming on our boats. We decided to remember this in the future when rafting!

We went aboard *Trident* for cocktails, which was pleasant. We had our bluefish for dinner, broiled with mayonnaise and onions, and it was great. Not a bit fishy. We had a noisy night, as the Marines ran loud generators on some trucks most of the night. We were up early at six a.m. and found it cold and drizzly. We got off by seven. I covered my poor tomato plant up so it wouldn't freeze en route. The tomatoes were almost growing while you looked at them. Something was eating the leaves though, so I thought I'd better spray. I also planned to re-pot it deeper if I could get soil in Beaufort.

We were delighted to remember that we had a mail stop that day. We talked to *Tug II*, who were just ahead and would meet us in Beaufort. We pulled in about eleven and docked at the lovely city docks. Colleen, Walter, Stan and I went shopping in the marina truck, which was fun. We got groceries and potting soil and so on. We went to the post office and got the mail, but there wasn't very much that day. We did get a note from Frank Rogers on the yacht *Lillian*, which was nice. We went aboard *Tug II* for cocktails. We finally had our fresh shrimp, which was great and collapsed into bed.

The next day was beautiful with no rain. We decided to lay over for a day. I finished my sewing for Althea and the pillow I was embroidering for Chrissy and got them mailed. I potted the tomato plant and it looked much happier. Colleen, Stan and I went to Bird Shoal, the island behind the anchorage not far from the marina and went clamming, but couldn't find any clams. We did get lots of oysters, so we came back and had a feast, oysters, grilled hamburgers, and key lime pie. We went early to bed that night with full, happy tummies.

We got up early, as Colleen and I wanted to go shelling on Bird Shoal before we took off that day. Stan ferried us over in the dinghy. We couldn't find much in the line of shells—there wasn't an ocean beach as we had thought—but just a huge tidal flat. It was pleasant exploring, though. We saw a darling baby pony with its mother. There were lots of wild ponies on that island, which date back to shipwrecked boats that first came to this country early in U.S. history.

We came back and left Beaufort regretfully around noon. It was such a beautiful place. It was blowing like crazy, up to twenty-five knots, and I was glad we were not doing the Neuse that day. To my dismay, we did cross to the bottom of the Pamlico Sound and it was rough. I was glad I had rigged for rough running.

It's funny though, I didn't mind it much after all. I guess perhaps I was getting more seaworthy, or at least my stomach was! After the Bahamas, anyway, nothing seemed bad. We pulled into Oriental around three o'clock and I leapt from the boat and into their beautiful laundromat. Oriental was a pretty little fishing village. The shrimpers were right opposite us. The marina was very nice and cost only ten dollars a night. Stan bought eight crabs for fifty cents while I finished the laundry. We boiled them and picked them and froze them for a super future meal.

Tug II traveled with us all day, as did *Ebisu*, and we all went out to dinner to celebrate Walter's birthday. We tried the Trawl Door restaurant, but it looked deserted—and didn't have the forty-three items in the salad bar that Walter wanted! So we went to the marina restaurant, which was very good, and we had a great seafood dinner. Later, we talked to *Circe*, who stayed at Whitaker Creek anchorage.

CHAPTER TWENTY-ONE

We were up early and left Oriental around 7:30, trying to beat the twenty-five knot winds predicted on the news. It was a terribly cold, dreary day and I feared for the poor tomato plant, but the Neuse wasn't too bad. It got a little worse as we went on, but was bearable. My tummy was glad to get off of it, though. We talked with *Tug II* en route and could see them near us. *Circe* and *Ebisu* stayed put back in Oriental.

It was cold all day and never stopped raining. We pulled into the anchorage just south of the Wilkerson Bridge and had a hot lunch—sausages, pancakes and eggs—which also heated up the boat thank goodness. My bread didn't turn out too well that day, as it was too cold for it to rise. I napped and had a lazy afternoon. *Tug II* stopped in Belhaven to let Tug One have a run and buy some cigarettes and she-crab soup. They pulled into the anchorage around five and we chatted for a moment via radio. Then, we watched the news, had dinner, and read in bed.

The wind changed in the night into the Southwest, after the weatherman had been saying Northeast twenty-five knots all day! He also had said we'd have a sunny day. He surely bombed out that day! We rocked a fair amount all night, but after I got up several times and assured myself that we weren't going to drag anchor, I slept pretty well. It was cold though, and I decided that that night I'd definitely wear my flowered Dr. Denton's. We got up the next morning at six to a rotten weather forecast, and winds were out of the Southeast up to twenty-five knots. Though, at least we had hopes of a following sea on the Albemarle Sound. While we were underway, I tried a sourdough French bread recipe, and had it rising in the engine room. I hoped that it didn't mind the noise and vibration!

We talked to *Tug II*, who had left early, hoping to find a comfort stop for Tug One, but with no luck. Someone reported on the radio that the dock north of the Fairfield Bridge was occupied, but they let Tug use the dock anyway, so he was probably not too uncomfortable. They invited us aboard for dinner that night. My French bread turned out pretty well. The Albemarle was fine in the beginning, but halfway across it began to a kick up and got pretty nasty before we were through. I didn't mind too much though, as I was asleep part of time. We came into Coinjock and the current was running strong. I tried to get my lines set and out in a hurry and I had trouble with that darn heavy spring line. In dashing around and yanking it, I hurt my back again. Damnation! We had a lovely dinner aboard *Tug II*, but I felt pretty miserable and had an uncomfortable night.

The next morning, we decided to go only as far as Great Bridge. Walt helped us get our lines off, as I couldn't bend. I stayed flat all day and took muscle relaxants and pain pills. We found that we could tie up all night at the little free dock and we did so. It looked like a very pretty spot and we would have liked to explore it more, but put it on the someday list.

We were up early the next morning and off to Hampton. I stayed below flat again all day. We had called ahead to Barney and Mary Gillespie and they had arranged for us to dock at their marina, which was the Sunset Marina. We pulled in around noon and it was so good to see them waiting for us. They left their Mercedes for us to use and it killed me not to go with the others to the shopping center, but I decided I better save my strength for the evening so I stayed flat. Stan brought back groceries and a new teapot, which we really needed. That evening Mary and Barney took us to the Hampton Yacht Club for dinner and we had a very nice time.

We had intended to start early for Ocracoke, but we discovered a leak in the port engine seal. In the process of fixing it, the mechanic cracked one of the oil injector pipes and Stan had quite a time fixing it. He had to get the new part, saw it off, file it down, and so on. We finally were able to leave and decided to go to Yorktown with *Tug II* instead of Ocracoke.

En route, the generator alarm went off and it shut down. Good grief! We called *Tug II* and asked them to get us a dock with electric. We pulled into Sara Creek, near Yorktown, which was lovely, and into the Yacht Haven Marina, which was really a beaut for $12.50 a night. My back seemed better, thank God!

We had a relaxed breakfast the next morning for a change and we watched *Good Morning America* on TV. The Strattons from *Tug II* were elated because Trudeau was defeated. They were Canadians and supported his opponent. It was sunny that morning, but as usual it clouded up by noon. We and *Tug II* headed out for Smith Island. It was kind of rough, but not too bad. I stayed below and Stan ran most of the way from below because it was cold and rainy (what else!). We pulled into Smith Island around four and docked at the city dock; if you could call it a dock! Smith Island was discovered by John Smith in 1608 and settled in 1628. It was a very interesting fishing village and it reminded me of Middle Bass Island in Lake Erie, where I spent my summers as a child. The children there went to high school on the mainland by boat and the people had an interesting accent that was hard to understand. It was raining pretty hard, so we didn't do much exploring that day.

We were up early the next morning because we had to vacate our spot at the dock by seven for the sailboats, fishing boats and so on to come in. We rafted onto *Tug II*. I sewed for a while, and then we walked around and explored between rain showers. My poor tomato plant! It had also turned quite cold. We bought twelve soft shell crabs and froze four of them. Colleen and Walter came over for dinner and we deep fried the crabs. I was disappointed, they didn't taste like I thought they would. Next time I decided I would sauté them. It was a fun evening and we all went early to bed.

Smith Island was beautiful, even in the rain, and we decided to explore more of the island. It was beautiful little town with gorgeous old houses. We were intrigued to see that each of the houses and yards were fenced all around. They also had their own little family graveyards in each front yard. I think the fences were important, because when you live full-time on a small island, privacy becomes very important. After we had walked around quite a while, we borrowed Colleen and Walt's bicycles and rode around.

My progress was a little erratic and wobbly! Stan steered me onto the sidewalk on the Main Street, feeling I was less of a menace to navigation there. We enjoyed seeing the old town and they had some gorgeous shops. The gourmet food store was a terrible temptation and the last thing in the world we thought you would find there. We bought the Sunday paper and *Cruising World* magazine, which had a report from the *Myann* and was such fun to see. They were really fulfilling their dream of cruising around the world in their sailboat.

We read the paper, and I sewed a birthday outfit for Christine. We resolved to come back there again. It was lovely!

The next morning was already 28th of May, and it was fun to just cruise at our own pace and not have a schedule. We left around 9:30 and cruised down the Tred Avon River to Easton, which was a gorgeous cruise! There were big estates all along the river. We tied up at the marina in Easton and got a ride into town. We discovered that our driver knew the Henrys and the Johnstons from Little Harbor very well. Such a small world! It was quite a long way into Easton and we were glad we weren't walking, as it was surely more than the advertised mile.

Easton was a beautiful little town with tons of gorgeous old houses and a nice-looking museum. There was an absolutely gorgeous fabric store, where I bought material to make Barbie a jumpsuit for her birthday. We wanted to have lunch at the pub, but it was closed, so we hitchhiked back to the boat. We had a quick lunch and then took off for Tilghman Island. It was a pretty cruise again.

We pulled into the Chesapeake House Dock, which was old, but okay. We spent an hour or so trying to get our power going, but finally gave up. We had an absolutely fabulous dinner there. I had the oyster special, which was oyster stew with two dozen oysters, oysters on the half shell, fried oysters and oyster fritters, plus some marvelous coleslaw. Naturally, there was no way I could finish all that!

Walter loved their coleslaw and asked for a second big dish served family style. This was our first experience with Walt's passion for coleslaw, or cabbage salad, as he called it, which we were often to experience in our many good times cruising with the Strattons. We hurried back, in the rain naturally, to catch the second half of a program that we really enjoyed on TV. Colleen's electric went off for a while, so she came over to watch with us. Later, we tried to reach our nephew Parker Orr, Jr. by phone, whom we were hoping to meet when we reached Annapolis.

We headed out early the next morning at 6:30 to go to a generator specialist at Herring Bay. Our generator wouldn't stop and *Tug II's* wouldn't start! We pulled in around eight and Stan, Walter and the mechanics started working and didn't finish until 6:30 p.m. I seemed to have gotten an eye infection and it was really starting to bother me, so I decided I would try and see a doctor when we got to Annapolis.

By the time they finished working on the generator, it was too late to head for Annapolis, so we decided to go out at six the following morning. *Tug II's* generator was fixed also, but at a very high price and Walt wasn't completely satisfied, so they decided to follow us later. We tried again to reach Parker, Jr. with no luck. We did get my dear friend Weezie and she planned to drive down to Annapolis the next day, or else come down to dinner with her husband Pat. I was really excited at the thought of seeing her.

We left as scheduled at 8:30 and it was a beautiful sunny day for our trip to Annapolis. I loved to see the crazy ospreys, who built their nests on every marker on the waterway. They were so sloppy and are made of big twigs that went every which way. The mama ospreys looked like harassed Phyllis Dillers. Maybe their nests kept slipping.

We pulled into Annapolis around 1:30. It was a gorgeous day and we enjoyed the cruise up there. We got a slip at the city dock, the same as last year, much to our delight. It was right in the middle of all the action! I ran to the bakery to get fresh strawberry rolls, and then hurried to the hospital, hoping I could get into see someone about my eye. I got in and out of there fairly fast, but I didn't know what to think. They had a minimum charge of fifty-six dollars! I almost turned around and walked out of the emergency room, but there were no doctors open on Wednesday in town, even if I could've gotten an appointment with one. I was seen by a nice doctor, who said he thought my problem was an allergy and prescribed some drops for me. I hoped he was right, because I didn't think it should have hurt that much if it was an allergy, but I decided to try the drops and see. Incidentally, the first question the doctor asked me was, "How do you get here from there?"

Weezie and her daughter Karen came down around noon and brought a darling basket of goodies—ham, cheese, crackers and so on. We went to lunch and had a wonderful visit. It was so much fun to have girl time with a dear old friend and her daughter.

Stan had worked on the generator all day. Something was still wrong with that miserable old piece of equipment and it was so frustrating! Especially since we had spent the whole day before having the mechanics work on it.

I managed to get in touch with Rosie Donihi, and the Hetteriches, but still no luck with Parker Junior. I was looking forward to seeing these old friends again.

It was so much fun being at the crazy city dock again. It was a little like being in the middle of the street. There were loads of midshipmen from the Naval Academy walking by, and they stopped to chat and we found several were from Cleveland. We wrote down their names and addresses and parents' phone numbers. We promised to call their parents and tell them that we had seen them when we got to Cleveland. We didn't manage to get our dinner that night until around eight because of many interruptions by passersby. We finally had to close the door and draw the drapes to be able to eat in peace!

The next day I did odds and ends of little errands around town while Stan worked on the generator some more and installed a new generator switch. I wandered around Annapolis. There was so much history in that town. Then, I came back to *Steelaway* and baked a strawberry pie. I thought my eye seemed somewhat better, but I was still having a lot of pain behind the eyes, which was kind of discouraging.

That evening, the Hetteriches and a priest friend, Father Bill, came for dinner. Bud and Gloria had been in a gourmet group with us in Cincinnati and were old friends. We had a pleasant evening and did dishes and got to bed at midnight. That was late for us, but so worth it! We woke up early to a rainy and misty morning, so we did some much-needed housekeeping.

We looked in a gallery in town and saw some of Zora Akins' paintings. She and her husband were the artists that we met in Chubb Cay when we were all stranded there. It was really neat to see her paintings. A little later, the Donahis came down for coffee and we had a fun visit. Rosie and Bob were always so great about seeing us when we were in Annapolis. After our experience with our boat dragging in a storm while we were away, we were a little leery of going to Washington!

We left Annapolis around noon and decided not to go to Baltimore and headed for Chesapeake City instead. It was a pleasant cruise there, in spite of being quite a misty day. The anchorage there was very nice. *Tug II* came along and rafted onto us. Another Grand Banks forty-two came in—the *Jerlee B. the Second*—and anchored near us. It was a very quiet night. There was no wind and the water was like a mirror and the no-see-ums were not biting! We went to bed early, because we planned a five o'clock departure the next morning. My eyes were still not feeling too good.

CHAPTER TWENTY-TWO

We were up at the first light the next morning and there was a very thick fog. It was cold, clammy, and sort of scary. We ran on the radar, communicating back and forth like mad with *Tug II*. It seemed like an awfully long trip, but overall not a bad one for the big bad Delaware Bay. We arrived in Cape May around 2:30 and tied up at the Cape Island Marina East. It cost us about $21.50 and had nothing in the way of facilities. We decided next time we'd anchor out.

I tried to get an appointment at the eye doctor's, but had no luck. They didn't have a courtesy car anymore either, and the place smelled like a fish factory. However, we got scallops at $3.50 a pound, which were delicious. *Tug II* picked them up for us from a nearby fisherman and *Hotspur* delivered them. *Tug II* was anchored out, but *Wild Hunter* and *Hotspur* were in there with us. We were very tired, so it was early to bed again, falling asleep to the sound of the soft rain.

It was up and off early again at eight o'clock for Atlantic City with *Tug II*, *Wild Hunter*, and *Hotspur* in convoy. It was another cold, dreary, rainy day and we ran from below a good deal of time. We had calm seas, except for a gentle swell, the kind that undoes me! We pulled into the Atlantic City Marina around two. *Hotspur* was already there and had slips lined up for us all.

Colleen and I did laundry and I read the Sunday paper. We had a lovely lazy, rainy afternoon. I tried to make a cake—pineapple upside down cake—but the cake mix was bad. I think it was mildewed and it was inedible. My eyes were maybe a shade less bothersome that day. *Wild Hunter* had a great recording of bugle calls, and they played taps for us at bedtime!

The next morning at 5:30, Tiger from *Wild Hunter* played reveille to get us all up! I'm not sure our neighbors really appreciated this. We started for Sandy Hook at six o'clock. *Tug II*, *Wild Hunter* and we were joined by *Serenity*, a fifty-foot Hatteras that was having trouble with their radar and radio and wanted to travel with us.

There was very little visibility and we had a steady rain. The seas were better that day and my tummy felt better. I certainly hoped that it would quit raining one of those days! *Hotspur* joined us also and *Nerissa* passed us by and waved. We finally came into Atlantic Highlands in the rain at about 4:15 and we all docked. I ran to the post office and got our mail. On the way, I spotted an oculist's office and made an appointment for the next day at 8:30 in the morning to have pressure tests and an eye exam. I was so relieved!

I was up early and at Dr. Rubin's office by 8:30. He said my eyes looked fine and he thought the trouble was my needing glasses for distance vision! I was so relieved and felt the weight of the world lifting off my shoulders. I had always had excellent distance vision, but apparently at my age that had radically changed. The doctor said my glasses would be ready in a few days. The sun was out and it was a beautiful day!

We rented a car and we went to the supermarket and stocked up on groceries. It was really fun to have a car and we did lots of errands. The other boats all left except *Tug II*, who stayed over because of generator problems. What else? Stan worked on ours all day, and then he fixed theirs! At least for the moment. We had a violent thunderstorm late in the afternoon and it blew like crazy for a few minutes, a real line squall.

By now it was the 6th of June and we had a busy day. We took advantage of the rental car and ran errands and accomplished quite a bit. My poor tomato plant didn't look too good, probably because it had been rained on too much. We picked up Tommy at the airport and he looked great and all ready to cruise with us to Cleveland.

The next day we had pea soup fog all day and it never did lift. We took a car and went over to Sandy Hook and had lunch in a darling restaurant called the Careless Navigator. We drove around a bit, but the beach didn't look too good in the fog so we headed back to the boat. I made a pair of slacks and picked up my new glasses. I couldn't believe how much better I could see! Hallelujah! And no more pain! Tommy worked on an art project and Stan read. We called our friend Tom Westropp and he said he was coming the next day. Stan and I both had terrible colds and we hoped that we wouldn't give them to the two Toms.

By the next day, Tommy had the community cold. It was foggy again that day, but not as bad as the day before. Tom W. arrived around 10:30 and we took off for New York. We enjoyed the harbor trip, but the visibility was poor. We took pictures anyhow. We arrived in Tarrytown around six and the sun came out and the evening was nice. The tide was very low though and we eased very carefully into our dock and just made it without an inch of water to spare.

We left Tarrytown early the next morning and it was foggy again. I made sourdough pancakes for breakfast from a starter that Colleen had given me, and they were pretty good. We ran to Kingston, which was getting to be practically our old home place! I was sorry that the scenery was not too good along the Hudson that day, because it was usually so beautiful, but we had a haze all day.

By this time, I had lost my voice and Tommy's cold was worse, but Stan's was a little better. We pulled into John Hoy's new location around four. It was a pretty spot, but there was no store or anything nearby. I missed our pretty little cove where we had spent so much time. We hoped to have John fix our darn generator for good this time. Talk about hope springing eternal!

We got up early and borrowed a car to go to town for church and shopping. After Mass, Tom W. picked up his rental car and we went back to Hoys'. We had a lazy day, mostly just sitting around in the sun talking. Tom W. left around four to fly back to Cleveland. We thought he had a good time in spite of being surrounded by germs. We hoped so.

It absolutely poured all day the next day without letup! John worked on the boat in the afternoon and while helping Stan to step the mast, it broke. So we knew we would have to stay over another day and get the darn mast fixed. We had to step the mast in order to go through the Erie Canal up river.

It was sunny, but very cold in the forties the next day. However, it was a lovely looking day. My cold and Tommy's were really bad and we all felt lousy. John got the part fixed and Stan got the boat ready to proceed towards the canal.

On June 13th, we took off at six o'clock. It was a beautiful but cold day for our start up the Erie Canal. We went through eleven locks that day.

They were pretty easy, as they were mostly up locks, my favorite kind. We stopped at the park at Lock 11 and tied up. We went through the Guy Johnson House, which was a very interesting piece of history. We got back to the boat and saw the *Caledonia* had tied up. They were Canadians, Catherine and Tom Henry, and we had met them before. They were on their way to the St. Clair River.

The next day was another beautiful day and we went as far as Illion. We stopped early enough so I could run into the fabric store and pick up some sewing supplies that I needed. The *Caledonia* had stayed with us all day that day. We had our first down locks that day, and it went okay. Tommy was getting very good at handling the Schenectady hitch, which was a big help to me. He was really good.

The next day, we went as far as Lock 23. It was another gorgeous day and I think we deserved it after so many rainy ones! The canal park was a gorgeous spot. We swam, sat under the trees for happy hour, and grilled hamburgers for dinner. We could see Lake Oneida up ahead and it was flat calm and pretty.

We left early the next morning and stopped in Baldwinsville to go to church and get some groceries. Then we went onto Lock 26. It was a very hot and humid day for a change. We were all alone there until the yacht *Felicity* from Grosse Isle joined us. It got suddenly very cold that night and we got an early start and went as far as Newark and tied up in a very pretty canal park there. There was electric there, but we couldn't make it work. However, it was warm enough that it really didn't matter. We had lunch, did some shopping and explored. They had a very nice clock museum there, which we enjoyed. We left and headed to Pittsford and the Halls' dock. We had a nice visit with Ruth and Sam and it was fun to see them again.

We borrowed the Halls' car the next morning and did some grocery shopping before we took off for Brockport. We saw the *Caledonia* pass by and we waved madly and then chatted briefly with them when we both stopped at the restaurant dock in Brockport. We agreed that we would meet in Buffalo. Then Tommy and I toured the university campus there, which was hosting the National Special Olympics that summer. Tom was a gold medal winner in the state of Kentucky and had hoped to go there, but the state could only afford to send a certain number of the gold medalists and Tom didn't luck out in the drawing. He still enjoyed seeing the place.

We stopped at Middlesport the next day to do a very large washing! It was so great to be able to hop on and off of the boat and right into the laundromat. No waiting around reading very old magazines while waiting for your laundry to be done. We had a funny experience that day going down the canal, when a truck up ahead tried to race across the bridge just as it was going up and didn't make it! He didn't fall into the water, but his truck ended up in pieces as he flew through the air when it landed on the bridge. It looked like something out of the Keystone cops! We tied up to a telephone pole on shore until a wrecker came and hauled the truck away and the bridge opened up again.

We also waited several hours at another bridge. We finally tied up to the bridge until an apologetic keeper came. They didn't always have a lot of traffic and they tended go to the local tavern for a few brews until some boat came along and blew its horn! Because of all the delays, it was nine p.m. by the time we pulled into the marina and we were very tired. Luckily, the *Caledonia* had made a reservation for us and we tied right up. There was a thunderstorm that night, but we slept right through it.

It was still storming the next morning and we debated whether to go on or not. We finally decided that we'd go on as far as Buffalo at about four o'clock and we could at least get the federal lock behind us. We got to the federal lock and they were holding it open for an enormous freighter. We had to wait almost two hours, but it was fun watching the huge boat go through. We were tied up next to *Caledonia*. Finally, both of us went through the lock together and we pulled into the Jones Boys Downtown Marina in Buffalo, which was gorgeous, although most of the electric outlets didn't work. We had a very late dinner again at nine o'clock and wearily fell into bed. The downtown marina was where the big observation tower was and we thought it would be fun to see it in the daytime someday. It had a gorgeous view of the Buffalo skyline.

We left Buffalo early in spite of the storm warnings and we had a rough trip to Dunkirk, where we anchored. It was very cold and rainy. We took the dinghy ashore and got groceries. This was a familiar spot and we anchored right under the Illuminating Company again, as we had the night of the terrible storm we encountered there.

It was horribly cold next morning! They had a record forty-seven degrees and a twenty-five knot wind, so we decided to stay put. We went into town again via dinghy and I got some wonderful material at the fabric store and sewed on Barbie's birthday outfit awhile. *Caledonia* was tied up at the outer dock at the yacht club where we had had such a bad experience. The Henrys put out two anchors to keep their boat from being thrown against the dock. We felt a shade safer anchored out, but Tommy was getting kind of restless I think.

The Henrys and their guests came aboard for drinks and we had a pleasant evening. We decided the wind had dropped a little the next morning and decided we'd leave. We stopped at Erie for fuel and it hadn't been too bad up to that point. However, it got very rough afterwards with those lousy northeast beam seas. The cabin looked like a disaster area. What a mess! One of my plants had been tossed right out of its pot by a huge wave. Tommy and I had gone into the cabin during the trip and were kind of scared. The TV had been tied down with a bungee cord again, but it looked like it wasn't going to hold. Fortunately it did, but I have to say it was one of the roughest trips we'd ever had.

Because Lake Erie is so shallow, it is notorious for sudden storms with very choppy waters. *Caledonia* got to Ashtabula about an hour ahead of us, instead of going to Erie, and reserved a spot for us at the Sutherland Marina. It was after dark and we had a tough time seeing lights and finding the entrance to the harbor, but were talked in by *Caledonia*. At night, lights that looked so familiar in the daytime were very hard to read. It was ten o'clock at night when we got there and we had a quick dinner and fell into bed.

The next morning, the 25th of June, which was Tommy's birthday and our anniversary, we finished the trek to Cleveland. We had a pretty decent day and it was not a bad trip. We felt we deserved it! We pulled into Cleveland around five o'clock in the afternoon and Chip and Cindy and the Chemas—Barb, Tom, Chrissy, and Steve—came aboard for Tom's birthday dinner! We were at our usual dock and it was heavenly to be here near all our family and friends.

CHAPTER TWENTY-THREE

Even though it wasn't in actual calendar days, we considered this to be the end of the second year of being liveaboards. It had been a year of seeing many wonderful new places, making new friends, and traveling many miles. It was a year of adjustment for us both. Stan had certainly mastered the many skills needed to keep the boat in good shape, learning a lot about weather, sharpening his navigating skills, which had always been very good, and maybe being more relaxed with the responsibilities of being the captain. He certainly became more skilled in handling me when I was scared to death. We no longer left the dock or the anchorage if the weather report was really bad and I didn't want to go. In return, I tried not to panic so much and I guess I was really just getting used to this life.

My favorite part of living aboard was getting to our destination and exploring the area, seeing old or making new friends, and getting off the boat. I decided I really enjoyed looking at water more than being on it! The long days of traveling to our destination could be pretty boring. Miles and miles of nothing but water to look at, or passing the same scenery that we had seen many, many times going up or down the Intracoastal also could be pretty boring. Luckily, I loved to read, write, do sewing and embroidery. It was also fun to communicate with the other boats on the radio. I did a lot of baking and household chores, which made the time pass pretty quickly as well. At any rate, much as I missed our family and old friends, I was happy to sign on for another year.

July and August were fun times with friends and family, as we were cruising to many of our favorite Lake Erie spots such as Cedar Point and Put-In-Bay. One trip we particularly enjoyed was with Chip and Cindy, when we went up to Mackinac Island in Lake Huron. We picked them up at Cedar Point and got them settled in the foreward cabin. We decided to head for Put-In-Bay for the night, but found it to be quite rough out there, so we went into Gem Beach instead. A lot of our friends were there and we were invited to brunch at the Islandview Apartments. We visited until it looked much calmer on the lake and we decided to head for Put-In-Bay, where we were able to pick up a mooring in the anchorage. We saw the *Coastal Queen*, which was the Chesapeake Buy Boat that we'd last seen in in Easton, Maryland with *Tug II*. Buy Boats are the ones that anchor in the harbor where the fisherman bring their catch in for sale. They were a long way from home. We had dinner at the Crew's Nest and then a quiet, restful night at anchor.

We left Put-In-Bay at 7:30 in the morning and headed for Detroit. It was a nice day, but we were glad we had a following sea, as it got quite rough before we got to Detroit. We enjoyed the trip up the Detroit River. We passed downtown Detroit with its interesting skyline and several pretty islands. It was intriguing to watch their morning rush hour traffic as we glided by in vacation mode. Just past Detroit, we stopped at the Municipal Marina, which was as nice as we remembered it from our former boating days. We tied up and decided to walk to the grocery store, which turned out to be a little scary as it had changed into a bad part of town. It started to rain quite hard, so we turned on the air conditioning because it was hot and muggy.

We left fairly early the next morning in a fog and crossed Lake St. Clair. I always liked Lake St. Clair, as it is a very pretty crossing, but because of the fog the viewing was not as sharp and pretty as normally it would be. We saw lots of freighters passing close by as the whole lake was buoyed for the freighters because it's so shallow. We talked to a U.S. Steel boat on the radio, which was a lot of fun for Captain Stan. They got a kick out of the fact that our boat was named *Steelaway* by a former U.S. Steel man.

We pulled into a gorgeous municipal marina around five o'clock in Port Huron. It had really been upgraded since the last time we were there. Chip and Cindy cooked hamburgers for us, which were very good. It was fun sitting on the deck, eating and watching life go by in the town. It rained most of that night.

We called Barbie early the next morning, and got a message that Cindy's dad was in the hospital for heart tests, so we decided to stay over a day and see how he was doing. We went to the store and explored the town and I got my hair cut. I should say scalped, as it was terribly short. Oh well, at least it would be low maintenance! Stan worked on our radar while we were doing all this. We went out to dinner that night at the Fog Cutter restaurant, which was on top of a tall bank building and it was lovely. We had a very good dinner and then got good news about Cindy's father. He hadn't had a heart attack and was being sent home from the hospital that day. We all went to bed very relieved.

We left Port Huron at eleven o'clock the next morning and it was a miserable day—rainy, windy, and cold. It started to clear up a little by noon, but it was fairly rough most of the way to Port Sanilac. We decided to pull in there. It was a lovely little port and had a great state marina. It was another one that had been much more developed than the last time we came this way. Chip taught a little boy from the yacht *Lemonade* to sail his dinghy. Then we walked the beach, and explored the town, such as it was. We got ice cream cones and the newspaper, which was a treat. Then we had a nice pot roast dinner by candlelight.

It was early—seven o'clock—when we left the next morning. We planned to run to Port Rogers that day and take advantage of the weather. However, the best laid plans often go astray and from Saginaw Bay on it really kicked up. We had a nasty beam sea with large rollers, so we decided to go into Harrisonville and arrived there about seven o'clock, which made it a long day. It was a lovely, sleepy little town. We were finding that all of the dock masters at these ports were so friendly. This poor man stuttered, though, and he had to say "H-h Harrisonville-H-h-Harbor" on the radio a hundred times a day. He never gave up and you had to admire him! Chip said it was hard not to answer back, "*S-S-Steelaway*!"

We were up to an early start at seven o'clock the next morning. It looked like a beautiful day and the weather report was good, but then so was it the day before! We passed two beautiful islands—Thunder Bay and Squaw. The water kicked up later, as usual, and was getting pretty fierce before we docked at the Rogers City Marina. They were having a Marine Festival and the place was really jumping! We picked the quietest looking dock and tied up.

We had called the Barrows en route to Rogers City and we called again to let them know we had arrived. Ruth and Al were old friends of ours from Cincinnati, who had a summer place at nearby Burt Lake, and we were looking forward to seeing them. They arrived shortly after we did and took us to their place at Burt Lake. Chip and Cindy elected to stay aboard and have a night to themselves. We had a super time with the Barrows and their place was really lovely. It was fun seeing Ann, Amy and Harry, and their daughter Lori Ann. We chatted until the wee hours and then slept in a lovely bed on a nice cool night.

We got the poor Barrows up at six o'clock the next morning and they drove us back to the boat, where we took off in the driving rain for Mackinac Island. It cleared up shortly though, and it turned into a beautiful day. We had a lovely run to Mackinac.

We talked on the radio with *Tradewinds*, who reserved dock space for us at the marina. We found the marina to be gorgeous and right under the fort. They played taps every night with two echoing bugles. I had forgotten how beautiful Mackinac was! There are no cars allowed on the island and we went everywhere by horse and buggy, bicycle or on foot. The fort stood high and dominated the island. It had been built by the British during the Revolutionary War, and also saw action during the War of 1812. We explored around the island a little bit and then had Mike and Jenny from *Tradewinds* over for a drink. We fell asleep to the sound of Taps.

We had breakfast the next morning at Yoder's Restaurant and met Vicky Yoder, who was the daughter of Dick Greiner, our landlord of sorts at the E. 55th Street Marina. Vicky and her husband had recently bought the restaurant and were having a great time running it. We promised her that we would tell her dad that we had seen them as soon as we got back to the 55th Street Marina.

After breakfast, we took a horse and buggy tour and then walked, exploring the island until our feet wore out! We hiked up the hill to the fort, which had been beautifully restored. We enjoyed wandering around with the map of the fort and seeing it as it had been many years ago. We had lunch on a porch looking out over the harbor above our marina and admired *Steelaway* below.

After a much needed nap, we went to the Islandview Hotel and had a delicious dinner. We strolled back to the boat, buying some of the wonderful fudge that the island was famous for. It was fun sitting out on the upper deck in the dark and watching the lights and the bustle ashore. We felt so privileged to be where we were and being able to share the fun with Chip and Cindy.

There was a lollapalooza of a storm that night! Much wind, thunder and lightning and it was still very rough and windy next morning, so we decided to stay an extra day in Mackinac. It was a gift to have an extra day on the island and since it wasn't raining, we made the most of the extra time.

We had a day to make up, so the next morning we left early and ran all the way to Harrisonville Harbor. It was fairly rough and a long day, so we were pretty tired when we got in. It blew like crazy all that night and it was very cold.

We had intended to go to Port Huron, but it looked so threatening that we docked in Port Sanilac instead. It rained and blew like crazy again all night. The next morning, the wind had died and it wasn't so rough, so we decided to do a long day and go all the way to Keane's Marina in Detroit. It had been cloudy and rainy all day, but not too rough for which we were all grateful. The next day, the winds were very high and it was much too rough to cross Lake Erie, so we stayed put there and had a lazy day.

We were greeted with the predicted high winds and waves the next morning, so we waited until almost two o'clock to leave. The lake was practically flat all the way to Mouse Island, where it kicked up some.

We had a funny experience on the way. Our radio was on as usual and we heard an S.O.S. call. A woman told the Coast Guard that she was alone sailing her sailboat and that she was pregnant and just about to have her baby. She said she was quite far from any port and she was unable to keep sailing the boat. The Coast Guard answered her immediately and asked for her location. She was kind of moaning and groaning and said she didn't know where she was. While the Coast Guard was trying to locate her, a nurse called on the radio and said she could help her deliver the baby by herself. By this time the woman no longer was on the radio and neither the Coast Guard nor the nurse could raise her. They kept calling on the radio, "Lady having the baby in the sailboat, come in, come in," but she didn't answer and they kept trying for a long time. It turned out to be a hoax, but the Coast Guard has to take these calls, because you never know when it would be a real emergency.

We went on to Cedar Point and had a farewell dinner at the CP steakhouse. John Firestone joined us and we had a pleasant evening. I hated to see Chip and Cindy leave, as we had been enjoying their company so much, and we reluctantly said goodbye and fell into bed.

We got up at the crack of dawn the next morning and headed for Cleveland. We had heard that big winds were coming very shortly, so we hurried on. It was flat calm and the whole trip was delightful. We got in just before the winds hit as predicted. The first thing I did was plug in the phone, a real luxury for us liveaboards!

One other trip that summer that we enjoyed was with our former Power Squadron from Canton, Ohio. We had kept in touch with them since we came aboard and they were very curious to see *Steelaway*. They were having a rally at Huron, Ohio and invited us to join them. We got up at six o'clock in the morning and headed for Huron. Tommy had come for another visit and was with us. We docked at Huron and immediately became the center of attention. We ended up having an open house on our boat because everyone was so curious to see it. You didn't see too many ocean-going boats like ours on Lake Erie, so they were curious to examine ours.

We were still having an open house next morning and were delighted to see many of our old friends, as well as meet some of the new members. The Squadron then headed for Vermillion and docked at the city wall and had lunch. Tommy and Stan went to a museum, and then we all went back to Huron and enjoyed the Squadron dinner at the Twine House. We came back to the boat after dinner, and who were sitting on a bench outside but George and Olive Miller, who were dear old friends from Mansfield. It was like old home week again, it was so great to see them.

We slept till eight o'clock the next morning, which felt awfully good. We had coffee and rolls with the Squadron on the dock and again more open house. We got to church for the ten o'clock Mass and got ready for a visit from Aunt Jo Fritzsche and the Fosters. It was so much fun to see them and we had a lovely lunch, most of which they brought! We took them for a short cruise to Cedar Point and back, but it rained, which kind of ruined it. We dropped them off back in Huron where their car was and after they left we decided to stay there that night, as it was really pretty miserable! We had a terrible time docking in the wind, rain and current. We finally did it with the help of a sailor who got our boat line for us. Unfortunately, this renewed my dread of going through the Erie Canal with just the two of us and all those down locks in the fall weather.

We left there early the next morning for Cleveland. There was still quite a bit of a swell from the night before, but it wasn't a bad trip and fairly short as well. I delightedly plugged in the phone!

We had about two weeks left in Cleveland and spent a lot of time with the kids and grandchildren. Chrissy and Stevie were delighted to have "overnights" on the boat and we loved this too! But before we knew it, the time had come to again head south. On September 10th we waved goodbye, unplugged the phone and headed for Buffalo.

CHAPTER TWENTY-FOUR

It was a pretty day, but the wind soon piped up and we had a huge following sea, so we pulled into the Grand River at Fairport Harbor and got a dock at the Grand River Yacht Club. It was so quiet, and a pretty, peaceful place and we enjoyed a nice restful day after our many goodbyes the night before. It was still blowing twenty-five to thirty knots out of the Northeast the next day, so we decided to lay over another day. Fairport is a lovely, sleepy, quiet old town and we took a walk into town to the post office and got stamps. I cleaned house, read a book, and wrote eight letters! That day the quality of light and air was definitely fall—which always makes me sad and nostalgic. But fall has always been one of my favorite seasons and I loved the beautiful colors.

At sunrise the next morning we started out. It was beautiful out and we had a good trip to Dunkirk. It took us twelve hours, but the water was really flat calm. We anchored in our usual spot and had a quiet dinner while enjoying the sunset. Unfortunately, as always seemed to happen in Dunkirk, the wind came up and blew like crazy. I think we were jinxed there! We didn't sleep too well because we were up checking the anchor a lot, but it was really an uneventful night and all was well.

We left early the next morning for the three and a half hour run to Buffalo. It wasn't too bad until the last hour. It was a good thing we left when we did, because the weather was rapidly getting worse. Hurricane Fred was coming! We went through the federal lock with no problems and pulled into the Smith Boys Marina around 1:30. We took a nap and then hiked to the supermarket. We said hello to quite a few of our friends.

At about eleven o'clock that evening the rains came! They had record rains for Buffalo. It leaked over my bunk in the middle of the night. So I went forward and slept up there. The river was very high and swollen by the next morning. We watched a lot of debris go by in the river and decided that we'd better stay put for the day. This gave me a chance to do several sewing projects that I was anxious to get to. I had planned on making most of my Christmas presents again. By the end of the day it looked like we would be held up here quite a while, because the canals were flooded and full of debris. Hurricane Fred had cut a big swath!

The next day was a gorgeous sunny day, but the canals were flooded and full of debris still, so we had to wait. We walked to the nearby town and did lots of shopping. I worked on my patterns and sewed a while. I read the book *Evergreen* by Belva Plain, which I loved.

We were still stuck the next day. So I sewed, using my new slacks pattern (who could believe that their thigh was bigger around than their grandmother's waistline when she got married!) And I fudged on the pattern and the pants were too tight. Too much good living that past summer I guess! I guess you really can't argue with the figures. We saw the Ernsts and the Christiansons and enjoyed renewing our friendship.

It was lovely and sunny again the next day, but cool. Elmer Ernst loaned us his car and we went to Mass, which was nice. Then the Ernsts invited us for supper aboard their boat, but later the event was moved to the Smiths' boat. Harold and Carol Smith were the owners of the marina and we had a very pleasant evening aboard their boat.

We spent the next day getting ready to leave. The debris and the water were supposed to be okay by the next day. We did lots of last minute chores and I sewed up some new beige slacks, which fit, thank goodness, and were very pretty. Whew! At cocktail time, Mike and Ann from *Miffer* came over. That winter they were chartering in Tortola, which was one of our favorite spots in the Virgin Islands. After dinner, Chuck and Betty Christianson took us for a ride in their car to check on the water in the canals. It looked okay and we thought it was so nice of them to do that for us.

We left the marina early next morning and went as far as Middlesport. It was a gorgeous day and a beautiful ride. We pulled into our usual spot around 1:30, had lunch, did laundry, and walked around. We tried to call Chip and Cindy and the Halls from Plowy's Saloon, which had the only phone in town, but had no luck. The wind started to blow like crazy and it got very cold in the evening, down to forty degrees! I got out my flannel sheets and the jammies with the feet in and was sure happy to have them!

We had another beautiful day and the weather warmed up enough to run the boat from the bridge again. We had gotten a late start because the bridge tender had taken an hour-long coffee break! I guess you had to look around in the saloons for them!

We pulled in to the Reed-Kents' dock around 4:30 and found the Halls were out-of-town, but due back that evening. We hiked into town and picked up a few groceries and made a phone call from a very noisy gas station. It got very cold towards evening and we turned the heat on. A note had been left for us from Walter and Colleen from *Tug II*. We had just missed them by five days, darn it! They said they were heading for Quebec and then south. Judging by the weather we were encountering, we thought they'd freeze to death! We resolved to leave for the south earlier next time.

The cold, as usual, broke records that night as so often it did when we were present, but it warmed up quickly in the morning. Sam Hall and a friend came aboard for coffee and we used Sam's phone to call Althea and were delighted to hear she would be coming down soon. I did some birthday and Christmas shopping in the Halls' lovely store and then we headed out. We ran from the bridge and the locks turned out to be a piece of cake. Halleluiah!

We stopped in Newark at 4:30 and after much fiddling around—and many quarters later—got their electric working. The outlets in the Erie Canal tended to be iffy, you never knew whether they would work or not. It would be a lot more expensive having to stop in a marina every night.

I walked into Singers and was so disappointed to discover they had no fabric available and not too many patterns. We sat on the bridge for happy hour and enjoyed the sun and the view while Stan grilled the first of our steaks for dinner.

We left early the next morning. It was cloudy and windy, but not too cold. It was a little windy in the locks, but we got through them without too much trouble. Our scenery was very pastoral that day. There were cows standing in the water, who watched our wake and ran when it got close. There were lots of herons, who seemed to be heading south. There were also lots of ducks, wild and tame. They quacked a lot as they glided along. Their wake looked just like ours! It was heavenly to be able to run from the bridge again and the locks were a piece of cake!

The next morning was Sept. 21st and we left early, feeling we were running out of time and needed to hurry south before winter set in. It was cloudy and windy that day, but not too cold. The wind bothered us some in the locks, but we managed to navigate them without too much trouble. We docked at the Lock 23 wall at Baldwinsville, an old canal town. We went to dinner at a nearby diner and had a good meal and enjoyed talking to the locals. They had a phone and we called the Motzkins and it looked like they'd be able to travel with us to New York City.

The next day was beautiful and sunny and we were able to make the 8:15 locking through Number 23. The goldenrod and purple weeds were gorgeous, if a little hay fevery. The cemetery behind the wall where we were tied up was old and peaceful looking. The leaves were falling from the trees and landing on our deck—and we didn't have a rake! There were a lot of evergreens mixed in with the scarlet leaves and it was pretty spectacular! We went through several locks and had to wait a while at each one. We had trouble again in Lock 19, the same as last time. The lockmaster let the water in way too fast, making it hard to control the boat and we were pushed all over the lock, trying not to hit the walls. Stan and the lockmaster had quite a shouting match while I tried to hide. We pulled into Illion at 7:30 and agreed it had been a rotten day!

We slept late the next day and went to ten o'clock Mass, so we didn't take off until noon. We were sort of recovering from the previous day. It was a gorgeous day again and we felt lucky to have it late in September. We had a long wait at the first lock though, because the water was very low and they were restricting the openings to save water. The lockmaster let us tie up in the lock so we did and had a lovely lazy wait, reading the Sunday paper in the sunshine. We went through several more locks, but had to wait a bit at each one. They needed to have deep enough water so the big boats could make it through. We pulled into the Canajoharie terminal at six, very tired, but it had been a nice day. We tied up under a bridge, helped by two local kids.

It was very cold that night and the canal was steaming and foggy in the morning. We waited until after nine, hoping the fog would lift. It was okay for a while, but then we were socked in again and we crawled along, not being able to see at all. I rang the bell every few seconds, hoping nothing was out there. I hate fog! It seeps into your bones and is so hard to breathe.

We went all the way to the next lock this way and tied up, waiting for it to lift. However, the lock tender told us we had to go through because he had a barge coming, so we went through. It was one of those low locks and we scraped the bottom. The fog was lifting as we went through though, so we could at least see where we were going!

We went through about five locks that day and we seemed to have trouble getting close enough to the lock wall. We caught up with the *Revenge* from Detroit and stopped around five at the Crescent terminal above the flight of five locks. Flight locks are the ones where you go right into one and come out in the next one etc. I was thankful that they would be the last ones! My shoulder and back both hurt from handling lines and running and jumping off and on the boat. I really missed Tommy! The Canal always started out like a piece of cake, but disintegrated rapidly as we went on. Some were so easy and some so bad, I never could figure it out!

The next day was a long and tiring one! The five flight locks were so close together and I had to work hard and fast as did Stan on the helm. We scratched up the boat quite a bit that day, having to move so quickly. Stan's paint job was like a child, and we hated to see it hurt. We finally pulled into Kingston about seven o'clock that evening and welcomed the sight of Rondout Creek. John Hoy came out to greet us on his dock and it seemed like old home week! The power was worse than usual at his dock!

John checked the transmission the next day and found that it needed new clutch plates. We had to postpone our trip to New York with the Motzkins and were worried they wouldn't be able to change dates. Al and Ann came to the marina to see us and left us a car! Joy! Ann took me shopping and I bought lots of neat sewing stuff. They took us out to dinner at a nice Italian restaurant and we had such a good time. It was a fun and relaxing day.

The next four days we ran errands, grocery shopped and I read and sewed as Stan peered over John's shoulder, learning more about engines etc. The Motzkins had us over for dinner and we had a great evening. These friends were such terrific people! On the 6th day, John put the transmission back. Hooray, but $600 was an ouch!

On the next day, Oct. 1st, we left Hoys' and went to the Motzkin fuel dock and picked up Al and Ann for the cruise to New York. Unfortunately it was a drizzly and foggy day and we hated for them to miss the fabulous view going down the Hudson River. We ran mostly from below and anchored near Bannerman's Island for a relaxed lunch. We stopped at the Tarrytown Yacht Club for the night.

We had a leisurely start the next day. After breakfast, we headed out. It was a very nice day and we were happy to be able to stay on the bridge.

Pope John Paul was in New York and the Battery would be closed to boat traffic the next day, so we skipped the 79th Street Marina and headed for Brooklyn.

We stopped in the Marine Basin, which was kind of a rundown marina. We had lunch and then Al and Ann headed back to Kingston. We hated to see them go, as we had certainly enjoyed their company. Stan found a barbershop outside the marina and got a haircut. He was amused because the barbers were just like those you saw in the movies with the Brooklyn accent. Everyone talked like Art Carney! The rest of the day we watched the coverage of the Pope's visit, which was fascinating.

The next day was another foggy, rainy, windy day so we decided to lay over and we watched the coverage of the Pope all day on TV. It was a really great spiritual experience and we were grateful for the weather for giving us a chance to do that. I made some phone calls and cut out fabric for Althea's jumpsuit and the day flew by.

CHAPTER TWENTY-FIVE

We left at 7:30 the next morning for Atlantic City. It was a long day, as we ran for ten and a half hours, and I was seasick all day. Those were the days when I wondered what on earth I was doing on a boat when I hated it so! I didn't really hate it, but I didn't like being seasick. Or scared. We anchored around 6:30 in the Atlantic City basin and had a quiet evening, which made up for the day. We tried to get more coverage of the Pope's visit to Des Moines, but we couldn't get TV, which was a disappointment.

We were up early the next morning and left the anchorage shortly after seven. We ran almost an hour in big beam seas before turning around and coming back. We decided to try that section of the Intracoastal, which we had never done before as it had the reputation of being quite shallow. It was an area that we always had wanted to see though, so we decided to give it a shot.

It was a really interesting cruise with picturesque and gorgeous summer homes. We lucked out on the bridges and didn't have to wait too long, even where they were repairing two of them. We ran to Ocean City and the Harbor House Marina, where we finally tied up after much difficulty because of the extreme tidal current.

That night we had a terrible storm with forty-knot winds and although we were docked, we bounced around like crazy all night and I was really frightened! I thought we were having a hurricane. The boat was leaping around like a bucking bronco the next morning and I was afraid to try and get off because I thought I would miss the dock and hit the water. Stan managed to literally toss me off and I walked around a little bit, but the wind nearly blew me over! I did find a grocery store and bought a newspaper. Ocean City was a booming resort in the summer, but pretty much closed down at the season's end. It was like a ghost town where the ghosts had blown away.

It continued to blow the next day and for the next four days. A cold front had moved in and the temperature went way down. We kept the ship's radio on all day and all we heard was the Coast Guard rescuing people. It definitely was not a day to be out there. One of the Mayday calls was from *Rag Doll*, which had been docked with us at Brooklyn. It was a bad day for sailboats!

That night I wore my flannel pjs with the feet and a wool stocking cap on my head and I still was cold under the covers. I could feel the cold seeping in through the walls beside my bunk. I wrote in my journal the next day, "It's still blowing, we're still pitching, and the Coast Guard is still rescuing boats like mad!"

It was the 9th of October next day and still cold and blowing. We were getting a little stir crazy, but I did a lot of sewing and in those three days almost finished the jumpsuit for Althea. We continued to listen to the radio and heard some harrowing stories. There were three brothers who had each taken their oldest son on a fishing trip and were missing. The Coast Guard was asking anyone out there to please watch for their bodies and they were still posting this watch several days later when we were able to travel again.

On Oct. 10th we awoke to bad weather. Again, my journal states, "It's a horrible morning! It's cold, rainy, foggy and blowing like hell from the Northeast and snowing!" But I was so excited because when I called *Tug II* on the radio, not really expecting to hear from anyone out there, but knowing Walter, who was fearless, just might be, we had a call back from *Sum Fun*, whom we'd last seen in a laundromat in Marsh Harbor! He said they'd been traveling with Walter and Colleen since they left the Rideau in Canada, but that *Tug II* had stopped at Catskill to work on their boat and to pick up their mail and *Sum Fun* went on. They were anchored in Atlantic City, and he said the anchorage was jammed. He also said he was going to stay there until the weather improved.

We talked to the *Traveler*, *Curlew* and *Sunsation*, all of whom were weathered in. Only a few nutty sailboats and *Tug II* were out there! Colleen and Walter were actually going to Cape May that day in the awful weather. Good grief! We tried calling them again and we got them. It was so good to hear their voice again after all those months. We said we'd keep in touch with them and hoped to meet them tomorrow in Cape May. The fog was really awful and we hoped that they'd be okay out there. That day was the worst looking day I had ever seen while living on a boat. Colleen was only a little bit braver than I was, and I felt very sorry for her out there and figured she was probably cowering below and praying.

The next morning it seemed like it might be an okay day to go. We couldn't leave till nine o'clock because the tide was not in our favor going out of the inlet. We called the Egg Inlet Coast Guard, who advised us to stay close to the buoys. We had to go under a bridge first and it seemed to take forever for the bridge tender to come and the Coast Guard finally called him for us. He was off the bridge, probably having a coffee break!

We made it out of the inlet okay going through giant swells. I looked to the horizon and thought I saw land—or a freighter—but then realized they were swells I was seeing! Horrors! We had good following seas as soon as we made the turn though. It was a nice sunny day and we were comfortable, thank goodness.

We chatted with *Sum Fun*, who was ahead of us, and prayed that we wouldn't see those bodies the Coast Guard was searching for. We pulled into Cape May and the harbor was serene and glasslike and rafted onto *Sum Fun* and *Tug II*. What a fabulous reunion we had, laughing, talking and catching up on each other's summer! It was so good to be together again. We separated and anchored around four o'clock. We had a lovely quiet night and it was heavenly not to be tossing around all night. *Yankee* pulled in just before dark and anchored near us. We hadn't seen them since the Conch Inn at Marsh Harbor. It was such fun to be hearing so many familiar names and voices on the radio and see so many friends anchored near us. We went to bed early since we all planned an early departure. It was not so cold either, but good sleeping weather.

It's hard to explain how quickly one makes friends when on a boat. We had a sense of adventure and love of travel in common, but there was an unexplainable camaraderie also because we depended on one another a great deal. We knew we could count on one another no matter what, and our friends would help, whether it was engine trouble or a real crisis. What we were doing compared to friends back home fast-forwarded friendships in the liveaboard world. We were different! Maybe friends and family back home thought we were crazy, but other liveaboards understood. We women perhaps needed the social contacts more than the Captains, who tended to be can-do people who were in charge. But that got lonely sometimes and they needed the brotherhood who understood what their responsibility was. And believe me that it was a lot.

Anyhow, we set the alarm for six, planning to travel with the others the next morning. We discovered our battery was really low and the port engine would not start at all. Stan decided the starter was bad and after conferring with Walter and Brian, he decided to put a new one in and the other two boats said they'd wait for us. Hooray, it worked, and the three boats of us set out for the Delaware Bay.

Cape May was mobbed with all the boats that had been weathered in, and there was a regular parade of us out of the harbor. The Delaware Bay was rough with a darned old beam sea! What else?! It seemed like an awfully long trip. It started to flatten out just before Atomic Island and I rose from my bunk and baked a pie as we came down the C and D Canal. It had turned into a cold, nasty, rainy day and as we pulled into the C&D anchorage. *Sum Fun* and *Tug II* talked us into docking at the Corps of Engineers dock, which we did. We even found electricity! That was a luxury on cold and/or rainy nights. Heat, glorious heat! We had the Strattons and the Smiths over for dinner and had a fun evening and went to bed late.

We had intended to leave for Baltimore the next day, but the weather was lousy and we decided to lay over a day. We walked around and saw some gorgeous roses in that somewhat isolated anchorage. We found the Canal Museum, which was very nice. In the afternoon the two Canadian boats – *Tug II* and *Sum Fun* – were boarded by Customs, which had an office there. They both had all the necessary documentation and passed inspection. I didn't know that the Canadians ran into that often because they were "foreigners." The guys were all working in the engine rooms and doing other chores again, while we girls drank wine and chatted, still trying to catch up on all the news.

I heard a huge flock of birds that morning and got up to see thousands of purple martins flying by, just as we had at Cape May the day before. We'd also seen flying wedges of geese and I guess lots of birds as well as humans were heading south! Stan reported later that our batteries were really bad and we needed to get new ones in Baltimore or we'd be stranded.

We got up and had an early start for Baltimore. We called our Cincinnati friends, the Hettteriches, who were now living in suburban Baltimore and told them we were en route. It was a windy day, but not too rough. We monitored a Mayday call on the radio between two sailboats that had collided, injuring one person. The Coast Guard rescued them as usual. It was an interesting trip into the Baltimore Harbor, but Lord was it cold! The wind chill factor must have been zero!

We tied up in the gorgeous inner harbor marina. We had never seen such a beautiful harbor! It had been completely done over and had parks, an amphitheater, stores, a science museum, an aquarium, old ships and the Constellation nearby. It was quite close to downtown and enjoyed by many in Baltimore.

The Hetteriches came and took us to their home, which was beautiful— and warm! We had a lovely dinner and super visit and stayed overnight. We had brought our laundry with us like college kids and enjoyed doing it in a warm and clean place!

The next day, Stan worked on finding new batteries with the help of Bud Hetterich. I drove Gloria to work and then did lots of errands. I mailed the October birthday presents (we had five at the time in the family!) and went to the bank, grocery, drug store, and department store using Gloria's car. I was able to find some much needed bras and felt it definitely was a public improvement! What a treat to have a day in a car! I almost felt like a landlubber. I fixed a casserole for dinner for the gang and enjoyed being with all the Hetterich children, who'd really grown up since our Cincinnati days. Afterwards, Bud and Gloria drove us back to the boat.

The next morning the batteries were delivered and installed, and when they were finished we explored much of the waterfront, especially the ship *Constellation*. Stan loves boats of any kind and I enjoyed the history of that one.

We got away again around noon. It was too cold to run from the bridge. We felt we needed to get south soon, as it was much too cold in that latitude! We pulled into Annapolis around 3:30 and tied up at the yacht club. Tiger from *Wild Hunter* had talked us into joining his yacht club in Boothbay Harbor, Maine, as it was very down to earth and best of all cheap! It was called the Down East Yacht Club. Walter always called it the Rising Sun Yacht Club, as the club pennant that we flew on the bow had a sunrise on it. At any rate, this enabled us to stay at any official Yacht Club for free, which was especially nice in Annapolis, as slips were hard to find in the city docks and we were leery of anchoring out after our storm experience.

I went into town and got a much needed haircut and ran a few errands. We went to dinner at the Dockside and had a great seafood dinner. We called Chip to wish him a happy birthday and also discovered that the reunion of our friends from Denison University, which we had planned to attend, had been cancelled so we were free to go on. I was sorry about the reunion, but also anxious to get farther south!

We did some final errands the next morning and phoned Althea, who said she was flying down to join us on the 3rd of November. I was so excited! We left Annapolis at ten and had a gorgeous day and flat calm seas to speed us along. We pulled in to St. Michaels around one and anchored in their beautiful serene harbor.

We watched the oyster tongers come in and unload their catch and Stan dinghied over to their ship and bought a whole scrub pail of them for $2.00! While the dinghy was down, we rowed in to shore for the first time in a long time and went to the post office and explored the town. It was lovely walking around the old, historic town in the gorgeous golden afternoon. I met a woman who told me that the beautiful brick house I had admired on the corner still had the black powder burns on its steps from where a cannon ball had bounced through the roof and down the stairs during the Revolutionary War. We returned to *Steelaway* and had an oyster orgy! For once in my life, I had all the oysters I could eat!! It was so peaceful and quiet that night that I slept like a rock.

We were up early the next morning and went ashore and did a few more errands and a quick trip to the museum. We had another absolutely gorgeous Indian Summer day and headed for Oxford, Maryland at about 12:30. We pulled into the public dock, tied up, and I made a fabulous oyster stew for lunch. At around 4:30, *Tug II* and *Sum Fun* came in and docked right below the Morris Inn and we decided to join them. We had happy hour on our boat and then a great dinner on *Tug II*. It was fun to catch up with our friends again! We saw the *Dragon* from Toledo, which we'd last seen at Hope Town in the Abacos.

We had a pea soup fog the next morning, which didn't lift till noon. I walked to the laundromat, but the dryer was out of order, so we postponed that and instead went through a nearby Grand Banks, which was gorgeous, but $189,000!

We took off around noon for the Solomons with *Tug II* and *Sum Fun*. We pulled in and made a dash to the store for supplies, and then hurried to our favorite anchorage, where the three boats of us anchored. Another trawler, the *Felicity*, came in and anchored also. No sailboats that night, which was unusual. We had a beautiful and serene night.

We took off for Smith Island on a gorgeous day. About one hour out, fog suddenly surrounded us. We couldn't see anything and the three of us slowed down and ran on radar. I had the helm while Stan had his eyes glued to the radar. All of a sudden, we passed a fishing boat, which came across our bow! We could hear his siren, but couldn't see him till he was forty feet from us! Scary!

Walter's radar went blank and *Sum Fun* didn't have one, so we tried to find them on the radar. They were behind us, then suddenly ahead of us. We were almost on top of *Sum Fun* when we suddenly saw their red Canadian flag. We decided to run in a triangle to keep track of all three boats. We were on the left bottom of the triangle of three boats and were trying to guide them. Even so, we frequently lost sight of them in the fog. We crawled all the way to Smith Island, where suddenly the fog lifted as quickly as it had come and it was a beautiful day again! Weird!

We tied up outside a fish packer and the other two boats rafted onto us. We all sat on the stern of *Steelaway* and had some stiff drinks as we talked about our adventure and Stan worked on the generator. We walked around the island a little bit, but soon had dinner and collapsed into bed.

The next morning was a lovely sunny day. Stan and Brian worked on the generator—again—while I washed my hair. We discovered that fuel prices were very good there, so we all fueled up and left about noon. I happily donned shorts for the first time in a month.

We pulled into Crisfield around 1:30. It was an interesting little fishing town on the mainland on the east coast of the bay. It seemed to be quite remote, although the children from the islands commuted there to school every day. We tied up at the town dock, but decided it was too rough there, so we went out and anchored in the bay. It was a lovely anchorage in the middle of the bay. We put our dinghy down so we could go back and forth. We did a little exploring and went into town briefly to use the phone and buy a pizza. We had a lovely and serene evening. S tan worked on the generator batteries some more!

We woke to a beautiful sunrise the next morning. We went into town to the hardware store and grocery, but discovered the supermarket had no meat, vegetables or frozen vegetables! We really were in the boonies. We got some new terminals for the battery in the hardware store and went back to the boat to try them out. I made one more quick trip back to the crab dock after Colleen called and told me that crab meat was $4.50 a pound! Then we upped anchor and all of us headed for Tangier Island. It was a really glorious day!

Tangier was a fascinating place and in many ways reminded me of Spanish Wells or Green Turtle Cay. There were no cars on the island, just a rubbish truck. Everyone rode bikes or mopeds. We walked around town and found it fascinating. Every yard was fenced in, and many had family graveyards in the front yard. It was customary there that when a child died, they buried it in the yard, often with a concrete vault above ground like in New Orleans. The Island was "dry" and primarily Methodist. We found the people were very friendly.

It was sunny and warm the next morning with a beautiful sunrise and we were off by 7:30. We had a nice run down the bay and when the sun was out it was quite warm. When it wasn't, it was cool and windy. As we were coming into the Elizabeth River we heard the *Sally Forth*, a thirty-three-foot Egg Harbor on the radio asking for help. They had fuel problems and we towed them to the Holiday Inn Marina. We got in around four, so I did some laundry, but I was tired, so Stan took me out to dinner at The Dock, where we had a nice seafood dinner. That surely did restore one!

Tug II and *Sum Fun* stayed put for the day, so we were the only people overnight in the marina. It was a little spooky, I must say. We woke early in the morning and headed for Hampton Roads, where a lot of the Navy ships were mothballed. It was very interesting to see and Stan told me the name of each one. We ran into a snag at a railroad bridge and ten of us were maneuvering around for over a half an hour while they fixed it. We finally all made it through and into the lock at Great Bridge. We thought it looked so nice in that area that we decided to stop overnight. There was a terrific shopping mall a short walk away and we found lots of stuff we had been looking for ages. We even bought some plants and came home and potted them. My shoulder had been hurting like mad for days and we tried to find a chiropractor, but no luck. We found the shore people to be very friendly and enjoyed chatting with them.

We were starting to hit "the fleet" traveling south and it was fun to keep running into friends like *Brandy*, *Night Wind*, *Blue Blazer* and *Barbalia* (who were from Halifax). Also docked with us that night were *Tug II* and *Sum Fun*. I baked sausage hors d'oeuvres and we walked down the dock and shared and chatted with *Tug II*, *Sum Fun* and *Miz Lou* who were from Bandeira, Texas and knew Stan's old girlfriend from there. Later, we met Stan and Rachel from Los Angeles aboard *Brandy*. She was British and they invited us to come over after dinner to see their boat and then we showed them our boat. Walter's electric went out on *Tug II* and Stan went to help fix it while I went to bed after a delightful day!

My arm was feeling better the next day, but Stan was having a little tummy trouble. It happened when we ate out a lot, especially seafood. It was another gorgeous day, but cold. We got a nice late start and dawdled along to Coinjock, where we got some mail, always a joyous occasion. How different from today where we can correspond via email and check it every day. We of course had never heard of email and managed pretty well with intermittent snail mail! We got one hundred gallons of fuel and a few groceries. I was delighted with the book exchange there and traded eight books. Then we headed down to Broad Creek at the head of the Ablemarle, a beautiful place that was total wilderness and really protected. *Sum Fun* was already there and *Tug II* shortly followed us in. Soon after *Brandy*, *Esca Maris*, *Wednesday's Child*, and *Blue Blazer* came in and anchored. It was the kind of anchorage I loved. A beautiful quiet and serene night followed a spectacular sunset, which I photographed of course.

CHAPTER TWENTY-SIX

We were up before the sun the next morning and off to cross the Ablemarle, which was not behaving too well! It was fairly rough, but calmed down when we got to the Alligator River, so I baked bread and lemon cookies. It was a long and boring trek down the Alligator-Pungo Canal. I always hoped to see an alligator there, but never did!

We came into the anchorage below Wilkerson Bridge around 3:15. This had always been a favorite of ours and was one of the most attractive places—probably because we were so glad to get there! *Sum Fun* went onto Belhaven but *Tug II* followed us in and anchored near us. They came over for cookies, bread and cheese.

We watched other yachts come in, including *Brandy*, *Barbalia*, and a new sailboat, *Avec Le Vent*. *Brandy* came in towing a boat that they had pulled most of the way down the Alligator-Pungo. It was dark by then, and the entrance was hard to see even in the daylight if you didn't know where it was. Walter shone his spotlight on them and Stan got on the radio to guide them in. We heard on the radio from poor *September Song*, who had veered right to avoid a barge and got hung up on some stumps and had to wait till morning to get off the darn things. The *Morning Watch* from the Royal Thames Yacht Club in London came in and anchored. The last time we had seen them was at Mackinac Island the previous summer! The yachting world was a small place in spite of the very long distances it covered! *Brandy* was the only other yacht from the USA, so Stan raised the Canadian courtesy flag on our ship in honor of all the Brits and Canadians. We had a quiet but very cold night and *Brandy* said they woke up to the sound of ice falling off the mast!

We took over the towing for *Brandy* the next morning and towed the *Eleuthera* into Belhaven, North Carolina and stopped at Jordan's Marina.

Brandy came in shortly after we did and talked to *Sum Fun*, who was already there and the two of them decided to leave and run south as fast as possible seeking warmth! We waved them off, and then went to the post office and store. It was sort of an unwritten rule that you never passed up a store, because you never knew when you'd see the next one!

Colleen and I split a pint of oysters while we had the chance. Then, we took off for Washington, North Carolina, which was a four-hour trip up the Pamlico River. We came through the Washington Bridge, which was hand-operated by a man on a treadmill who pushed it open by brute force! It took him at least ten minutes, not a day job you would want I shouldn't think. We docked at the town docks with Walter and Colleen. It was a pretty waterfront marina right in front of the city and had free water and electric, which was a treat!

The next day was Sunday, so we were looking for a church and Mass times. We got directions, borrowed Walter and Colleen's bikes and took off. We rode about fifteen blocks and finally found the church. It was a small church with a terrific community spirit. A young African-American seminarian gave a wonderful homily and we enjoyed the Mass. We rode back and I could surely feel it in my legs, no longer a landlubber here! It was such a pretty day and we invited Walter and Colleen over for a French Toast and Bloody Mary brunch. Then we read the Sunday papers and had a lovely, lazy day. Daylight savings ended that day, so we went early to bed.

Another gorgeous day with a nice breeze followed and Colleen and I hit the stores. I got a lot of birthday and Christmas shopping done and almost felt like a landlubber. That evening lots of people strolled around the dock and gazed at our boats. They were very friendly and intrigued with our strange lives!

We got an early start the next morning at 5:30, with much groaning on Colleen's and my part! We watched the man push the turntable again to open the bridge and we were on our way. It was another nice day and not too windy, and we hoped the Neuse River wouldn't be too bad. No such luck! It was nasty, with a following sea and not too much beam sea, but we were tossed around a lot and things were flying around the cabin.

We finally got across and pulled in to Cedar Creek in a pretty little cove. *Tug II* was with us, as well as *Wish Stream* and *Sea Biscuit*, whom we had last seen at Oxford, Maryland. Since it was Stan's birthday, I baked a chocolate cake and grilled some Cornish game hens and had the gang over for cake and ice cream. It was an awfully windy night, but the anchor held well. We were obviously getting to be pros!

We were awake at five again, awakened by roosters crowing. We hadn't heard that sound since the Bahamas! We left the anchorage around eight, as we had trouble with the salt water pump on the deck, which kept blowing fuses. Stan decided it had a bad terminal and rewired it and we were on our way. It was another warm sunny day again and we thought we were far enough south at last!

We passed *Windstream* en route and heard the captain had the same tummy bug Stan had had recently. We came into the Beaufort dock around eleven and docked with some difficulty because of the wind and current. I was so happy to be back there. The anchorage was jammed and many boats were forced to anchor in the channel.

It was always busy there because it was a popular jumping off place for boats crossing the Atlantic or heading for the Caribbean, as well as the usual Intracoastal traffic. The Coast Guard caused a good deal of consternation at happy hour when they came and chased all the boats in the channel away. It wasn't safe for them to be in the channel, but sometimes there was nowhere else to go.

I cleaned house and worked on my correspondence and then headed for the A&P and dragged back a pretty big load in my granny cart. We went to the Fish Net for dinner and I had so many scallops on my plate that I had to take a doggy bag home. While we were sitting out on the bridge, three "trick-or-treaters" came by from one of the boats. They were going to celebrate Halloween no matter what and had terrific costumes. Luckily, I had some cookies for them. Life does go on!

We woke to an absolutely glorious day. Beaufort was so neat, a very salty place because so many transatlantic boats were there. We wandered around, talking to some of the people aboard and a yacht came in next to us that had made the crossing seven times! I went and did some more Christmas shopping and found some darling little ornaments for our small Christmas tree. We waved goodbye to *Tug II*, who went on. We hoped to see them at Charleston or Camachee Cove. Walter was anxious to get to Camachee because he was going to haul the boat and paint it.

We called our friends Harold and Bessie (now Linda) from the Rogers Marina in Fort Lauderdale and they came and picked us up and guided us to their new dock in Atlantic Beach. The current was so bad that we had to wait for it to slack to get out from the dock. It took us about a half an hour to get to their place.

It was lovely, a brand new dock at the back of their friend Charlie's yard. There was room for us to dock and they got us all settled. They were just three blocks from the ocean and it was really nice. I think they didn't really like cruising, but loved the ambiance of living aboard, and this was an ideal set up for them. Linda had found a job as a waitress in a restaurant and they loved it there.

Harold and Linda took us to dinner at Linda's restaurant and we had a great dinner. Afterwards, they took us to their club, Christy's, and I learned how to play pinball. It was fun until the music started, and it was so loud we couldn't think. Linda brought us home at eleven and I'm afraid they thought us real party poopers.

We spent several days with them and enjoyed seeing them again. Linda had a car! Bliss! She drove me all over and we did a lot of shopping. I have to say that when we later sold the boat, I was really "shopped out" and haven't liked to shop since, but while aboard it was a treat. When we got back, I walked to the beach and it was beautiful. It reminded me of Hilton Head and I walked for an hour or so, but had to get back because I had bread rising. Meanwhile, Stan and Harold had found us two great bikes! I was thrilled because this gave us transportation when we were docked.

The next day was the 3rd of November and the weather looked threatening, but it was warm until noon. I rode my bike and had such fun while Stan installed a new head in the guest bathroom. This was surely an improvement and it certainly was nice to have one that worked! He also built a new platform for the head, so we were all set for when Althea came. I cleaned and got the guest cabin ready for Althea. It started to blow and rain around noon and the temperature dropped rapidly. We changed from shorts to jeans and were still cold!

We had been feeding the ducks and Canada Geese and did they ever make a racket. I tried feeding them cereal, but they were junk food junkies and preferred bread. It rained all afternoon and I cut out and started to sew a skating outfit for Chrissy. I thought it was going to be really cute. She wanted it for ice skating up north.

We left late in the afternoon to pick up Althea. The airport was in the boonies and I thought we'd never get there. We picked up Althea and she looked wonderful in spite of a bout with bronchial pneumonia. We picked up some steaks on the way back and headed for Jim and Charlie's, where they were having a cookout. I also took a pumpkin pie along. There were lots of people there who were very friendly and we had a good time. Althea went to Christy's with the gang, while we went home and collapsed.

The next day was a cold but sunny day and we quickly turned on the heat. The tide was very high, so we could not leave until eight o'clock in the morning. We had a cold, short, and uneventful trip to Beaufort. Docking was a little difficult, as usual in the wind, but we tied up next to the boardwalk, which meant we were on display. Stan and I took a bike ride, while Althea slept. Then Stan and Althea went to a football game, while I stayed home and read the Sunday paper and started cooking a pot roast. After dinner, Althea partied with the gang who went to Christy's and Stan and I went early to bed.

It was very windy the next day so we decided to lay over. I rode my bike to the chiropractor's office, which turned out to be a good idea as my shoulder felt much better after his treatment. I rode back and took Althea out to lunch at Clawson's, which was fun. Afterwards, we explored Bird Shoal, which Althea enjoyed a lot. We had a good time, but it was cold!

We left Beaufort the next morning about nine o'clock or so and it was a gorgeous day, sunny and warm. I was so glad to have some warm weather for Althea. We soon changed into shorts and went up on the bridge. Stan was not feeling too well again and I was starting to worry about him.

We pulled into Mile Hammock Bay around two o'clock. It was really pretty and peaceful in there that day. There was scarcely any Marine activity at all. A trawler and several sailboats had followed us in, and Bob from the *Pole Star* came over for drinks and ended up staying to help Stan fix the generator fuel pump. Althea and I had been smelling diesel fuel and it turned out that we did have a leak! Luckily, they got it temporarily fixed so we could have a hot dinner that night and hot coffee the next morning. It was an absolutely gorgeous starry night, and so pretty and peaceful.

We were up early and off to Wrightsville the next morning to get a new generator part. While Stan was working on that, Althea and I went walking and got groceries. I found shrimp for $3.50 a pound and we got two pounds, realizing later that we should have gotten more, as they came with the heads on and had horrid creepy feelers! However, Althea chopped off their heads and we had a feast. After dinner, Althea didn't feel well and I thought she might have pleurisy. Stan complained that he felt terrible too, with a headache, backache and upset stomach. I feared we'd gotten some bad shrimp!

We were up early and took off soon after seven o'clock. It was a nice sunny day until about two o'clock or so and warm while the sun was out. We were hoping to get to the Waccamaw River that day. We passed the *Michael Stuart* and waved hello. Althea was still not feeling too well and had a pain in her side. Stan, however, was feeling better. Darkness hit us early and we had to run about an hour in the dark, including going under the Locasta Bridge. It was pretty scary and I didn't like it.

We pulled into the Waccamaw Cove around 6:30 and anchored. It was one of our most favorite anchorages and there were only two boats in there. We had a nice steak dinner by candlelight, without the generator, as we cooked on the grill. It was a beautiful calm and starry night. We slept until 7:20 the next morning, and had a pancake and bacon breakfast and took off around 9:10. It was a warm day again, thank goodness, but cloudy and with sun breaks in and out.

We heard on the radio that we had just missed *Tug II*. They had left there just the day before, so we hoped to catch them in Charleston. Going through the tidal marshes that day was beautiful. We stopped in McClellanville, planning to stay overnight, but they had a dredge in there and the whole marina was messed up. So we left and went to an anchorage just below McClellanville, which turned out to be a truly lovely place. We put out our new crab trap while a sailboat came in and anchored near us. We had a beautiful sunset and it was warm enough to sit on the bridge and enjoy it. It was a quiet, quiet night, crystal clear with beautiful stars and moon.

We were up at six o'clock and greeted with a gorgeous sunrise. We could see a storm on the horizon, but were lucky enough to miss it all day. We pulled up the new crab trap and had tons of crabs and one snail! We kept four of them and threw the rest back. The excitement of catching our own crabs had somewhat worn off when faced with the labor of "picking" them! That was one meal where the labor of preparation probably used up more calories than eating them.

We headed for Charleston, and again luckily kept missing the rain. We loved the cruise past the waterfront in the pretty sunshine. The history went back so far in that part of the country and it looked just as it might have back in the Civil War days. The homes were stately and beautiful and they all faced sideways for the shade and had lovely huge porches.

We were surprised at Ashley's Marina to see Bob and Sally Bayless on the yacht *Fantasy*. *Brandy* and *Esca Maris* were also there. We got tied up and took a bus into town, where we had a great lunch again at the Colony restaurant. Then we took a horse and buggy sightseeing tour, which was super, but soon headed home because it had suddenly turned cold. The warm boat certainly felt good! Althea's chest was bothered by the wind. We cooked our crabs for supper and they were superb! We watched TV and stayed up late for us, until ten o'clock! It rained some more in the night.

We slept until eight o'clock the next morning. It was cloudy out and looked ominous, but we decided to go on and head for Beaufort. We passed the *Renown* with Susan and Dorothy aboard and slowed down to chat with them. They told us that they had to stay in the States that year because Dorothy is going blind in one eye. We passed about six sailboats and no power boats. *Blue Blazer* was one of the ones we passed and we waved hello like crazy. The rain turned into a real drizzle and we ran from below to be inside. Later in the afternoon, we saw a shrimp boat and Stan bought two pounds of shrimp for two dollars, so we had a big shrimp boil and it was super! We watched a movie on TV, and went to bed late.

We were up early to a cold and dreary rainy day. We trekked out to the supermarket, which was not in a very good part of town, but got our groceries. It was Veteran's Day and we couldn't get our mail, darn it!

After Althea and I went shopping for a gold belt to finish her new outfit, we left around eleven so that we could get into Harbour Town in Hilton Head at high tide. We docked at the finger docks. We had seen dolphins frolicking on the way, much to Althea's delight. After docking, we went window shopping, enjoying Hilton Head's lovely shops.

Later while we were enjoying cocktails, we saw a big rat running up the line and aboard the ship next to us! This was often a problem on docks, particularly in tropical climates, and we hurried to spray our lines with the strongest stuff we had. Friends of ours, who had a rat that they just couldn't seem to trap, finally put an open bag of garbage on deck and captured the rat when it entered the bag and hurried to take it off the boat and far away! Rats were very hard to get rid of, and loved to travel with you, so we put that marina on our list of "don't dock here marinas." Cockroaches boarded boats the same way, and all we yachties had traps all over our boats. My favorite is the *Roach Motel* which fortunately had few visitors! Cockroaches really freaked me out! It was another reason why we loved to anchor out!

We went to the Calibogue Café for dinner, which was a treat. The next day, we went on bikes for a long ride around Hilton Head, which had lovely bike trails that smelled of pine and was such a pretty place.

We sadly put Althea in a limousine for Savannah, then headed out for Skidaway Island and got in around noon. Marg Miles and her daughter, Lynn came to the boat and took us to their lovely home. After lunch, Stan and Lynn went back to the boat and Marg and I had such a good visit. Seeing an old and dear friend was such a treat in our new life!

The next day, Stan worked on the boat while Marg and I toured Savannah. It was fun being shown the town by Marg, who now was "a native." We had dinner at their house and went back to the boat, where we discovered three big crabs and a flounder in the crab trap!

It was a beautiful sunny, but cool day, so we took a long, long bike ride around the island. I worked on Chrissy's skating outfit and picked crabs for salad at the Miles' that night. Bob and Lynn came and picked us up for a delightful dinner at their home.

CHAPTER TWENTY-SEVEN

We left the next morning for Queen Bess Creek, one of our most favorite anchorages. En route, we passed six of our friends' boats, all hurrying south. The *Michael Stuart* anchored near us and Liz and Jim rowed over. We really admired them, as they were en route to the South Pacific! They were very knowledgeable and experienced sailors, and I envied them their courage! I was such an "ocean coward" that I couldn't imagine crossing the Pacific. Stan would do it at the drop of a hat, but would want a sailboat. You'd really have to do that for such a long crossing because of the fuel requirement.

We were up before the sun the next morning, watching the porpoises frolic and feed. I loved hearing them breathe, which was possible in Queen Bess Cove because it was so unbelievably quiet. We watched the sunrise, which changed from a lavender to a vivid rose. Those mornings were the ones that make liveaboarding so special. We caught five huge crabs overnight in the trap and gave them to Liz and Jim. After sharing coffee with them, we reluctantly left the cove and headed down the waterway. We passed five friends' boats and all waved madly. The rush south was really on!

We had a call on the radio from our special friends on *Fayaway*. They said they were heading south to the Bahamas after Thanksgiving and would see us there. We had a call from Dave and Nancy Davis and they met us at the Frederica Bridge, escorting us into the Golden Isles. There, we discovered that Tim was the new dock master, as Dave had resigned. We had dinner at Dave and Nancy's and Bob and Gita came over and we had a delightful evening with old friends.

We slept really late the next morning and didn't get up until 9:15. Pat Collins loaned me her car and I had a wonderful time going into St. Simon's for groceries, banking and window shopping. You'll never know how much you value a car until you don't have one! The Davises and the Collinses came over for dinner that evening and we had a fun time. Stan had spent all day fixing a salt water pump on the starboard engine. It was fun to be back at the Golden Isles, where we felt right at home. Sadly, we found that Tim and Cindy had divorced. We thought they had been such a nice couple. It was good to see him again though.

The Bakers came down the next day and showed us their new house, which was beautiful and right in the village, which was a super spot. We took off soon after that and stopped at Fernandina to fuel at low tide. We were way below the dock and took on two hundred gallons of diesel. As we were going down the waterway, we heard from several of our friends again. We anchored in a lovely cove below Fernandina, and were delighted to find that we were going to have it all to ourselves. Sort of like owning the world. We had a lovely peaceful evening and I worked to finish Chrissy's skating costume.

We left in a fog the next morning, which didn't lift until we stopped at Fort George. We dinghied ashore and enjoyed seeing Don Juan's house, which I had read about in one of Eugenia Price's books. As we tried to put the dinghy back aboard, the block broke, so we had to tow the dinghy all the way down the dreary Tolomato River to St. Augustine. As we were going down, who should call on the radio, but *Sum Fun* and we had a great chat with Brian and Walter, who were waiting for us at the marina in St. Augustine. We pulled in at about 5:30 and saw the gang waiting for us on the dock, and who else should we see there but *Tuktu*, whom we had last seen in the Bahamas! It was so great to see Bill and Dianne again! Walter and Colleen's boat was up on the ways, but she planned on cooking a turkey for Thanksgiving. I said I would do some pumpkin pies and a salad. We knew we were getting south that night because it was so warm and I kept shedding covers all night.

Thanksgiving was a gorgeous day in the eighties and we opened up the boat, rejoicing in the warmth after so many cold days. When it's cold, it's really cold on a boat! Dianne and Bill loaned us a car, so I hurried to the grocery store and got supplies for the holiday.

What a nice place the Camachee Cove Marina was. It had a great laundromat and shower and toilet facilities, which were so important when one's boat was up in the air while on the ways and one doesn't have a working bathroom! They even had a bench you could sit on while making phone calls, and we had to do that so often that we appreciated the comfort. I made my pumpkin pies and visited with Dianne while Stan helped Walter with his electrolysis problem and Colleen roasted the turkey. Their boat was back in the water, but Walter was very worried about it because he was getting a lot of unwanted advice.

The holiday was a typical "boat" one, as neither Stan nor Walter told Colleen they had turned off the electricity to find the electrolysis problem, so the turkey was not roasting! We didn't have dinner until eight o'clock and the guys were suitably chastised. Colleen did the turkey, dressing and giblet gravy, while I cooked broccoli with cheese, a spinach and orange salad, and the pie. It was truly a feast and a great Thanksgiving. That night, we slept with the companionway doors open and watched the stars.

We were at Camachee Cove for three weeks, which was fun. The week we spent up on the ways while Stan painted the boat wasn't even too bad because of the nice facilities, a car and our good friends. Well, not for me that is. Stan had the job of sanding and painting the forty-two foot-boat, which was a really hard job. Luckily, our time in fresh water over the summer had made most of the barnacles drop off. The view from our high-in-the-air perch was wonderful.

Unfortunately, the weather turned cold, breaking all records of course, and the wind seemed to creep right through the walls. I grumbled as I got out the long underwear, flannels and wore my wool stocking cap to bed! Bill and Dianne loaned us a heater, which helped a lot. We couldn't use the sinks because we had no running water, and I washed a few dishes and the coffee pot out in the ladies room. We did eat out a lot with our friends, which helped a great deal. I put on my wool gloves and did a lot of sewing, making my Christmas gifts. The dirt and clutter were awful, but that too did pass!

Boy was I glad to get back in the water and hooked up to electric and water! We were at the C dock this time, which was close to the laundromat and phones. Stan spent the rest of the time varnishing, the eternal chore, and painting our head, which looked terrific.

In that time, I sewed three nightgowns, two starfish and bluehead pillows, finished Chrissy's skating outfit, and started a shirt for Chip. I did all the Christmas cards, finished my Christmas shopping, wrapped and mailed everything, baked three kinds of Christmas cookies, washed all the rugs and bedspreads, and attempted to clean up all the dust and dirt. Whew! Stan's ulcer was flaring up, which worried me, as he was working much too hard. The marina people broke one of our teak rub rails while we were on the sling being raised up onto the ways, and that had to be fixed, which required extra time.

We did fun things too. We went out to all the local restaurants and enjoyed the seafood and steaks. We went into St. Augustine to the cathedral for the Messiah concert and to Jacksonville with Bill and Dianne to shop. Stan and I also drove to Melrose, Florida to see our good Cincinnati friends, the Webers, who had recently moved there.

We also had many drinks and dinners with Colleen and Walter and many other friends who stopped on their way south. And of course, we loved the music on Bill and Dianne's *Tuktu*. Bill was a terrific organist and we spent many happy hours enjoying his playing and Dianne kept me supplied with magazines and books.

I loved the shore time and all the amenities, and sort of hated to leave, but we looked forward to seeing all the boat people we knew going south and onto the Bahamas. Having a car at my disposal was like being a landlubber, but I was ready to go onto the next adventure.

CHAPTER TWENTY-EIGHT

It was a horrid rainy day, but we left Camachee Cove anyhow, waved off by Colleen, Walter, Bill and Dianne. It was cold and Stan mostly ran from the bridge, while I stayed below working on Chip's shirt. When we pulled into the Daytona Municipal Marina, we saw *Sum Fun* docked nearby and were disappointed to discover they weren't home. The marina had lots of pretty Christmas lights and most of the boats were decorated and it began to put us in a holiday mood, no matter the weather.

We knocked on *Sum Fun's* door the next morning and Brian was up and came over for coffee. We chatted till 9:30 and reluctantly left in more gloomy, cold, wet weather. The day kept getting rainier and Stan mostly ran the boat from above, as there were lots of tricky sections and he could see better from above. We made the Cocoa Beach Marina and were glad to turn on the heat and be cozy. This was pretty much the pattern as we went south.

The Indian River had big waves that kept pushing us out of the boat channel, but I loved that part because there were so many uninhabited islands. They were full of feathery green pines, shiny bush foliage and mangroves. There were tons of pelicans, both brown and white, plus egrets and herons. Signs along the way warned us to watch out for manatees, but we never did see any, much to our disappointment.

We had to wait a lot that day for bridges to open, which was hard for Stan, as the big waves kept tossing the boat around as we waited. We were glad to anchor in the Vero Beach harbor. The wind kept blowing harder and harder, so finally we set out another anchor about ten p.m. I hated doing that in the wind and darkness. I was always afraid that Stan would get caught in the chain or line, plus because of the noise we had to use hand signals, which were hard to see in the dark and we could misinterpret each

194

other. Sort of a nautical charades game but with higher stakes! Anyhow, after we'd done it, I was glad because we slept much better on a wild night with a howling wind.

We got to Miami, docked and headed for the airport to pick up Tommy. He arrived and we headed for McDonald's, where we were the only non-Spanish speaking people. Then we went to the Altschullers' and had a good visit. We had arranged for family to send Christmas packages there for us to pick up and save for the big day. Barrie and Althea's packages had arrived, but Chip and Barbie's hadn't, much to our disappointment. As always, Joe and Virginia came to the rescue and said they'd send them by Greyhound to Fort Myers when they arrived, where we had Christmas reservations. The packages arrived at Altschullers' the day after we had left, naturally!

We spent a day at Sandpiper Bay, waiting for better weather and getting ready to cross the Okeechobee. Tom and I looked for alligators, but couldn't find any. It seemed to be a quest for Tommy on that trip! We gave up and swam at the pool, which he really enjoyed.

We left the next day and went down the St. Lucie Canal. It was very pretty and kind of like the Erie Canal, except for being tropical. We planned to go from the east coast to the west coast of Florida via the Okeechobee Lake. Tom and I kept watch for alligators. At the St. Lucie Lock, they handed us lines, not the usual way but backwards. It wasn't exactly the piece of cake the Waterway Guide promised, as they rose us up by only opening the gates a little way and the ensuing surge of water and turbulence was like riding the rapids! Tom and I struggled to hold the stern line, but finally got it around a cleat.

The rest of the trip to Indian Town was uneventful and we arrived at the marina there. The setting was beautiful and pastoral and our dock was nice. The dock master invited us to a dinner they were having there that night. Some boys at the marina had found a water moccasin and a man from the marina shot it three times, but it was still moving. The dock master said it wouldn't die till sundown and I respected local knowledge enough that I figured he was probably right! Tommy has a fascination with snakes, so this was almost as good as an alligator! Then some sky divers came down right in the marina! One landed right where the snake was, ugh!

We had seen a bearded young man in a canoe with a sail on it on the Intracoastal in Georgia and lo and behold, there he was again! We talked to him and found he was from San Francisco and had launched his craft in the Chesapeake and had made it this far. We enjoyed talking to him. Tom and I then put up our Christmas tree, which looked beautiful and made our main salon look very festive. We were getting the Christmas spirit!

We went to the Christmas party and everyone was so welcoming. We sang carols and enjoyed a lovely buffet dinner. While there, we met the man who wrote the section of the cruising guide on the area we were in. To a yachtie, he was a celebrity! He gave us some good tips for our journey across the Okeechobee. It had been such a nice day!

We got off at eight the next morning and found the cruising to be very pretty. We tied to a piling in a beautiful spot to have lunch and to fix the autopilot, which was acting up again. Then we went through another lock into the Okeechobee. I don't know quite what I thought the lake would be like. Sort of mysterious or something, but I was disappointed. We went quite straight across and so couldn't really see much of the shoreline. It was rough, although not for a boat our size, but we had a beam sea, which I hated as it always made me feel quite queasy!

Anyhow, we came to the other side, which was where we met the Everglades, and that was gorgeous and what I had hoped to see. Tommy and I were still looking for alligators. We cruised through that gorgeous part of the country and saw many ranches, which somehow I hadn't expected in Florida. In one place, we saw an egret riding on top of a cow, which was an unusual cowboy! We saw lots of those birds clustered around and on the cattle and learned they are called cowbirds, what else?

We came to Port La Belle and pulled into the marina there. It was being developed like Sandpiper Bay and would be gorgeous when finished. Meanwhile, it was a nice marina that had beautiful sunsets and was blissfully quiet. Best of all, they had "beware of the alligators" signs and Tom and I began looking, but were unsuccessful. The dock master said they really did have them, but we had no luck.

It was very foggy the next morning, so we dallied till 10:30 before we proceeded down the canal. It was not quite as pretty a section as the day before, but the day was warm and we enjoyed it. Shortly thereafter, we went through our last lock. We decided those locks were very weird, but the lockkeepers were very nice. The final lockkeeper asked if I wanted to make a key lime pie and we all said yes and he gave us a lot of key limes!

We just made it under the Fort Myers Bridge before it closed, and into the marina there. It was very nice and right on the waterfront. It was there that we heard a tourist say, "Oh look, there's a boat from Cleveland!" Her companion replied, "Do you know how many millionaires there are in Cleveland?" Didn't we wish!

We enjoyed exploring Fort Myers, a very pretty town, and walked quite a distance to church. There wasn't too much open on a Sunday, so we window shopped. We checked with Greyhound to see if our packages from the Altschullers had arrived, and they hadn't. We were starting to get worried because it was the 23rd and we were running out of time!

On the 24th, we went to the grocery store and did some last minute Christmas shopping. Tommy was delighted because the local TV station came to the marina and took pictures of the boats, which were decorated for Christmas, and said they'd be on the six o'clock news! Best of all, our packages were delivered by Greyhound and we blessed the Altschullers and Greyhound!

Later, we went to a very nice marina Christmas party and had a good time. We met lots of interesting and nice people. Back at the boat, we followed our Christmas Eve tradition of each of us opening one present, and then called Cleveland. The family Christmas Eve party was at Chemas' as usual, and we called to wish everyone a Merry Christmas. I tried not to be blue, but I did so wish we were there too.

We opened our gifts the next morning, went to church, and had our turkey dinner. I hate to say it, but I think that was the hardest day I ever spent on the boat. I fought back tears all day because I was so homesick and trying not to ruin the day for Stan and Tom. I was vastly relieved when the day was over and we went to bed!

The next morning, we called Gail and Jack Shannon and they came over. It was great to see them again and they invited us to come over to their house for a few days. We took our boat to their dock in Cape Coral, which was right behind their house! They were right across from the beach and had a heated pool in back. Bliss!

We had a great time the next three days. We went swimming, beach walking, shell hunting and the guys went fishing. We also took their small boat into Naples and had lunch at the Tin Factory, a very nice restaurant. We enjoyed getting to know Gail and Jack better and this was the start of a very special friendship, which is still going strong today, many years later.

We left for Sanibel the next morning. It was surely pretty cruising country getting there. The Intracoastal comes very close to many islands there, which were a pretty shade of green and sheltered tons of birds. We had the bird book and binoculars out a lot. The Sanibel Marina was in a lovely setting, shaded by pines and close to the beach. Tom and I did a lot of beach walking, shelling, and swimming. He was intent on getting a good tan before he had to go back to school. Stan took him fishing in the dinghy and he caught a large catfish. Stan had to nail it to the dock to clean it (ugh!) and then I cooked it for lunch for him.

On our last day there, Tom and I spent the day on the beach. It was pretty, but not very wide and there were an awful lot of people there. It was famous for its shelling and Tom and I both got stiff necks from staring down while looking for shells. Back at the boat, Tom decorated for New Year's Eve and we looked very festive! Our party was fun, but it was a struggle to stay awake until midnight after all that sun!

We left Sanibel and cruised to the Captiva South Seas Plantation, which was gorgeous and very plush. It was sort of like Hilton Head, with a beautiful marina, twelve pools, a nice beach and great shelling. We found some good shells, and while walking around, we discovered *Gamecock Two* was there and stopped to chat with George and Betty Day.

CHAPTER TWENTY-NINE

Stan had not been feeling very well since we were at St. Augustine, and I was worried about him. He became very ill and George Day loaned him his car to drive to Tampa to see Dr. Norby, whom we knew from Cleveland and was the Shannons' doctor. The doctor discovered that Stan had a very bad ulcer, which was on the verge of perforating and wanted to hospitalize him, but Stan refused. He didn't want to leave Tom and me alone on Captiva, which was really quite isolated. Dr. Norby reluctantly agreed, as long as he was confined to the boat and was absolutely quiet. He had to have a very special diet and medicine till Jan. 18th. I don't know how he made it home, but he did and went right to his bunk.

He was NOT the world's best patient, in fact he was the "impatient!" The diet was hard, all bland and soft baby food-type stuff, and the marina store ran only to cocktail food. George drove me to a grocery so I could stock up. I worried that the ulcer might perforate and we were so far from civilization out there, but was comforted by having a helicopter pad quite close to us in case of an emergency.

I was trying to keep Stan quiet and Tommy entertained and it was quite a task. Tom and I beached it a lot, shelled, rode bikes, and swam. He also went fishing and caught six fish and we had them for lunch. People invited us over to their boats, but we didn't stay long as I didn't want to leave Stan alone long, or he'd be painting varnish or working on the generator, which were strictly forbidden activities!

The Shannons came over in their trawler on the 9th and seeing the situation, insisted on taking our boat over to their house and docking it. Then I drove Jack's car back to Captiva and he and Gail took their boat back to Cape Coral while I drove back. They had to return to Cleveland, but insisted we stay at their house while Stan had to recuperate. They were so wonderful to us! They hadn't known us long, but entrusted us with their house and car and it surely was easier to manage back in civilization and with a car! We were so grateful!

Tom and I had a good time in Cape Coral. With a car at our disposal, we could drive all over and explore. We went to Jungle Larry's and enjoyed his show and saw lots of alligators! Mission accomplished! It was a big help to easily go to the grocery store and shop for Stan's diet. He was pretty good about quietly sitting and reading by the pool or sitting on the deck of *Steelaway*, conveniently docked in the back yard.

The weeks went by quickly and it was time for Tommy to go back to school and he had plane reservations in Tampa. I drove with Stan sitting quietly because he wouldn't let me do it alone and he was forbidden to drive. As a treat for Tom, we stopped at Busch Gardens and drove the jungle trail and saw all kinds of animals, which we all enjoyed, then headed for the airport. We waved Tom off and headed back to Cape Coral.

Stan was awfully tired, so I called our friends the Webbs, who lived at Holmes Beach and they invited us to stay in their Ocean Beach Club, which was right on the beach. We had dinner and a nice visit with them and collapsed in bed. The next day, I drove back to Cape Coral and was relieved that the trip hadn't seemed to hurt Stan.

We had a few quiet days before the 18th and our appointment with Dr. Norby. I got the boat stocked up and ready to go. After tests, the Doctor pronounced Stan in good shape and said we could go on! Halleluiah! I wondered if all the work and worry over the generator and all the other systems that went wrong in our great adventure had caused the ulcer. He had worked so hard at Camachee Cove and had so many responsibilities. We were so fortunate that this had happened where it did and that we had the Shannons to help us in so many ways.

Fog held us up a little on our day of departure, but it lifted and we enjoyed a beautiful day. We headed south using the autopilot and the gulf was calm. We had to stop twice to fix the darn thing and decided we needed a new sprocket as soon as we could get one. It was so good to be underway again.

We saw a flight of eight geese, who were flying in a straight line barely skimming the water top. They would glide in unison and then one by one, starting with the leader, flap their wings and then resume gliding. They were the Rockettes of the Gulf! We passed Naples and Marco Island and thought they looked pretty. The colors of the Gulf of Mexico were beautiful that day—aqua, blue, green and sapphire. The water looked more like the Bahamas, but not as clear.

We played our Christmas gift tapes from Tommy up on the bridge, as it was a long day and we were out of sight of land for a while. We had some patches of fog, but it wasn't pea soup and not too bad. We ran on a compass course into Indian Key Light and headed for Everglade City, but we were tired and the sun was setting so we decided to anchor.

What a beautiful anchorage! It was so quiet and not a soul around. We were in the ten thousand islands of the Everglades and felt as if we were very far from civilization. They were bright green mangrove islands, many with sand beaches. The sunset was spectacular, followed by one of those quiet, black velvety nights with a million stars and a sliver of a new moon. The only sound was the lapping of the water as the tide came in. I surely hated to turn on the generator to cook, but we used it quickly, turned it off and relished the total peace.

I stepped on the scales the next morning and was delighted to know I had lost 6 ½ pounds and weighed just 111 ½ pounds. Would that I could do that thirty-some years later as I write this! I got up early to see the sunrise and it too was spectacular.

We had beam seas that day. Ugh! We just went as far as the Shark River as the wind was coming up and Stan didn't feel like battling those seas for four more hours. We pulled in behind Shark River Island in the Everglades National Park and oh my, was it gorgeous! There were mangrove islands everywhere and we saw lots of herons, ibis, egrets, cranes, water turkeys, and cormorants.

The *Doris G.* was anchored there also and we were delighted to discover they were fellow Cincinnatians. Stan fished and caught lots of catfish, which he threw back as we didn't like them much. Two rangers came by in their boat and came aboard for a few minutes to visit and we had a lovely quiet afternoon. We tried to get the Super Bowl on TV, but we were too remote. However, we did get it on the radio. The Rams almost won, to our delight. We headed to bed and had such a quiet night again. The sound of the fish jumping around us was thunderous!

We were up early the next morning to a glorious sunrise and managed to get under way by seven o'clock. It was another beautiful day, but the crab traps were everywhere, which required much vigilance. We got *Odyssey* on the radio and they told us that *Tug II* had generator problems and was in Boot Key and we decided to join them.

Who came on the radio then, but *Sum Fun*, who had heard us and said they were in Boot too and told us come on in. We found out that *Ebisu* and *Freedom* were also there and it began to look like we were in the Bahamas, but without the gin clear waters and beautiful colors. Boot Key was a nice harbor, a hurricane hole actually, and we anchored between *Sum Fun* and *Tug II*. We went for a swim while Stan pulled about forty feet of crab trap line off the props!

We went to the fuel docks and when we discovered diesel was just eighty-three cents a gallon, we took on three hundred gallons. Now we were pretty well set for the Bahamas, at least in that department. *Tug II* gave a welcome back cocktail party for us and *Sum Fun* and *Odyssey* were there. We rejoiced to all be together again!

We were all up at sunrise. I discovered I'd put a pound on since the cocktail party! Darn! We dinghied into the dock and walked into Marathon, which was Florida ticky-tacky, and to the Ferro Blanco Marina. We went to the dive shop and bought me a Bermuda jacket for snorkeling. Then, we went back to the boat and had a swim. It felt so good to be swimming again.

We were up early the next day because the guys wanted to go fishing, but *Odyssey*, who was organizing the expedition, found high seas and had trouble getting to us, so they decided to try again the next day. Luckily, the guys were all around, because suddenly a water line on our bar sink broke and water was cascading everywhere! Walter and Brian helped Stan fix it, while I mopped up and then cleaned the cupboard, which was way overdue. What a mess! Never a dull moment on a boat!

We had a lazy afternoon and visited Gail and Jack now that *Odyssey* was anchored nearby. We planned on having the gang, plus *Ebisu*, over for cocktails, but had to cancel when a bad storm came up. Everyone was scurrying around putting a second anchor out. It's kind of fun to watch a storm when you're safe in an anchorage!

It was calm the next day and the guys went fishing. I was having a nostalgic desire to have a landlubber's "ladies luncheon" and invited the girls over to *Steelaway*. We had a great time and the fishermen came home only a little too early. It was fun to get away from "our world" for a while.

The guys caught a lot of fish; Stan had a big mackerel, which made a nice supper. I went into town with Brian, Norma and Gail and started getting supplies for our run to the Bahamas. I also took advantage of land lines to try and get various family members. The gang, plus *Ebisu*, went aboard *Odyssey* for drinks and concluded a long busy day.

We were going to get an early start the next morning, but *Tug II* had problems and we didn't get underway until ten. *Sum Fun* joined us for the run to Islamorada. We had a nasty beam sea and I was seasick for three and a half hours. We finally pulled into Islamorada, which was a beautiful place that looked like the Bahamas, pretty water colors and all. We first mates were all angry at the captains for taking the outside passage, just to save ten minutes. I was not the only seasick one!

We swam in the beautiful water and later Stan and Walter took us out to dinner to make amends. It's funny how a good dinner calms one down! We again enjoyed Walter's love for coleslaw, as he proceeded to eat a whole family sized bowl of it.

The wind came up during the night and the anchorage became rough, so we three boats decided to head out at seven. The radio had a severe weather bulletin out and we had rain and wind off and on all day, but it wasn't bad. It was an awfully long day though, but pretty scenery through the channels and the Keys.

We didn't pull into Angelfish Creek until after five and had a terrible time getting the anchor to hold. Walter, as usual, was hanging on his little dinghy anchor with no problems at all. We tried three times, as did *Sum Fun*, before succeeding! It was a beautiful anchorage in the Mangrove Channel. Later, around nine o'clock, we started to drag again, as did *Sum Fun*, so we both hauled anchor. *Sum Fun* went back to our first anchorage in Angelfish Creek, while we anchored behind Pumpkin Key. We had no problems that time and had a quiet night, except we kept getting up to check to see if the anchor was holding.

We slept a little late the next morning, but headed out to pick up *Tug II* and *Sum Fun* and headed for Pennekamp Reef, where we stopped to snorkel. There was a bronze statue of Christ, thirty feet under water, and the snorkeling was supposed to be fabulous. We were almost there when we hit a coral head, which scared us to death, but turned out to have just nicked the keelson. We anchored and tried to snorkel, but the waves were big and I came back aboard as did Colleen. Walter fished and caught a lot. I wished the dumb ocean would stay flat once in a while, but it's not the nature of the beast! Stan enjoyed the snorkeling, but said he'd rather dive it, as it was calm under the water.

We went on to Hurricane Harbor at Key Biscayne, which was gorgeous. It was a sheltered cove with lovely homes all around. Walter brought over some of his fish for dinner, which were delicious. We discovered we could get Miami TV, which was fun and we could watch *Good Morning America* the next morning. It really was the only way we could keep up with the news, except when we were able to get the occasional newspaper. We did enjoy keeping a little in touch with the world!

Around nine the next morning (after *Good Morning America!*), we headed for Miami and had a great day cruising along the coast. We arrived at the Miamarina, which was one of our favorite places. It had a lovely view of the city and the water. We could all provision there for the winter in the Bahamas and when the weather was right, make the great crossing. *Blue Blazer*, *Mandarin* and *Auriel* were already there. Colleen and I walked into town and hit the department stores and I bought a much needed new bathing suit. We went through them fast in the tropics, as we practically lived in them. Stan and Walt borrowed a car and went shopping for engine parts.

The next morning began the great provisioning! Walter's friend, Arped Papp, offered us the use of his car. It was exhausting as well as expensive, as we bought a ton of stuff. Ken and Rosemary from *Blue Blazer*, Walt and Colleen and Stan and I went to the stores and I could not believe we bought twenty-five huge bags of groceries between us! Then, we went back in the afternoon and bought fifteen more bags and twenty cases of beer! Bahamian beer was horrible. I feared for Arped's car with all of that stuff and the six of us!

The next day we did more provisioning (!) and finally decided we had enough. *Blue Blazer* came over for drinks and we had a pleasant evening. We tried to finish getting ready the next day, but there was so much to do. I was embroidering a pillow for *Odyssey* that I wanted to finish, and we were having trouble getting a new credit card for the radio telephone and we couldn't make phone calls without it. We went to church in Miami and had a choice of English, Spanish, French or Haitian Mass.

I had a sleepless night worrying about the crossing the next day. Only *Blue Blazer* would be crossing with us, as all the others were going to Cat Cay and we were going to West End.

CHAPTER THIRTY

We woke at four a.m. and jumped off across the Gulf Stream at 5:45. We were delayed at the railroad bridge because it was down. They finally opened for us and we headed into the ocean. We had a gentle three-foot swell abeam (ugh!) and the wind was slow in swinging around to the southwest, so I was seasick for a while. The ten-hour trip seemed to take forever before we had a following sea and I could sit up and see land. Before we got to West End, the seas were eight to ten feet, so coming through the reef was scary. A trawler in front of us looked like it was going to broach, but thankfully it didn't! We got in, docked and heaved a big sigh of relief. One good thing about the trip over the Gulf Stream was that the autopilot that Brian had helped Stan fix worked beautifully all the way, which was a big help.

A sailboat came in next to us and told us that they had left West Palm at two a.m. and their engine had conked out halfway over! They attempted to sail across the reef and went aground. A small boat pulled them off and helped them dock here. The first mate was a wreck!

We'd heard lots of scary tales about crossing the Gulf Stream. The scariest I ever heard was from a sailor who was sailing over with two other boats and hit bad weather. The boats were trying to stay together and his boat started to sink. There was no way the other boats could get close enough to rescue him, so he put on a life jacket and went overboard holding his dog. It was a dark moonless night and the other boats couldn't find him in the huge waves. They searched for several hours and were about to give up and call for help when one of their searchlights caught the gleam in his dog's eyes and they quickly rescued both. That captain surely loved his dog, with good reason!

We slept late the next day and had a lovely lazy day, which we really needed. We did some housekeeping and then rode our bikes to the beach. The Bahamas radio network had good reception there and we tried to get Charlie's Locker, which was a message channel for the yachties. We hoped to hear who else made it across, but had no luck.

We got an early start to Great Sale Cay and went aground again trying to navigate the West End Channel, but were able to get off by ourselves. The waters in that neck of the woods were shallow and we tried to "read the water" as well as use our charts. The former often worked better than the latter. It was a beautiful day though, and we pulled into Great Sale around 2:30 and anchored beside *Blue Angel* and two other sailboats.

We sort of hurried to Green Turtle Cay the next day because we had arranged to meet the Crossets and Temples, who were renting a house in White Sound. We broke one of our rules there, which was not to ever say we'd get some place on a certain day because the weather, a systems problem, or something else, always happened to make it impossible! This time, we were in luck, a rare occasion!

We anchored, got in the dinghy and spotted them coming towards us in their dinghy. We had a great reunion and went to their place, which was called the Deck House. It was a neat house with a deck on the top, which had a fantastic view over the harbor. We had cocktails and watched the macaws that flew in every night. They were gorgeous creatures with at least six primary colors on each one. One looked like he had long red underwear on, another orange and a third one chartreuse. They flew in every night around five to join us. Such a treat! It was so good to see these dear friends again also.

We puttered around the next day, doing chores until the Temples and Crossets came out to *Steelaway*, and we had a spaghetti dinner and drinks and watched the required sunset. The next day, we took our friends to New Plymouth and explored the really charming town. We found the famous Miss Emily's Blue Bee Bar, a local landmark, but didn't go in because we were shopping for a picnic. We bought some bread and cold cuts for a boat picnic and headed for Pelican Cay.

The weather suddenly looked ominous. Wind, black clouds, and drizzle appeared, so we changed course and went to Manjack Cay instead for our picnic. After lunch, Dave and Dick fished while Stan took us girls ashore in the dinghy, where we found a beautiful oceanside beach.

We went back to White Sound in a grey drizzle and went out to dinner at the Green Turtle Club. It was a fun place and our dinner was outstanding and the ambiance great. It was a popular vacation spot for Americans. Martin heard Stan's story about the time he heard someone on the radio ask how the lamb was at another restaurant was and replied, "Terrible," which was true. Martin was amused, but said to me, "Please keep him off the radio!"

We were having generator problems again, so reluctantly said goodbye to our friends, but said we'd see them again when they went to Treasure Cay to catch their plane home. We went to Marsh Harbor and the Conch Inn Marina. It was fun to see Wally, Phyllis, Maureen and Barbara again. We docked instead of anchoring, so I could get groceries and do some laundry. Stan worked on the engines and the generator all day, while I replenished our supplies.

We left around noon of the next day and went to Treasure Cay. We picked up a mooring, put the dinghy down and went ashore. To our pleasure and surprise, who was the marina manager, but Paul Welter, whom we had met the year before during our long stay at Chubb Cay. We had a long chat with him and he said he and Laura were both working for Treasure Cay, she as activities director. Treasure Cay was a very popular, plush, resort and has the most beautiful beach in the Bahamas. A huge crescent of white sand, framing water of brilliant shades of blue, green and aqua. You could walk out a long way before it became deep.

We took on water, all you could use, for two dollars! That was a true bargain in the Bahamas, where it was usually five cents a gallon at least, and we needed two hundred and fifty gallons. We swung at anchor and had a quiet night.

We picked up the Crossets and Temples, who had arrived via ferry and cab the next morning, and headed for Guana Cay, one of our favorites. Wouldn't you know it started raining as soon as we got there, and it rained all day? Now, I know I'm not responsible for the weather, but somehow, when you're hostess, one feels like it and our friends had pretty lousy weather the week they were there.

Guana was another resort, much smaller than Treasure Cay, but cozy and has a gorgeous ocean beach and one of the best dining rooms in the Abacos. We had lunch and trekked across the narrow island to the ocean in the rain. We decided it was going to rain all day, so we left for Marsh Harbor. We shopped the Conch Inn's fun boutique and later had dinner there, which we all enjoyed. They were famous for their conch burgers and grouper dinners.

Our friends left early the next morning and I had the Conch Inn do the laundry, preparing for our next round of guests. Needless to say it rained! We taxied to the Abaco International Airport, which was about the size of a garage, to pick up Althea and her friend Dorie. Mackey Air was early, so they were waiting when we got there. I was so excited to see them! They were so worn out that they had a drink and went to bed. It was a good day to do this, as it was windy and rainy.

We left for Guana the next morning and anchored there. It rained off and on, but we explored the club and the beach and they loved it. We found some wonderful homegrown tomatoes at a local market and enjoyed those. It got quite windy and the anchorage was getting rough, so we upped anchor and went to Man-O-War Cay, which had a hurricane hole harbor and it was comfortable there. They were broadcasting gale warnings, so we stayed aboard and decided to explore the town the next day. The gale never did materialize. They missed often, but we had to take them seriously, because if they did come we wanted to be ready.

It was sunny the next morning, so we took the dinghy into town and explored the town and spent time on the beach. The girls, coming from cold wintry Chicago, were anxious to get tanned, not a problem there. We saw the Lanes from *Star of Maine* anchored near us and invited them over for a drink. Laura Welter had given me lots of lettuce at Treasure Cay because it was very scarce there and a real treat. I wasn't using it up fast enough though, and shared it with the Lanes.

We left for the Island Marine, where we got our scuba tanks filled with air and headed for Sandy Cay, where Stan and the girls wanted to scuba dive. There was quite a swell, but they went snorkeling on the reef, which was one of the most beautiful in the Bahamas. I snorkeled a bit, but the water was really cold, so I stood watch while Stan and the girls tried scuba diving. It was Dorie's first dive, other than with her lessons, and she was nervous, but enthralled with the beautiful reef. We called it a day and went to Little Harbor, which we were dying to show to the girls. What a beautiful day we had and what fun with our special visitors.

The girls were pretty zonked out the next day from all the previous day's sun and water. It was hard to keep guests from getting badly sunburned from the tropical sun because they all wanted to be out there after coming from cold snowy climes! So we slathered on sunblock and went exploring and beachcombing. Althea, Dorie and I hiked to Bookie's Cove on the ocean beach, and they were fascinated with that bit of paradise. The girls were both excited about exploring the studio the next day.

We all were early up to watch the sunrise there, which was always spectacular. We dinghied ashore and went to the studio and the girls were enthralled! It always was exciting to see Ran's work and he spent a lot of time with the girls. They bought a lot of stuff and Dorie fell in love with an expensive mermaid plaque and bought it. We promised to ship it to her when we got back to the States because of all the problems involved in trying to ship from the Bahamas.

Dorie was an artist and Ran wondered if she would be interested in an apprenticeship in his studios. After a long talk and tour of more of the studios, both girls were seriously considering coming down for a year and living in a tent so Dorie could apprentice and Althea write a book. Sanity eventually prevailed, but the thought of living in that exotic place enthralled them! We know, because later that winter, we almost bought land on top of the harbor and planned to build a house and bring Tommy down to live with us.

We saw Libby and had a nice chat with her and she took the girls through her school and the house, which they had built for themselves mostly out of items found on the Atlantic beach or nearby woods. After lunch, Stan and Althea snorkeled for a while and then we went for a walk, leaving Stan to varnish. We saw Ran again and he invited us back to his house for a lovely tea that Margot prepared. We had a nice visit and both girls were floating on cloud nine! Stan's varnish, as always looked great.

We left around noon the next day after having a nice chat with John and Jean Chambers, who lived in "No See'ums Bight" and went back to Sandy Cay. It was too rough for me to snorkel, so I kept watch on the boat. Dorie was a little nervous, which worried me. The three of them dove in and went under. They were gone a long while, when I saw Stan surface and signal me to bring the dinghy to them. I thought something was the matter and I hurried over to them. He was a long way away.

There was a strong tidal current, which had taken them a good distance and they were having a hard time swimming back against the current. Luckily, the engine started right up and I zoomed over to Stan. I got Stan's weight belt and tank off and got him aboard. He said the girls were okay, just behind us and trying to swim to *Steelaway*. Dorie suddenly surfaced and she was exhausted, so we hauled her aboard. In the meantime, Althea couldn't find Dorie and started to swim back to find her. Fortunately, she surfaced to see if Dorie was up and we quickly pulled her aboard, also totally exhausted. As they all staggered back onto the boat, my comments were, "Well, I hope the three of you have this out of your systems for a while!" and "Some people sure have weird ideas of fun." We left for Marsh Harbor and anchored out for the night.

We were up early and the girls went to pick up the mail and groceries while Stan and I took the boat to the Government Dock to get water. While we were there, Frank from the *Northern Loon* called and asked us to bring two batteries for Judy Page and she would give us free dockage for a couple of nights in return. We had a pretty queasy trip around Whale Cay, which was pretty normal for that trip, and it got quite rough (which it usually did) before we pulled into Green Turtle Cay.

Frank and Tommie helped us dock at Judy's pretty place. We took the girls to dinner at the Green Turtle Club and Martin's eyes lit up when he saw our pretty ladies and he said we were to sit at his table, which was a special honor. He had a bunch of young men from Chicago and was delighted to provide some feminine companionship! We had a fun dinner and Martin latched onto Althea and a doctor from Chicago did likewise with Dorie.

There were a lot of young people there and Martin offered to take everyone to the ocean beach in his boat. We begged off and went back to the boat to bed. They all had a ball and the girls crept in around four o'clock in the morning. The girls had a wonderful time and for the next two days were besieged morning noon and night with invitations. We visited with Frank, Tommy and Judy and enjoyed the quiet while the girls played!

The third day, we went to New Plymouth with the girls and they loved it. We saw the macaws several times flying to the Deck House roof while in White Sound. We left on the 28th and went to Powell Cay and anchored. We were trying to show the girls all of our favorite spots. The wind changed direction and it was rough, so we upped anchor and went to Treasure Cay through the White Passage and anchored. The girls went to the beach and I caught up on my correspondence and got a disastrous haircut. I wouldn't need another all winter!

The next day, we beached it and then did some shopping in the boutique while Stan varnished. The girls rested up! We were invited to a cocktail party at the resort and who should show up, but Martin and Allen, much to the girls' delight. All came back aboard the boat for dinner and had a good time. Then the young people went dancing to celebrate Leap Year's Day. Needless to say, we went to bed! As we were moored when they came back, Althea jumped in the water and swam to the boat and took the dinghy to shore for Dorie.

We left around noon, after topping the tanks for Hope Town. It was blowing very hard when we got there, so we set out two anchors even in that sheltered anchorage. We got word on the radio that there was a message for us and it would be delivered the next day, as it was so rough. There was much speculation as to what it could be.

It kept blowing harder and harder and the radio was sending bad storm warnings for our area. Man-O-War got hit hard and we braced for the oncoming storm. Our anchors were holding well, but there were a lot of boats anchored there, including a big yacht from England. We worried about somebody dragging into us. It was a wild night with nobody getting much sleep, as the winds were fierce and we'd keep getting up to check the anchors—and everyone else's as well!

We went to Mass the next morning in the tiny library and Father Jim said Mass on the checkout table. The signs posted outside said the Mass time was "When Father done reach," which generally was the case.

Althea and Dorie had gone on ahead to the Harbor Lodge, where the champagne brunches were held and got us a table. They enquired about the message they were supposed to get and discovered it was a "thing," not a message. It hadn't arrived due to the bad weather, but would be there tomorrow. Such frustration for the girls! We had a great brunch with lots of champagne and then headed for the post office, where the phone exchange was to call my sister Barrie and wish her a Happy Birthday.

When we were dinghying back to the boat, we noticed the wind coming up again and that it was getting rough. We heard over the radio that the wind was increasing rapidly and boats were dragging all over the place in the harbor. We had a wild night with winds gusting up to fifty knots. I stood watch until 11:30, and then went to bed. Stan was up off and on all night, checking the anchors. We had two of them out again.

It was windy, but sunny the next morning and we stayed put until the girls' "message" came. It turned out to be a lovely bottle of French champagne from Martin. We left for Marsh Harbor and it was rough, but not too bad. We anchored in the harbor until the Conch Inn had a dock for us. Althea and Dorie shopped in the boutique and bought lots of stuff.

Martin and Allen surprised us and came over by boat and stayed for dinner, a very festive occasion with Martin's champagne.

The next morning, we took the girls into the dock by dinghy and by taxi to the airport. The girls were told they had been undercharged for their ticket and after much confusion, anteed up fifty-four dollars apiece and the plane finally left. I was sad to see them go, but I imagine they had many tales to tell back in Chicago about their exotic vacation! We brought *Steelaway* back to the dock, cleaned up a little and mostly loafed the rest of the day.

CHAPTER THIRTY-ONE

We went to the phone exchange and called Barbie, who told us that Parker and Joan, (Stan's brother and wife) were at Treasure Cay! We were so excited and spent the rest of the day trying to get a message to them, but no luck. We would just have to go over there and find them.

We met a couple there from the yacht *Kristine*, who had been paged by Charlie's Locker with an emergency message. The radio in the Bahamas was like a giant party line and boats all over the Bahamas were calling them to make sure they got the message. They had, and luckily it was something they could take care of there. That reminded me of Walter's privacy method. When he called us, I would answer saying, "Switching," and both of us would switch to Channel 8 where we could talk and not have the whole boating world hear!

I went to the Rub-A-Dub-Dub Laundromat on the waterfront and it was so awful I almost felt sick, but I did two loads before the machines stopped working. I thanked God for the Conch Inn, who did the sheets and towels!

We were all set to go to Treasure Cay the next day and discovered the miserable generator wasn't working again! We had a message from Parker saying they'd meet us at five there and we decided to take off anyway. We were able to get in touch with Paul Welker at Treasure Cay and he said he'd hold a dock with electricity for us, so we were in luck.

After we got there, we saw Frieda Douglas from *Mandarin*. She was a friend of Parker and Joan and knew where their villa was, so she took us there. Was it ever great to see them! We went back to our boat for cocktails and then to the Spinnaker Room for dinner and we had such a nice evening.

Parker came over the next morning and helped Stan fix the generator (hooray!), while Joan and I beached it. It was a lovely day and the beach spectacular as usual, so we really enjoyed our time together. The guys went to play golf and later we went to Parker and Joan's place for drinks. We then went to the buffet for dinner, which was very good. They even had lettuce! What a nice day!

Parker and Joan spent the next morning with us and had lunch. We went to the beach for a while, and then sadly said our goodbyes and headed back to Marsh Harbor. I hurried to the store and then to the Rub-A-Dub-Dub, which was totally gross! I decided I'd rather wash clothes in a tub on the deck than go back there. We could get the towels and bedding washed quite reasonably at the Conch Inn, so I could do the rest.

We had quite an experience the next morning at St. Francis De Sales church. An exiled Haitian Bishop said the Mass in Creole to the beat of a drum. The Haitians were all dressed up as usual, the children with bright ribbons in their hair. The service lasted two hours! I was amazed at how much of the sermon I could pick up with my high school French.

The bishop would ask them questions and they would answer or comment. Then, he repeated the whole sermon in English! He told them (and us), that despite all the Haitians had suffered, and the discrimination they had endured in Marsh Harbor, that they had sinned because they had not tried to establish community with the black and white Bahamians (who wouldn't accept it if you paid them—my comment).

Then, he had them all come up to the altar and swear on the Bible that they would try to be true Christians and would try to establish community rather than stay to themselves. Wow! They were such gentle, hardworking people, and had such a hard life, barely scraping by, and the Bahamians were so awful to them. They were true Christians; they always shared what little they had with those who had none. It was a fascinating Mass, if long. Stan said we'd probably made up for the Masses we'd missed!

Alice Farinacci from *Andiama* and I went to the Catholic school so that Alice could take photos for a social studies unit she was putting together. She and her husband John were from Cleveland, where she taught at Orange School, and was on leave for a year so that she and John could cruise with their boat. John was a retired principal of Heights High and conductor of the Akron Symphony. He had built *Andiama* himself in a warehouse. They were very interesting and fun people and we became close friends.

St. Francis school consisted of a bunch of small buildings like wartime barracks and each served one class. Four nuns, Father Jim and several lay teachers did the teaching. The "cafeteria" was sort of a screened porch, where the nuns served a lunch of a jelly sandwich, cupcake and soda for seventy-five cents, bought by the affluent Bahamians. The Haitian children sat under trees and had nothing. Alice and I were so upset seeing children go hungry that we wanted to run to our boats and bring back bread and peanut butter, but were too cowardly to offend the nuns, something I regret we didn't do to this day.

Their equipment was adequate I'd say, and Alice took lots of pictures in and out of school. They had a very nice activity center with a library, headed by a very dynamic Sister Elsie. We sat in on quite a few classes and I must say, if nothing else, the Haitian kids were getting a good education.

The following day, our friends the Steelhers arrived from Cleveland after a terrible flight. They ended up in Nassau before finally arriving at six p.m. on a flight due in at 1:20. We had given up on meeting people at the airport because they practically never arrived on time, and we could never get any information as to when—or if—the flight would arrive. We just told everyone to get a cab to the marina and we'd be waiting there.

They were game for partying, so we walked up a hill to Maureen and Barbara's house, which was beautiful. It was on the highest point of the island and had a fabulous view. It was a fun cocktail party and almost all the boating crowd was there. Bill and Judy were very friendly and outgoing people and I think they had a good time. We did take pity on them though, and left early, as they'd had a long day and we all fell into bed.

The generator went on the fritz again and we called a local repairman and he actually fixed it! Incredible! I really did hate that darn thing and we depended on it so much over there in the Bahamas, where we anchored out so often.

At any rate, we got going around noon after visiting on *Andiama*, with the Cleveland connection enjoyed by the Steelhers and Farinaccis. We headed for Little Harbor and arrived at four and anchored.

It must have been a spring or neap tide, because we watched five or six boats go aground. The entrance there was very narrow and we only went in or out at high tide. Sailboats particularly had trouble, because they drew a lot more water than power boats. We needed seven feet under us and they needed at least ten, depending on the size of the boat. You really had to read your charts in the islands, because it could be dangerous. We had gotten pretty good at reading the colors of the water and that could be helpful too, sometimes more so than a chart!

We explored with them and toured the lighthouse, cave, and Ran's shop, where they bought the famed Little Harbor belts. They were distinctive, leather with a cast-iron bronze buckle, and anywhere you went, anyone who'd been to Little Harbor recognized them. It was like a little secret club. We did the ocean beach and then walked up to the top of the island next to Chambers' house and enjoyed the view. Little Harbor was such a little jewel! The guys were tired and went to bed early, but Judy and I sat up half the night talking. It was such fun to link with a fellow Clevelander.

The next day was gorgeous and we set out for Treasure Cay with its beautiful beach and picked up a mooring. Later, we went to the Spinnaker Room and had dinner.

Guana Cay was our destination the next day and we anchored to snorkel the mini-reef. Bill especially enjoyed snorkeling and seeing all the pretty fish. Stan dove down and brought up a sea biscuit for me and some starfish for Judy. We showed her how to hollow it out, so her luggage wouldn't smell like rotten fish when she got home! We swam on the beach, then anchored and had dinner aboard and enjoyed a serene, quiet evening.

We left Guana for Hope Town the next day, and it was quite windy, but not terribly rough. We anchored in the harbor and went to explore the town. It was kind of a fun place, with lots to see and do. We walked the ocean beach for a while then headed back to the boat.

We went to Mass Sunday morning, sitting on the beach under a huge tree facing the harbor, and then introduced Bill and Judy to the champagne brunch, which they enjoyed a lot. We dinghied over to the lighthouse, which was a beauty, and I picked some wild dill from beside the path. They enjoyed hiking up to the top, where there was such a great view of the harbor and Hope Town.

We left for Marsh Harbor the next morning and the Steelhers finished some shopping, had a conch burger, and sadly left for the airport. Stan worked on some varnishing, while I stocked up the larder, changed sheets, and did some laundry. We had Alice and John from *Andiama* over for drinks, and then went back to their boat where we met some teacher friends of theirs, plus Bud and Fay from *Honeydew*, who were so nice.

After Mass the next morning, we took off for Little Harbor with Alice and John as guests. They were dying to see Little Harbor, but didn't want to try and get over the reef with their deep draft boat. En route, John rigged some deep sea lines for us and we trolled along behind *Steelaway*. All of a sudden, I felt a big tug on my line and I reeled in a fourteen pound mutton snapper just as we were about to go over the reef into the harbor. I needed John's help get it aboard because Stan had his hands full. It was a bright pink and other colors and had to just flop around on the deck till we anchored in the harbor. John cleaned it and grilled it for supper, and it undoubtedly was the best fish I ever ate. We had enough left over for another meal. It was my first ocean fish and I couldn't wait to try again!

We showed the Farinaccis around all the wonderful parts of Little Harbor and they fell in love with it too. Alice particularly enjoyed seeing Libby's school and the view from the Chambers' house, and the two first grade teachers had a great time comparing notes. We invited Libby and Roger Henry over for dinner and had such a pleasant evening.

We explored around a lot the next day and spent quite a bit of time on the ocean beach. We found big plastic-wrapped bundles of what we thought was marijuana. *Honeydew* had joined us and enjoyed Little Harbor also. Farther down the beach, we showed them the pieces of the booster rockets that had fallen down when the rocket from Cape Canaveral jettisoned the booster. It was such fun to share our beloved Little Harbor with Alice and John!

CHAPTER THIRTY-TWO

We had more guests coming and so needed to head back to Marsh Harbor, which we did and anchored out. We dinghied ashore to return the Farinaccis to their boat. I did the usual re-provisioning, laundry, and bed changing, which by now I had down to a science! It surely helped to have the Conch Inn do the sheets and towels, although I heard that a new laundromat had opened, which was clean and pretty good mechanically. At least they gave you a free do-over when your machine died! It was kind of a long walk from the dock, but it was worth it!

We dinghied into the dock the next day and waited for George and Peggy Brandle to arrive. They were old friends (Stan's boss actually) from our days in Cleveland, and boaters themselves, which was always a help. They arrived around four o'clock and we went back to the boat and got them settled. We had a quiet evening and went early to bed. We were in our fifties in those days, and were surprised to learn that George was sixty-nine. He looked great, as did Peg.

We had one more guest arriving and waited until Mary Kay Ransdell, a dear friend from our Mansfield days, arrived at four o'clock the next day. We got her settled in our cabin, as Stan and I had volunteered to sleep in the salon.

Andiama went with us to Guana. The wind had really piped up and the anchorage was quite rough. George got quite seasick and we decided to renege going aboard *Andiama* for cocktail hour, and instead the five of us went ashore to celebrate my birthday with drinks and dinner at the club. I had a great lobster dinner, as did Mary Kay, and I felt very birthday-partied!

It was still rough when we went back to the anchorage, so we went back to Marsh Harbor and anchored. Seasickness with guests was a problem that I could certainly relate to, as we usually anchored out rather than docked. I must say though that my inner ear or something had gotten used to the constant movement of the boat and I rarely got seasick anymore unless we had a horrible beam sea or I was scared to death.

Andiama decided to wait till the next morning to move, as their boat was a huge concrete thing, and John hadn't had much experience docking before they came to the Bahamas. When he did dock, all hands ran to help and it was a Chinese fire drill!

We got up early for "bring your own palms" Sunday. We loved the idea that everyone was supposed to go out and cut their own. They certainly were everywhere, and Stan brought along his knife to cut some on our way to church with the aid of several young enthusiastic little Haitian boys eager to help. Father Jim had us gather outdoors in the schoolyard. The altar was heaped with palms, which he blessed, and then led us into church accompanied by throbbing jungle drums and the singing of Creole hymns. It was a beautiful Mass and our guests enjoyed it.

We headed for Little Harbor, but it was blowing hard and we decided to go into Hope Town and anchor. We went ashore and explored the town and walked on the beach. It was a lovely day.

However, George didn't feel very well and Stan took him back to the boat.

We got up early so we could show them the lighthouse, which really was neat. We were waiting for the sun to come out so that we could leave for Little Harbor. Part of the way there, we had to go through Lubbers Quarters, which was shallow and tricky, and it helped to have the sun out so we could read the water. However, the sun didn't cooperate and it was still rough, so we decided to wait until the next day.

We girls decided to go ashore into town. I wanted to get some tomatoes, so we headed for the little grocery. A sign on the door said it would open later. I know from experience that later meant when they felt like it, so we decided to go to the beach and come back "later." The sun kind of popped in and out, but enough so that the girls could get a tan, and we had an enjoyable afternoon.

We stopped at the grocery on the way home and they were open and did have tomatoes, so I bought some for our supper. You would think that in a warm climate they'd grow more, but they were generally as hard to find as lettuce. I realize it's probably too hot to grow real lettuce but tomatoes?

The only place we consistently found lettuce was in the supermarket at Marsh Harbor and it was flown in from the States and cost the world.

We were able to go to Little Harbor the next day. It wasn't the world's greatest day weather-wise, but our friends were running out of time. En route, we had a radio message from *Sum Fun*, who were in Little Harbor on their way home from the Exumas. We had a great reunion when we got there. They said they really enjoyed the Exumas and we decided we should go there the next year. Our guests loved Little Harbor. It was a little bit of paradise!

The next day was cloudy, but we girls and Stan went to the ocean beach and waded and went shelling. We found some beauties and then Stan found some gorgeous tulip shells. Then we went back to the studio and Mary Kay and Peggy shopped and bought the de rigueur belts.

When we dinghied back to the boat, we found George really sick. His blood pressure was so high that we were afraid he'd have a stroke, and he was having great difficulty breathing. We couldn't get across the sand bar for a while until the tide rose some more. We realized we had to get help and Stan decided to barrel over the sand bar. We bumped several times, but did get over, hearts in our mouths. It was dark by then and you just don't run at night in that part of the Abacos.

Libby had suggested we call Dr. Pfeiffer at Marsh Harbor, whose call sign was *"Perfect Match,"* as he lived on his boat. We had no luck reaching either the doctor or Wally at the Conch Inn Marina, but got a call from the yacht *Porfin* saying they were at the Conch Inn and had a doctor aboard. We did reach David Gale, who called both Dr. Pfeiffer and Wally, and both said they would be waiting on the dock when we came. *Sum Fun* called and said they had a pretty good doctor at Hope Town, which was closer, but we decided it would be best to go where they were expecting us.

Thank goodness Stan was an excellent navigator, and we ran on radar mostly, but did use the powerful searchlight we had when going through Lubbers Quarters, which is dangerous at night and it was pitch dark. We all heaved a sigh of relief when we passed Hope Town and got into more open waters.

As we approached the marina, we had a very hard time seeing where it was because of the many lights on shore. I got on the radio and called "Any boat in the Conch Marina, any boat in the marina. We're coming in with a medical emergency and can't find the marina against the shore lights, please have someone go to the end of the docks and wave a flashlight!" The boat that had a doctor aboard came back and said someone was there and we saw the flashing light and got right in. They even had someone with a flashlight standing on the dock Wally had saved for us.

As we slid into the space, they caught our lines and as I was tying up one of the men said he was the doctor and where was the patient? I sent him aboard and sank to the deck in relief! We discovered the doctor was a cardiac specialist vacationing aboard a charter boat! How lucky can you get! Dr. Pfeiffer came and we directed him aboard also.

Both doctors agreed that George needed to double his medication, gave him a shot and wanted to give him valium to quiet down his apprehension. Peg had a fit, but finally agreed and put him to bed and the rest of us collapsed with relief! The doctors said they'd see him again in the morning. There wasn't a hospital in the Abacos, so he would have to be flown to Nassau if necessary.

The next day George's temperature was down, but his blood pressure still very high so the cardiologist suggested we stay put for a while. Peg insisted that George was fine and "they wanted to continue their vacation," so against our better judgment, we left for Man-O-War Cay, which was not too far from Marsh Harbor.

Stan stayed with George while I took the girls ashore in the dinghy. We spent the afternoon at the beach, which was a very nice one, and Peggy snorkeled the reef and we got that off her bucket list. Dinner was late because we had to be towed back to the boat when the dinghy engine quit halfway across the harbor. Luckily, a friend came to our rescue in his dinghy. We didn't sleep too well that night, as George struggled to breathe all night. At five o'clock, Stan told me that at daylight we were heading back to Marsh Harbor because he didn't want to be responsible for George dying over there!

En route, we called Dr. Pfeiffer, who met us at the dock and said he felt George needed to go to a hospital in Miami. Wally helped me get to Bahamas Air, who had a flight about to leave, but would hold it if the Brandles got right to the airport. Mary Kay and I packed their things in a mad rush, while Peggy dressed George and Stan got a cab and we practically threw the poor guys into the taxi. They did make it to the airport in time and got to Miami, where the doctors thought it was probably the change in altitude from high up in Denver to sea level in the Bahamas. They did make it home to Denver and George had no more trouble, thank God!

We felt so sorry for Mary Kay because we had to leave every place so early, but bless her heart she said she'd still had a great time (if a little different)! Stan was really exhausted from all the drama, so we stayed put in the marina. Mary Kay and I shopped around and explored Marsh Harbor. The Farinaccis invited us aboard *Andiama* for cocktails and we enjoyed the camaraderie so much. Mary Kay was a musician and a choir director at her church, as well as a high school music teacher, and had much in common with Alice and John. We then had dinner at the Conch Crawl, which was always good. It was a pleasant ending to a nice day.

There was terrible wind and rain the next day, so darn it, we couldn't go anyplace else! And all the stores were closed because of Easter. But Mary Kay and I rode bikes all around the area, and had a good time catching up on news of our mutual friends in Mansfield. Incidentally, the only other homes in Little Harbor besides Ran and Margot's, Pete and Debbie's, and the Henrys' were owned by two couples from Mansfield and Mary Kay knew them both! Talk about a small world!

Yellow Bird invited us for cocktails that evening with several other interesting couples, which was fun, followed by dinner at the Conch Crawl. At least Mary Kay was meeting some very interesting people. Jerry Hart from *Yellow Bird* was a published writer and well known in boating circles and Lucy from *Song* was singlehanding her sailboat all over the world. I so wished it wasn't Mary Kay's last night.

CHAPTER THIRTY-THREE

We were up early and got Mary Kay a cab to the airport. We were very tired, so decided to have a lay day and just relax. I did our usual re-provisioning and laundry and realized that I was beginning to feel like I was running a B & B, but I really loved having all our guests. We went to church for a very long Mass, over one and a half hours! Father Jim read Shel Silverstein's *The Giving Tree*, while the little kids acted it out. Then, he had them make butterflies (a symbol of Lent) out of bright colored crepe paper, assisted by the adults, and pin them on the cross. The Farinaccis and people from the *Frannie W.* were there and we invited them back over to *Steelaway* for Bloody Marys. It was fun, but we were still tired and loafed the rest of the day.

We were anchored out and had invited Brian and Norma from *Sum Fun* over for a steak dinner to thank Brian for helping Stan work on the generator, which was ailing. I had everything ready when the generator stopped again! It was becoming our nemesis! Brian and Stan worked on it until almost eleven, when we had our overdone dinner! I hated that darn thing. So necessary, but so unreliable!

Several of Alice and John's children were visiting and wanted to see Hope Town, so we took them over accompanied by Trish (a teacher at St. Francis) and her visiting sister. It was a very rainy day, but we put on rain gear and at least we were doing something!

Two days later, the darn generator was on the fritz again and we went back into the marina. Brian and Stan worked on it all day again while I gnashed my teeth. We knew we'd have to get a new one when we got back to the States and that was going to be a major investment! Bummer! We did see a space rocket going overhead at sunset and it was a gorgeous pink streak in the sky that lasted well after dark. Those things did make up for a lot of the frustration we experienced some days!

It was a beautiful sunny day next morning, and we took off with *Sum Fun*, *Nerissa*, and several of Farinaccis' kids for Tahiti Beach, a new place for us. It was on the far south tip of Hope Town, an isolated sandy reef that was so pretty and had superb shelling. We found some beautiful shells we'd never seen and were so excited to find that neat place. We went back later, and anchored in Hope Town Harbor for a while until we went back to the marina to drop off our guests.

It was blowing like crazy the next day and the generator was on the fritz AGAIN! Stan fiddled with it for a while and I sewed a new pair of shorts and baked bread while he worked on it. He thought he had it fixed and we went into the Conch Crawl for lunch to celebrate. We got back to the boat and it wouldn't work again. I felt so sorry for Stan! I know he wanted to throw the blasted thing overboard. We had about decided that we needed to head back to the States and have it majored. I didn't know it then, but I think this was where Stan decided that maybe we'd had enough boating and that we should go ashore for good. He was really tired of spending so much of his time fixing things.

The next morning, we took a bunch of friends over to Hope Town after Mass for the champagne brunch. En route, we saw *Andiama* aground on a sand bar and stopped to pull them off. We all went to the brunch and had such a good time. Afterwards, we took *Andiama's* guests aboard and back to Marsh Harbor. *Andiama* came in shortly after and we helped them dock and tie up.

We discovered *Tug II* had come in and we were so excited to see them! They invited us over for a roast beef dinner and we had a great reunion. It was so good to be with them again! When we left them that evening, it was blowing thirty knots and we decided we'd better babysit the generator, so we left the dock and went out and anchored. I mended a pair of shorts and Stan fussed with the generator again till we went to bed.

It was a wild and stormy night and we didn't sleep too well. Stan was up at five the next day and worked on the generator, while I fell back to sleep on the gently rocking boat. It was cool, windy and rainy. I awakened feeling peppy, so while Stan worked, I baked bread, altered my slacks pattern, sewed, wrote lots of letters, made a cake and a lamb stew for dinner! Stan finally thought he had the monster fixed for good! Stan slept almost all afternoon, which was good; the monster had worn him out! And I discovered that I functioned best in cooler weather. All told it was a nice day.

I must explain here that when in the Bahamas, it is almost impossible to find a competent mechanic. Except maybe at Man-O-War, which was a working boat island where everyone was named Pinder. Stan had literally taught himself to read complicated manuals and fix just about anything. Nothing ever broke down at a convenient place or time; it seemed that we were always in the boonies where no one had a clue!

Walt and Brian were also good at that, like so many other ship captains we knew. To liveaboard, the captains had to be that way. We'd seen many liveaboards have to give up that life because they couldn't do it. If they lacked navigation skills and emergency maintenance abilities, they couldn't last at that lifestyle. That skill stood us in good stead when we went ashore. Stan could fix almost anything and saved us hundreds of dollars in repair bills over the years.

The next day was pretty and sunny. I dinghied ashore and into town and did some chores. There, I stopped and talked to the crew from *Windstream*, whom we hadn't seen since Oxford the previous fall. They had been in the Exumas and had come to Marsh Harbor because of an abscessed tooth, and went to Stan's dentist who was pretty primitive. We went back to *Steelaway* and invited Alice and John out for Bloody Marys, which was most enjoyable. We went to the Government Dock for water and left for Little Harbor. We caught a mooring and had a quiet, relaxing evening and slept like logs.

We slept till seven. The generator started a little reluctantly, but it did start! Don Chambers radioed us to tell us they had bought a Grand Banks back in the States and we invited him to come aboard later and see what ours was like. Shortly after that, we heard a Mayday on the radio from a cigarette boat saying they needed a boat to rescue them. Pete, who generally did the rescue work there, was in the States, so Stan volunteered to go and several sailors from *Pegasus*, which was anchored nearby, went with him to help. I stayed ashore and went to Ran and Margot's breezeway, which overlooked the ocean. Everyone was most hospitable and offered refuge. I was feeling very scared and shaky, as it looked awfully rough and windy out there. Wow, what a wild day that was! Everyone on shore was so great.

I climbed the hill to the Chambers' house to tell them why *Steelaway* wasn't in the harbor as planned, and found them glued to the radio listening to the rescue. The boat in trouble had no idea where they were and Stan was questioning them and checking radar to try and figure out where they were. He asked them to radio if they saw *Steelaway*. They told him they could see a sailboat on the horizon, but not *Steelaway*. Stan figured out by radar where the sailboat was, and where they probably were, and eventually found them a ½ mile from shore, not the seven or eight miles offshore that they thought.

The boat then threw *Steelaway* a line, but Stan said it was much too thin and would break. They didn't have much time, as they were being washed ashore, and it was a desolate and most inhospitable shore—coral cliffs and uninhabited. One of the men on our boat threw them a stout line and they missed the catch. Worse still, the line went under *Steelaway* and wrapped around the prop.

One of the men from the little boat was a diver and took a knife and went down. All this was happening in ten-foot waves and Stan worried the boat would hit the diver on the head while he was under it. Fortunately, he knew to always keep a hand on the keel above his head, so he moved with the boat, and he emerged safely, line in hand. They quickly fastened the line to both boats and started back to Little Harbor.

Two of the men were so exhausted that they just laid down on the deck. The trip back was slow, with six-foot head seas. I was watching from Debbie's deck, where I had eaten lunch. They were approaching the ocean exit when it looked like *Steelaway* was wallowing right where the huge waves were shoving them ahead. I was panicky and called them on Margot's radio. Stan answered and said they were okay, but that they needed to shorten the tow line and they were trying to get ahold of it again!

There was a huge following sea always going in that entrance, and we rarely went that way. They had an eye on the lighthouse just ashore, which marked a huge reef, and they were lining up the two boats to make the run in. I was so scared that I couldn't watch anymore, so I went back down to the dinghy to wait.

Roger Henry came down and told me that they were passing the lighthouse and almost into the harbor. It was not only low tide, but was an extra low spring tide. Stan was so tired after six hours of work that he decided to barrel across the sand bar and of course went aground! I went aboard and we put out two kedge anchors with the help of Bud and Fay from *Honeydew* and Don and Ken Chambers, so we'd hold still until the tide came in to help us float off. The Chamberses towed the cigarette boat to their dock, while I put our boat back in order and Stan's helpers returned to their boat. When we got off the sand bar, the Chamberses helped us tie up to a mooring that Libby and I had secured earlier in the day with a yellow canoe.

I forgot to mention that while the rescue was going on, one of the women from *Pegasus* called me and said she was worried because it was taking a long time and her husband was a diabetic and needed to eat and drink at specific times. I called *Steelaway* and told Stan to tell him there was orange juice in the fridge and plenty of food so he should take whatever he needed. That radio was really a lifeline in many ways!

I went ashore and up to Margot's to tell her we wouldn't be coming to dinner, as Stan was exhausted. We went up to the Chambers' place for a drink. We watched a glorious sunset from their deck with its fabulous view over the harbor and ocean and marveled at how it shed its rosy glow on the anchored boats below us. What a lovely peaceful ending to a hard day!

CHAPTER THIRTY-FOUR

We slept till seven the next morning and were delighted to know the generator still seemed to be working. Knock on wood! We had been thinking of buying some property at Little Harbor and Debby came and took us to look at some really prime real estate that was for sale. Debby and Pete, and Margot and Ran owned all the land around the harbor and were very particular whom they sold it to, so we were flattered that we made the list. So far, that had only been the Henrys (who were Debby's parents), the Chamberses, and the Crawfises from Mansfield. A few apprentices lived on boats anchored in the harbor, or had built little shacks out in the woods. It was very isolated there with no roads, electricity, phones, and everything had to come from Marsh Harbor. You had to have a cistern for water and it was sometimes salty. They had generators (eek!) for electricity and ran them at certain times, so there was peace and quiet, but we were used to living with generators, when they worked that is!

Debby took us up to the land. It was at the top of the cliff, on the right, shortly after you passed the sand bar. The view was incredible! It looked out on the harbor, the lighthouse, and the ocean. The back part went all the way back to the Bight of Old Robinson, where there was a little half moon of a sand beach and a little dock, which we could enlarge. There were gorgeous flowers up there and the soil was good for growing things, but we'd have to fence the vegetable garden so the wild boars wouldn't tear it up.

There was an old shack up there that we could live in while our house was being built, but I bet we'd be there a while, knowing the Bahamas and how hard it was to get anything done by USA standards! We envisioned living in that small vibrant community and bringing Tommy down to live with us. We would sell *Steelaway* and buy a smaller boat to get to Marsh Harbor, for instance. But I wanted to be sure we could afford frequent trips to the States and have plenty of room for the family to visit.

We had a lovely day at anchor there. Many people radioed us and complimented Stan on the rescue. The radio was really one's newspaper, TV news, and all the comings and goings, and gossip were there. Almost everyone had the radio on all day, and that's why we had the "switching" thing going with Walter. A little privacy there.

We shelled on the ocean beach, swam and went visiting on various friends' boats. We went aboard *Honeydew* for happy hour and met Eleanor and Frank Lyons from *Putter*, who were charming. They were Californians from Los Angeles who were chartering.

April 14th was a lovely day and Stan went fishing with the crews from *Honeydew* and *Putter*. I packed myself a lunch and hiked to Bookie's Cove. I hiked miles down the gorgeous beach, seeing no footprints but the sandpipers' and my own. I found some nice sea fans to add to my collection. When I got back, I worked on my shells for a while until Stan came back and said we were invited over to *Honeydew* for drinks and fish stories.

We took the Rues and Lyons on a hike to Bookie's Cove and it was neat. No one was in sight anywhere. They found lots of shells and we saw a piece of a space capsule. There was so much interesting debris to be found on the beach, some of it like crystal net balls all the way from Portugal. They were a beautiful aqua color, but not found too often anymore and were considered a real prize. I think Portuguese fisherman had switched to something plastic.

When we returned back to the boat, I was at the kitchen sink peeling potatoes when I looked up and a huge boat was slipping by. I couldn't believe they could get over the sand bar guarding the entrance! They docked in front of Ran's studio and I saw it was the *New Shoreham*, which we'd previously seen in the North Channel of the Georgian Bay and again in Oxford, Maryland.

It was a small cruise ship with maybe thirty passengers and it surely seemed strange to see it in that really "off the beaten track" place. The world just doesn't come there. The passengers debarked and we talked to the Captain, who was Marcel Albury from Man-O-War. Apparently, the company hired a Captain from the area who had the local knowledge needed to navigate unknown waters. They took people all over the place. Marcel complimented Stan on his rescue the other day. We talked to a lot of the passengers who were enjoying their cruise very much. Ran's studio sold lots of stuff, which was good, but oh dear, outsiders in our special world!

We invited the Rues and Lyons over for drinks and were having a good time when a huge line squall came through. We heard next day that we had three inches of rain. Our guests stayed until 8:30 and still got soaked going back to their boats in their dinghies, which they had to bail out! We bailed about two feet of water out of our dinghy the next morning.

We spent several more days in Little Harbor and took friends on exploring expeditions, shelling, and up to the Chambers' house to take pictures from that perfect place. Of course, the sun went immediately behind a cloud! *Tug II* came in and we met Walt and Colleen's daughter and her boyfriend and had the gang over for dinner. Libby finally took me on a long-awaited hike to Winding Bay to see the space capsule. We took a lunch, as it was a twelve mile hike! We walked through the woods near the shore and suddenly emerged to see the most beautiful half moon of beach I'd ever seen!

The water was that lovely assortment of colors typical of the Bahamas. There were two little cays in front, making it a sheltered spot. The beach was fringed by palm trees and it really looked like a spot in the South Pacific. We ate our picnic lunch and swam in those beautiful waters. Libby said it was an unknown cove to most of the world because it was uninhabited all along that coast and there were no roads. The only way to reach it was by boat or hike like we did. Only a few people knew it was here, as the cays in front hid it from view by water.

We looked at the space capsule, which was awesome. It was an enormous thing, fifteen feet long and black. It almost looked like a submarine. It really made you think, having that stuff falling from the sky! I felt sort of like Chicken Little! The walk home seemed long, as my knapsack was so heavy with stuff I had collected en route.

As we neared Little Harbor, we saw smoke from a fire that the Haitian who worked for Ran had started in order to clear a plot for his family's garden. Ran let them live in the abandoned lighthouse, as they had no place else to go. They subsisted on bananas and fish. The little money Mano made was sent to his family in Haiti. Libby mobilized us to put out the fire—there were no fire department or fire hydrants there. We had to put it out by beating it with large rugs! Man was I tired when I got back to the boat!

We left early the next morning, towing the Johnstons' boat to Hope Town, where we met Debby, who used it to get back to Little Harbor. We then went onto Marsh Harbor. We had lunch with the Farinaccis and Strattons and I loafed the rest of the afternoon, as I was really tired from the day before! The frosting on the cake was having dinner aboard *Andiama* with John's famous spaghetti.

The next day we were busy re-provisioning and doing the ever present laundry. I liked the new laundromat there. It was almost as good as the ones back in the States, even if I had to walk a mile pulling my cart to get there. I stopped at the post office and I had five letters, a red letter day literally! Tricia, one of the lay teachers at the school, came for dinner and we had a nice evening chatting. I think she was a little homesick and we cheered her up.

We had kind of a harrowing morning the next day, running around and refueling, as we wanted to get away early to go to Green Turtle Cay. To top everything off, my bikini strap broke as we were going out of the harbor! As we came around Whale Cay, who should we hear on the radio but *Odyssey*! It was so great to hear their voices again.

We stopped in New Plymouth and rafted onto *Tug II* while I made a flying trip into Miss Emily's Blue Bee Bar to get a tee shirt. We both went to Green Turtle with *Odyssey* close behind us and docked. Gail and Jack had Bonnie and Arthur Songler with them, who were going to boat-sit *Odyssey* while the Shannons made a flying trip home. The Songlers' sailboat, the *Ho Hum*, was de-masted and damaged on their last Gulf Stream crossing and they were getting back in the saddle again so to speak. They all came aboard for cocktails and Colleen brought her famous conch fritters. We decided to go into the Green Turtle Club for dinner and had a great time. There was much kidding with Martin about Stan's lamb call.

We all got an early start the next morning. We were headed for Treasure Cay, the Shannons to Marsh Harbor and the Strattons to Powell Cay, where they were jumping off for the States. We had an okay trip around Whale Cay, but then it got horribly rough. We weren't rigged for rough running and water poured in all over the place and our stateroom windows leaked. Bummer!

We came into the harbor at Treasure Cay and got a mooring. I mopped up and we slept awhile. We had the Welkers over for dinner and it was fun to see Laura and Paul again. We told them of our possible plans to build a house at Little Harbor and Paul said we were crazy. He told us that we would lose our minds going through all the regulations and aggravations of trying to work with the Bahamian government while trying to build and live in Little Harbor. He said that we had the ideal setup now, and if we wanted to spend time in Little Harbor, we should buy a mooring and stay in comfort on our boat. The more we thought about it, the more we were afraid he was right. We were really afraid of rocking the boat taking Tommy out of the school he'd known for so long and putting all of our eggs in one basket. There was much to think about.

We left Treasure Cay early the next morning after taking on water and headed for Marsh Harbor because the generator was leaking oil. Groan! We saw Brian and Norma after we got there and were sad to hear they were headed for the States the next morning. The Shannons were going to fly back to Cleveland in two days and it seemed like all our buddies were headed back to the good old USA. The Farinaccis threw a sort of going away party for a lot of the gang and there were about twenty people there including the Smiths, who owned the marina, the Conch Crawl and the Inn. It was a happy and sad occasion.

Stan got the generator fixed, thank God, and we had a kind of quiet day. Bonnie and Arthur left the dock and anchored out, as did we. They were to take care of the Shannons' boat till they got back. It was kind of a grey and cool day, so I worked on a sampler for my niece Mary Katherine Snider and just kind of puttered around. It was nice to have one of those days once in a while, especially when the generator was working. Later, Bonnie and Arthur came aboard for cocktails.

Alice and John came aboard early the next morning and we headed out to New Plymouth. We tied up at the dock and explored for a while, then went to Pelican Cay to snorkel over the reef. It was a gorgeous day and on the ocean side it was calm as could be, and the water clear as crystal. Alice was fascinated, as it was her first reef and she loved it!

John caught our supper, a large mutton snapper. They were such pretty fish that we almost felt guilty eating them. Note the "almost!" It made a great meal grilled on the stern. Before, that we went back to Guana for lunch, then spent the afternoon exploring and shelling on the ocean beach. Later, we went back to Marsh Harbor where we anchored and had our fish dinner. Bonnie and Arthur blinked a CQ message to us, and Stan, who had been a radio operator on a bomber in World War II and worked with Morse Code, had fun answering. They planned an excursion to Hope Town the next day.

CHAPTER THIRTY-FIVE

We did go to Hope Town the next day. Bonnie, Arthur and Alice took the dinghy ashore to explore the town while Stan and I loafed. We were beginning to feel like full time guides to the charms of the Abacos! We tried to go to Mass, but it was a day where Father hadn't "done reached." We all went to the champagne brunch and enjoyed it as usual. I took Bonnie, Alice and Arthur up into the lighthouse while Stan and John rested.

John was not feeling well and we worried about him, so we returned to Marsh Harbor. We took a long nap, I finished a book I was reading, and worked on a sampler until bedtime. We were sleeping soundly when a lot of noise woke us up. We discovered that a large CaribShell freighter was trying to make its way into the harbor in the pitch dark and it scared all of us to death. There were a lot of boats anchored out there and three sailboats had to pull up anchors and move, which was not appreciated in the middle of the night. It was a circus for a while! Finally, the vessel went firmly aground and everyone heaved a sigh of relief and went back to bed.

The next day was a lazy one because all of us at anchor were tired from all the nocturnal activity. The Chamberses radioed us that they had picked up their new Grand Banks in the States and were coming into the harbor to show us the yacht. They rafted on and we went aboard and oohed and aahed over that beautiful boat. I must say that Stan and I were more than a little envious when we viewed their new generator.

Shortly afterwards, the wind came up and blew like crazy. We were supposed to go over to *Odyssey* for happy hour, but after much consultation with Bonnie and Arthur we decided to stay put. We never knew when we'd drag anchor, or worse, when another boat would drag into us! The CaribShell freighter tried to get out of the harbor at high tide, but had no luck. It finally made it out at midnight, thank God. All of our boats were at the mercy of that big, hulking, clumsy monster.

We left there and went to Green Turtle, where we anchored out. Al Lang from the Deck House rowed over and invited us over there for drinks, which was fun. The parrots arrived on schedule and delighted Alice and John. We hadn't previously met the Langs, who were the owners of Deck House and we enjoyed getting to know them. We all went into the Green Turtle Club for dinner, which was good as always. Martin was still trying to talk Althea into staying there for a year and writing her book. She would be his hostess at dinner and other times, but would have plenty of time to write. However, Althea's answer was still no.

We took Alice and John over to Treasure Cay so that they could go to the dentist there, who apparently a little more "modern." We had lunch at the Spinnaker and saw the dwarf from the TV show *Fantasy Island*. We also heard rumors that Perry Como was filming one of his shows at Green Turtle, as well as at Treasure Cay. He did, and we saw it on TV a year later and felt superior because it was our stomping grounds that he liked so well.

After the dentist, we took the Farinaccis to Baker's Beach, which was beautiful as always. There was no wind and the water was crystal clear and calm. We got some starfish and saw a whole school of rays swimming around. We were anchored out, so we took the dinghy into the beach. That beach had the reputation for being a nude and topless place but there was hardly anyone there. We only saw one nude and one topless sunbather. No one was on the gorgeous beach and we shelled a while. In the late afternoon, we anchored in the west harbor of Guana, which was serene and lovely. We had dinner aboard and watched a beautiful sunset, which was a perfect ending to a very nice day.

We went into the dock the next morning early and I did some grocery shopping, picked up the mail. We said goodbye to the Farinaccis and Songlers and headed for Green Turtle. It was windy and wet and we had a yucky beam sea for a while, but Whale Cay was a piece of cake for a change! It was nice, and we docked at Green Turtle about two in the afternoon. We were amazed to see a big fancy Chris Craft there, and it turned out to be our friends Rux and Phyllis Schuch from the Roger's Marina, whom we hadn't seen in two years! They had chosen the name *Freedom*. They both looked great and the same as ever. It was fun catching up on their lives.

The next day was busy with packing for our trip to Cleveland for Chrissy's First Communion. Martin ran us over to Treasure Cay and we caught the plane there and had a smooth flight to Miami and then to

Cleveland. It felt really weird to be back ashore, but we had a great time in Cleveland with family.

Stan flew back to Treasure Cay and the boat, while I flew to Bloomington to spend a wonderful week with my sister. I left there and flew to Frankfort, Kentucky, where I rented a car and spent the weekend with Tommy. It was parents' weekend at the Stewart School, so there were lots of activities, as well as good family time with Tom.

I then flew to Miami and my plane was late. I was afraid I'd miss my flight, but found a great skycap who retrieved my luggage and took me in a cart out the door and over the tarmac to my plane. I was really anxious to get home to Stan and *Steelaway*. After all that rushing around, we sat on the plane for ages while the flight attendants went up and down the aisles counting heads. After they started doing it for the fourth time, some passenger called out, "Helen Hayes is in the john," and we all laughed like mad. Finally, we arrived at Treasure Cay and Stan and Martin were waiting for me.

Steelaway looked gorgeous as we approached. Stan had been varnishing the whole two weeks I was gone and she shone in the sun. After I unpacked, Stan asked me if I noticed anything different. I pondered awhile and said, "Well everything looks beautiful." Then he told me he had quit smoking! I was really impressed and not a little grateful that I had missed the crabby stage. How lucky could I get?! He'd been smoking two packs of Camels a day for twenty-five years or so and this was a big change!

Gail and Jack were at Green Turtle also and we all went into dinner together. Martin was sad that Althea had said she definitely wasn't coming to live there for a year. She liked her life in Chicago. We were sort of happy that she hadn't elected to live the mañana life in the tropics.

We left fairly early the next morning to get around Whale Cay. It was very rough and I was scared and seasick. Gail was very scared also. Nasty piece of water that, and you had to go around it, as there was no other way. We anchored off one of the beaches at Guana and explored, then anchored in the North Guana Harbor for the night. The four of us went into the club for drinks, but cooked dinner aboard.

Chip and Cindy were coming the next day, so we got an early start to Marsh Harbor. It was a wet and rough crossing, but luckily a quick one, so we docked and started the chores of getting ready for guests. Stan did fueling and so on, while I stocked up the pantry. We had breakfast with the

Farinaccis, then went out and anchored till Chip and Cindy's plane arrived at 5:30. It was so good to have them aboard! They loved going out to the boat in the dinghy and being anchored. It was kind of a new experience for them.

We left early the next morning for Little Harbor, accompanied by *Odyssey*, who had the Farinaccis aboard. It was not a bad trip except for the giant rollers at the North Bar channel. Luckily the kids loved boats and didn't get seasick! We went beachcombing after we all anchored and swam a while and generally loafed.

We had several small showers, but they went quickly. In the late afternoon, Pete opened his pub and we all went there. It was a bar built into the shore in the half of an old boat and was legendary in the Bahamas. Pete didn't open it much anymore, so we felt flattered that he did for us!

We went to Bookie's Cove the next morning with the kids and Gail and Alice, while John and Jack fished. It was a beautiful day, but very rough on the ocean side where we were. We hiked, swam, shelled and showed the kids the required pieces of a spacecraft. Margot and Ran came over for tea and we had a pleasant afternoon. Ran then took the kids through the foundry and his studio. Chip and Cindy then enjoyed exploring on their own on foot and with the dinghy. We loved having the kids share our special Little Harbor!

Alice, Gail and I went to Johnston's cave the next morning, while the kids went back to the foundry. Then, they explored the lighthouse, walked the beach, sailed the dinghy and generally had a fun day. We went over to *Odyssey* for happy hour and then Chip grilled chicken on the stern of our boat, which was wonderful! We saw some fluorescent minnows swimming around after dark when we were sitting on the flying bridge and they were bright green and blue flashes in the water and really neat to see.

The next day dawned hot and with no wind at last! We left Little Harbor early at high tide and went to Tahiti Beach to shell hunt. Since it was high tide there, we didn't find many good ones and it was hotter than Hades, so we went to Hope Town and anchored. Again *Odyssey* was with us and anchored nearby. We went to the beach and swam to cool off after showing the kids the lighthouse and town. The water was quiet—very unusual on the ocean side—and crystal clear and cool! After a long swim, we headed back to the boat and Chip cooked some marvelous chicken for us again.

We left early that next day and went to the beautiful long beach at Guana. We took a large canvas with us to sit on, as the sand was really hot. We swam a lot and Cindy found a beautiful Hawkseye Conch, to her delight. We saw a baby shark swimming close to shore and followed it for quite a while. We ate our picnic lunch—not much sand in it—and had a delightful morning.

We went back to the boat and the kids sailed the dinghy for quite a while. Chip and Cindy took us out to dinner at the Guana Club. We had crawfish all around and enjoyed a delicious dinner. Cindy and I had one Guana Grabber apiece and boy did that grab us! It was such a fun day all around!

The kids and I explored the tiny town of Guana the next morning and went back to the beach for a while. Then, we headed back to Marsh Harbor and the Union Dock for water and groceries. There were charterers there who were about to leave and they gave us all kinds of great fresh food! We anchored near the Conch Inn and got our mail.

The Farinaccis and Shannons came over for drinks and then Chip grilled hamburgers for us, which was a treat. We saw four dolphins feeding around the boat after dinner and Chip and Cindy got in the dinghy to play with them. They followed them all over and the dolphins even dove right under the dinghy!

The next day was "flat ass calm," so we headed around Whale Cay to Green Turtle and docked at the Club dock. Martin had a rescue call and took the kids with him. They rode high up in the tuna tower, which was exhilarating and they loved it. Our boat was great, but not fast! Later, we took the kids to Pelican Reef and they had a fun time snorkeling.

We showed Chip and Cindy many of our favorite places like New Plymouth and had one jewel of a day at Baker's Beach. The ocean beach was glorious, calm and colorful and we spent almost the whole day there in the water and had a picnic lunch. We anchored later at Man-O-War and watched a vivid sunset. It was so hot the next day that we didn't spend much time exploring and took off and anchored at Tahiti Beach at low tide for some superb shelling. We ended up at Little Harbor and it was mobbed, with seventeen boats anchored!

We were experiencing the Florida invasion! When Floridians heard we were going to the Bahamas in December, they said we were crazy, that it would be too cold and we should go in the summer when they did.

Luckily, they all stayed home in winter, which was good. When they did come, it was crowded and awfully hot and we definitely felt we had had the better time of year and were all fleeing home to the States. If the kids hadn't been with us, we probably would have been heading back to the U.S. in late May.

Summer is the Bahamas' rainy season and it rained six and a half inches that night and the next day! We had several leaks, but fortunately none in critical places like above beds! It was kind of good to have a lazy, cloudy day to let all the sunburns quiet down. We spent another day at Little Harbor, as it was the kids' favorite place, as well as ours, and they did much hiking and exploring while they had the opportunity.

On the 17th of June, we sadly said farewell to all our friends at Little Harbor. Debby asked me if I'd be interested in going into the pillow business next winter with her and Lita and I replied that I'd love to. Lita would do the drudgy appliqué and I would do the artistic part of the embroidery. It sounded like a great idea and I'd be thinking of ideas all summer.

It was Chip and Cindy's last day, and so we headed to Marsh Harbor, stopping at Tahiti Beach for some last minute shelling. We docked at the Conch Inn and took care of many chores, then had a farewell dinner at the Conch Crawl.

We went to Mass the next morning and said farewell to Father Jim and Chip and Cindy left on the noon plane. We hated to see them go, as they were such good boat people, but knew we'd be seeing them eventually that summer in Cleveland.

That evening, we chatted with a boat that had come in and were delighted to find out they were from an area of Cleveland we knew well. They were new liveaboards, having started in March, and were having a very traumatic first year. We invited the Shannons over to meet these fellow Clevelanders, and both of us shared some experiences with them and hoped to see them again. We also entertained some Annapolis midshipmen, who were on a summer cruise aboard two sailboats.

CHAPTER THIRTY-SIX

Gail and Jack were flying back to Cleveland the next day, and they gave us lots of fresh food, which was great because we were provisioning for the crossing. We completed our provisioning and started the trip back to the States. We got as far as Green Turtle that night and docked in front of Martin's office to say our goodbyes. I was sad because I felt that we might never be coming back there again and we did so love the Abacos, with their lovely cruising and the wonderful friends we had made. Stan's and my conversations on leaving the boat seemed to be leaning in that direction. We went into the club for one last Goombay Smash. Drowning our sorrows?

We were up early the next morning to a hot day and headed for Great Sale Cay. We anchored and swam to cool off. The anchorage was crowded and we wondered if Florida had been totally emptied of boats! One got such a different feel to the Bahamas that time of year, probably because of the serene weather and the sheer number of boats. The water that day was all shades of blue and aqua, with pinkish lavender highlights on top. I wished once again that I was an artist and could paint the scene with water colors.

We had a gorgeous run to West End the next day. It was glassy calm and we could see the bottom as if we were snorkeling. We couldn't resist stopping, shucking off our clothes and skinny dipping in the crystal clear water. We also tried out the new trolling rod that Jack had given to us and promptly caught a barracuda. However, I think we were probably moving too fast, because we didn't get anything else. All too soon, we pulled into West End and tied up. We got our mail and did some shopping, but it was hotter than Hades and we ran the air all night.

We were up at 4:30 the next morning to head for the States. The weatherman had promised flat calm, but alas he was wrong! It was dark and rough and thoroughly miserable. I hadn't rigged for rough weather and the cabin was wet and a mess. I was seasick for about half of the way across until it finally calmed down. We arrived at Spencer's Marina around noon and docked and I quickly turned on the air.

We spent a week there, as we had to put in two new heads to meet the USA regulations. $2,000 ouch! The new heads burned up the contents before dumping it in the water, which certainly was more ecologically correct and was now required in the U.S.

Boy was it hot that week! It was ninety-five degrees every day and the humidity about ninety percent. We ran the air conditioning day and night and were so grateful to have it! I rode the busses to a shopping center and found a market that delivered, which simplified life. I had tried walking in the ninety-five degree heat with a knapsack and could hardly make it.

Tommy arrived on the 25th of June and we celebrated his birthday. He was going to ride with us up the Intracoastal for a while. We did a bit of sightseeing, but were happy to leave when our work was completed. We stopped at a buoy in Hobe Sound for lunch and a swim. That really felt good, as we didn't use the air while running. A nice breeze sprang up, but the sky was looking ominous, so we hurried to Peck Lake and promptly went aground. We were able to back off and tried again, coming much closer to the sand bars, where we found deep water and anchored just as the storm broke.

It rained for several hours, but then cleared and Stan was able to grill our steaks and they were great! It was a hot and muggy night and the no-see-ums were out in force. We decided after a restless night that we would spray both ourselves and the screens before we went to bed.

Peck Lake was really just a big cove, and when you went ashore you could climb the dunes to the ocean beach. We had tried swimming in the river, but it was like a hot bath. Tom and I climbed to the beach the next morning and had a refreshing ocean dip.

We decided to stay another day in that neat place and enjoyed walking the beach, swimming and generally having a lazy day. Stan discovered tracks of the large sea turtles, which were made when they labored up the beach at night to lay their eggs. It was the season when they do that, but you had to go out in the moonlight late at night to see them, and I swear the bugs would carry you away! Flashlights were not allowed. Each turtle laid about one hundred and fifty eggs, all the while crying enormous tears, poor things.

We were surprised at noon when suddenly a flotilla of small boats arrived. We discovered that it was a very popular spot for the "locals," and we could see why. That night, we sprayed ourselves and the screens and had a good night's sleep in spite of the heat. The heat was especially bad when the wind died down, which it did every night.

Tom and I took a quick swim the next morning and hurried back to the boat when we saw a storm coming. We took off for Sandpiper Bay, trying to stay ahead of the storm, but no luck. It poured, and when it stopped and the sun came out, it was like a Turkish bath. With great relief, we pulled into the marina and plugged in the air conditioning and it was sheer heaven! It rained off and on the rest of the day and steamed outside. It was so nice sleeping with the air on and savoring a cool, dry bed.

It looked threatening the next day and did rain a lot, so we stayed indoors and had a cool day. I felt rejuvenated. The heat had taken a toll. Again, while Tom and I had a swim in the marina pool, it stormed. We took on fuel when it stopped and headed for Frances Langford's marina, which was very nice, very pretty, and had a pool. We had dinner that night at the Outrigger Restaurant and enjoyed our day so much.

Tom and I had a swim the next morning and shortly after, it rained again, so we decided to have another lay day. It rained again all day, but we walked down the road in rain gear about a half a mile and found a grocery store and a great ice cream parlor, where of course we indulged! When we walked back, the harbormaster gave me some tomatoes from his garden. I did some laundry and we enjoyed our day, in spite of the weather.

We left Langford's and headed for the Moorings at Vero Beach, where we anchored and rowed ashore. By now, we had decided that we were definitely going to sell the boat and go back to being landlubbers. I was very ambivalent about this, as I think I was finally settling into the yachties' lifestyle and was willing to sign on for another year at least. One day, I'd think it was too soon to go, because we had so many places we still wanted to see, and I wasn't sure Stan really wanted to do it. Then, I'd think of the parts I didn't like. The extreme boredom of long runs, particularly the Intracoastal, the days of seasickness, although my inner ear had adjusted fairly well to the constant motion, wanting to see more of the family, and wanting a home base that didn't move! Most of all, I would miss the wonderful friends we'd made and the special camaraderie we enjoyed because of our lifestyle. Stan, however, insisted he wanted to do it, so we started thinking about where we wanted to live when we came ashore. The Golden Isles and St. Simon's attracted us, as well as the Carolinas and we decided to look into those places. We thought we should check out Vero Beach, although we didn't think we wanted Florida.

We found a saleswoman who showed us around. We saw a beautiful development, but we felt was too expensive for us, so we went back to the boat and headed for Eau Gallie. It was a long hot run and we got caught in the rush hour traffic at the bridge and had a very long wait.

We finally got into the anchorage and who greeted us but the Pelleys, who were living there aboard their boat. They had long given up the cruising life and still hadn't decided what to do or where to go. It was fun to see them and we tried to cover the two years or so since we'd last seen them. We docked at the marina to get electric, as it was hotter than Hades as usual. I could see why Pat hated it. The electric, like at so many marinas on the Intracoastal, was lousy. We could only run the air if we turned everything else off and there were no circuit breakers on the dock, so everyone kept blowing fuses.

Stan rode his bike over to Indian Harbor Marina, where the Farinaccis were aboard *Andiama*, and came back in their car! We went over to visit and decided to move over there the next day. They were temporarily permanent residents there, while they made trips to Cleveland and handled some business before they went cruising again. Shortly afterwards, they left the boat and moved ashore.

It was very hot the next morning, so we moved over to the other marina at eight o'clock. The electric wasn't great there, but we could juggle systems enough to manage. It was the 4th of July and we were invited to raft onto *Itchi Ban* and *Andiama* out in the river for dinner and to watch the fireworks. The highlight of the evening was some marvelous homemade ice cream.

The next two days were beastly hot and terminal boredom was setting in, mitigated by fun visits aboard *Itchi Ban*, *Andiama* and several other boats that we had met in various parts of our travel. An evening out with the Farinaccis to the Dragon Lady Restaurant was much appreciated.

CHAPTER THIRTY-SEVEN

The Farinaccis loaned us their car and we took Tommy to Disney World to celebrate his birthday. As always, it was hot! Ninety-seven degrees! We quickly learned that the best way to beat the heat was to be at the park at opening time, retreat by noon to the air-conditioned hotel room and rest till five or so, and then go back and play till almost midnight. We stayed two days and Tom had a great time, as did we. When we got back, we discovered we could only run one air conditioner and one burner on the stove, but at least the boat was cool!

Two days later, we headed back up the Intracoastal to New Smyrna. The heat really got to us, especially Stan, who had a miserable summer cold. He and Tom stayed up on the bridge and I spelled them occasionally. It was 100 degrees that day and we were really happy to pull into the marina, which had adequate electric. We turned on both air conditioners and blissfully relaxed!

Marineland was our next stop and we could only use one air conditioner, but were happy to have that after a long hot day on the bridge. We had a storm that evening and the temperature really dropped! It was the best weather we'd had since returning to the States. Tom and I walked in our bare feet on the beach after dinner and thoroughly enjoyed that. We actually slept with the windows open that night and no air. Bliss!

We took Tom to the first show at Marineland the next morning and it was great as always. It got very hot at noon, so we headed out for a very hot run to Camachee Cove near St. Augustine. We had talked to Walter and Colleen from *Tug II*, who were there the night before and were looking forward to seeing them again. The marina had great electric and we could run both conditioners and cook too! Wow!

Walt and Colleen came over for drinks and we had a great reunion. One of the things I liked best about our life was running into good friends at one place after another. It was always a celebration. It's hard to explain, but it was so special. I guess it was because it was often a lonely life and friends were a joy.

Walt drove us into St. Augustine the next morning to show Tommy the town. We did quite a bit of sightseeing, especially the fort, which was wonderful. Walt picked us up and we had a lovely lunch at the White Lion Inn. I'd gotten Stan's cold, which slowed me down some. Luckily, Tom didn't get it.

We packed Tom up and Colleen and Walt took us to the airport in Jacksonville, where he caught his plane back to school. I think he'd enjoyed his stay a lot in spite of the heat. We had dinner at Sailmakers and then went back to the boat where we watched the presidential convention until midnight.

We went to town several times with Walt and Colleen and restocked the ship, which was a big help for the rest of our trip. They really showed us the town and we enjoyed the time, as we knew it might be the last time we spent with them for a long time. We did laundry and all the essentials before we took off.

It was a sad time, as we realized we would miss *Tug II* a lot! On our last night, I made fresh peach pie and we had oysters as well for a farewell dinner with our friends. A few tears were shed. Once again, we wondered if we were making a terrible mistake in leaving that life!

We had an uneventful trip to Fernandina, except for an encounter with a barge that was having difficulty turning into a channel across from the inlet. Stan was in one of his "right, even if you get killed," moods and passed it on his portside, nearly giving us all a heart attack! Boy, did that Captain ever swear at him. We walked around Fernandina, stopping at the post office, and put four hundred and fifty gallons of diesel in the tanks. Groan!

We headed for St. Simon's the next morning and arrived around three. We had called Nancy and she came down for dinner. Dave was en route to Santa Domingo on a towing job. We had a great visit, catching up on all the news of our boating world. Nance loaned us her car the next day and we did the grocery routine, got a great haircut for me, and met with a realtor who took us around looking at houses. We went to Nancy's for a lovely dinner and enjoying seeing Quita and Bob Davenport again. Once again, we said a sad goodbye to a place we loved and dear friends. We were considering settling there when we became landlubbers though, and that was consoling.

We were up and gone again early the next morning to catch the 8:30 opening of the bridge. It was another hot, humid, and rainy day. We went aground near Hilton Head, but were able to back off. The sailboat *Teal* was unable do so, but we were able to pull them off. As we were continuing, we saw a Grand Banks coming towards us and it was *Gamecock*! We waved like mad and had a good chat with them and they said, "See ya next fall," which we again knew we wouldn't be doing. Bummer!

It continued to be very hot and humid and we were happy to pull into Beaufort and turn on the air. That wonderful marina allowed us to turn on both air conditioners. Heaven! The reason we needed to go to the store again was the smallness of our fridge and the fact that the fresh stuff was used up fast. Stan went with me, as the store was in a bad part of town, and we picked up the necessities. We ate the last of our shrimp and went to bed, lulled by the sound of rain.

It was still raining the next morning and we started early to get under the bridge, which we could do if we took our aerials down. *Teal*, who had docked and came with us, had to wait for the bridge to open, as sailboats couldn't get under, so we went on ahead. It rained all day, but we ran from the bridge most of the time, as it was nice and cool up there. We came to the Belle Isle Marina and docked. It was a beautiful place with all the amenities and best of all, decent electric! I'd reached the stage where electricity was an important part of my life. We went out to dinner, which was a treat.

We decided we needed a lay day, so we stayed over the next day. It was a lovely day and we rode our bikes under the towering live oaks, did laundry, read the paper and had a lazy day and felt rejuvenated.

There was a pea soup fog next morning, but we did get off around nine in the rain. What else? It did rain off and on all day, so we decided to dock at the New River Marina. It had REALLY tall docks with tall poles way above us and no one there to catch lines, but we docked liked real pros even with a strong current running. I walked down the road to the fishermen's docks and bought several pounds of shrimp and we had a shrimp peel for dinner. At Wrightsville Beach the next night, I bought three pounds of shrimp with the heads on for $2.30 a pound. I decapitated them and filled the freezer, saving the heads for the crab trap.

The next day was gorgeous and cool and we made good time in spite of having to anchor in the river at Camp Lejeune for an hour while the Marines practiced shooting and landings. We swam and loafed while we waited. We arrived at Spooner's Creek Marina, which looked lovely, but had iffy electric. Their water was also bad and they told us not to take on any. However, they had a nice pool and a great restaurant and we had dinner after a swim. It was a cool night, so we opened up and slept well.

We left at eight for Beaufort, the other Beaufort, and were delighted to see Jeb waiting for us to dock. That great marina was always one of our favorites! We strolled into town, picked up the mail and had a beer at the dock pub. I was very excited because the next day Barbara, Tom, Chrissy and Stevie were coming. Stan painted while I provisioned the next morning before our guests arrived.

Barbie, Tom and the children arrived the next day and we were so happy to see them. We swam off the stern of the boat, which the kids loved, an activity that kept them happy many hours during the week. We had a shrimp peel for supper, a new experience for the kids. They also were fascinated with our crab trap, which obligingly yielded up ten crabs and two toadfish that first night. They pulled it up so often to look for new catches that I was surprised that the crabs could crawl in. We were rapidly using up our shrimp heads and chicken bones from the freezer.

The first day of the week we went to the Shackleford Banks, where there was a beautiful beach. We swam, shelled and explored the dunes looking for the wild ponies that lived there. We saw many ponies and herds of wild goats, as well as a smelly dead shark on the beach. It was hotter than Hades on the dunes, as it was in the upper nineties all week long, and we were glad to plunge back into the water. Unfortunately, Tom badly sunburned his feet, which hindered him all week. You really had to watch that tropical sun, but it was hard to convince people of that.

We returned to our dock each night and everyone enjoyed the shops and places to eat along the docks, especially the ice cream shop, which we patronized almost every evening after dinner. The kids discovered the candy and junk shop stores and went there as often as allowed until their allowances ran out.

We cruised to Cape Lookout three times and it was super. There were absolutely gorgeous beaches and dunes and the best shelling we'd seen since the Bahamas. Chrissy found a gorgeous huge moonshell for her collection. The black and white lighthouse was a famous one and was very interesting to see.

One of those days, the Power Squadron had a rendezvous there with many boats. One of their boats was in trouble and we towed them into the spit and they rafted onto us. Stan helped them fix their engine and then we visited and found out they were from Cleveland! As always, we discovered mutual friends and caught up with news from Cleveland and our friends. It really is a small world—a true cliché.

One of the highlights of the cruise was passing the pirate ship *Meka*. Stan pretended to attack them and Stevie fired his gun and threw clamshells at them. Stan raised our pirate flag to declare battle. *Meka* fired their cannon several times and the kids were enthralled. The sailboat *Meka* was actually a summer camp experience for boys to learn sailing a big ship, which we didn't tell our kids, so they enjoyed the pirate experience. They docked near us and that night told Stevie that "He'd had a direct hit and to watch out the next night as they'd get him in battle!" Steve was so excited he couldn't sleep and at six in the morning he pulled a chair up to a porthole to see if they were going to attack yet.

That night, the marina sponsored a pirate battle with *Meka*, another pirate ship, *Morning Star*, and the *Iris* against the waterfront. They passed out hundreds of balloons to be filled with water and to be used as ammunition and the town prepared for the attack. It was hysterical! The ships sailed past us and threw their balloons and we fired back. There were a lot of misses, which floated in the water and Chris joined others who jumped off the boats and retrieved them to be fired again. Stan gave a play-by-play description on the loud hailer while we were ducking hits. The shore batteries threw balloons, buckets of water and sprayed hoses and everyone got soaking wet. We laughed until we ached. It was so much fun and the kids as well as adults had a ball. We had several more days of exploring, but none topped the pirate battle!

CHAPTER THIRTY-EIGHT

We sadly said goodbye as our week ended, but were consoled knowing we would be seeing them soon. We were heading up the Intracoastal to Oxford, Maryland and planned on selling the boat there.

It was as usual hot and humid as we traveled on. As we headed to Coinjock after crossing the much hated Neuse River, it became hotter and hotter and the nine-hour day was really a long one. For some reason, I felt more nostalgic than usual as we covered territory where we'd had so much fun traveling with *Tug II, Sum Fun, Odyssey, Brandy, Blue Blazer,* and others. It seemed strange not to be on track with the other live-aboard boaters, and I was beginning to realize that I was going to hate it when the fall trek started south through the Chesapeake and we weren't there.

We awoke to another beastly hot day and decided we were too tired to keep going, so declared a lay day. Stan wanted to work on the autopilot, which was balky at best, and I cleaned a bit and worked on my article for *Yachting Magazine.* I borrowed the marina car and went shopping.

It was a delightfully cool day, so we left for Norfolk reveling in the cool breeze. It was the 16th of August by now, so we were anxious to get to Oxford. We were held up by lots of bridges and were quite late in getting into the marina in Norfolk. We also had a hard time docking between the wind and the current and finally had to go into the next slip down, which was fine with the marina.

We slept with the windows open, which was a treat. The weather the next morning didn't look too good, so we put off our run until the next day. We rode our bikes into the historic district of Norfolk, which was beautiful, bought a newspaper. We discovered that we had the wrong church time, so we rode back to the boat and came back later for Mass at ten.

We were sound asleep with the boat open when at 1:30 a.m. I heard footsteps and voices outside the boat. A voice said, "There's our transportation home," and I thought "There go our bikes!" Two guys jumped on board and ran forward. I leaped out of bed shouting, "Get off this boat," and hurried forward to blow our very loud horn to get the security guard's attention. Stan emerged from below saying "What the hell is going on?"

The guys were scared and ran off the boat and we heaved a sigh of relief. They dropped a heavy log running off, which they obviously were going to use to break in and steal some of the pricy equipment. The security guard never did show up. He probably was sound asleep! We went back to bed, but didn't sleep too well.

Stan got us started at six the next morning, over my protests, for the eight-hour run to Onancock Creek, where we anchored. It was very isolated except for some huge attractive houses. We put the dinghy down and explored a little. There was a small, pretty little town. We walked around it for a while, enjoying the pretty houses.

Then, we went back to the boat and headed for Tangier Island where we docked at Captain Parks, where we had been before with *Tug II* and *Sum Fun*. That of course made me very nostalgic again, so we walked into the little town on Tangier, enjoying seeing the telescope houses. We loved seeing all the houses and yards fenced in. I suppose if you live on a small island with lots of people, you need to stake out your territory. Also, it gives you a measure of privacy, even if it is just illusory. I suspect everyone really respects everyone else's privacy, as all the gates were firmly closed. The people there seemed quite prosperous. Seafaring must have paid well.

There were jellyfish in the water everywhere, so we didn't feel like swimming. This was par for the course during summer in the Chesapeake, and why we saw so many pools right on the waterside. It was cool that night and we actually slept under blankets.

We had a short run to Oxford the next day and went to Shanahan's Marina, which we had been told was a good place to sell a Grand Banks, as he was the local dealer for GBs. John was not there and we were told to just tie up and we could talk to him the next day.

We rode our bikes around the charming town and fell in love with it.

We stopped at the post office and met Lynn, the post mistress, who was so nice and friendly. She told us that we had mail at Bates Marina, which was where we originally had planned on staying. We rode out there to pick it up. It looked like a nice place to stay, but was really in the boonies. Then, we biked in to the Masthead Restaurant and had a great dinner. We met the manager, who told us she had spent the past winter in the Exumas. She also asked me if I'd like a ride into the supermarket in a nearby town of Easton, as she was going there that day. I was eager to go with her, as Oxford had very few sources for groceries.

We met with John the next morning and realized he didn't spend much time at the marina. He didn't want to work Fridays, Saturdays and Sundays. After a long talk with him, he offered to let us stay at the dock and to pretty much sell the boat ourselves if we would work for him, answering his office phone and taking messages for him. He had a phone put on our boat and we were allowed to use it whenever we wanted to. What a treat that was! Now we didn't have to trek to the pay phone booth every time we wanted to call the kids, etc. Also, signs went up on our boat and we were in the Grand Banks registry. It was kind of weird, but great for us. We ended up staying there a month before selling the boat.

We enjoyed our time in Oxford and really got to know the town and the very friendly people. It was a popular retirement town for the Washington area and we made some great friends. The postmistress was our buddy and helped us send Dorie's sculpture from Little Harbor. If it weren't for her, Dorie would never have received it, as the Chicago post office said it had never arrived. Lynn had sent it as a special delivery that had to be signed for at each step en route including Chicago and she had documentation of the whole trip there, so Chicago finally found it stuck on some shelf!

Lynn said she had a friend who was interested in buying a Grand Banks and she sent him over. He came and loved the boat, but we felt he was overwhelmed by all the systems and didn't know too much about seamanship. We knew only too well what happened to people who weren't mechanical so to speak, so we weren't surprised when he didn't buy it.

We kept busy answering the phone and getting involved with the volunteer library and the Episcopal Church. There was no Catholic church in town, so we went there a few times. I did some needlework for their bazaar, which was fun. We met Jane and Carl Kaiser, delightful people who had retired there and they took us around a lot and had us to dinner at their house. The work we did for John required very little time, and we were so grateful to have the excellent accommodations we had.

It became very hot again, over one hundred degrees, even in September. It did feel a little claustrophobic, as we didn't go out during the day unless we had to. I worked on my pirate article and some other articles for boating magazines. I sent stuff of with query letters to *Boating* and *Yachting* magazines, typed resumes and lists for the boat, worked on my embroidery, read a lot of books from the library to keep myself busy. We had several people look at the boat, but hadn't sold it yet. We were getting a little depressed and again wondering if we'd made the right decision. Stan did a lot of cosmetic work on *Steelaway* and the days went on.

Time went on and the heat spell broke and we opened up again with joy. Bike riding gave us a lot of much needed exercising. The friends we'd made in town gave us the needed socializing. I'd discovered that John Shanahan's Mother and two sisters had graduated from Trinity College in Washington, D. C., where I had gone to school, and she came to call one day bringing fabulous cookies.

I discovered a book in the library, *All in the Same Boat*, which was a story of a family who sailed around the world. The wife and daughter's idea of heaven was "to get ashore as often as possible." The author's description of great scenery was "something not mucked up by having water around it!" I chuckled as I remembered my answer to Granddaughter Chrissy's question of where did we want to live? I replied that when we moved ashore, the only water I wanted to see was in a bathtub! I do love to look at water; I just don't want to be on it! I wonder why men don't feel that way? It must be something genetic.

I had a letter from Gail, who was back aboard *Odyssey* in the Abacos. She told us the sad story of the *Kalia*, a boat we had often seen in Marsh Harbor. It was the home of a Detroit couple our age that were doing the liveaboard thing like us. Their bloodstained, bullet-ridden boat was found drifting in a remote area of the Bahamas by a small boat that said there was a decomposing body in the dinghy. By the time the Bahamas Defense Force got there, probably days later, the body was gone. Gail said Nassau was trying to hush it up, but it was all over the yachtie world. They had decided not to go to the Exumas that year.

Time went by again and I received a very nice rejection letter from *Yachting* saying they liked my article, but couldn't use it. I later sold them an article that was in their November issue after we had gone ashore.

We did have a few showings of the boat. One of them had an

appointment at two o'clock and arrived at 6:30 p.m. just as we had given up and started dinner! They liked the boat though, and we thought they might buy. Another couple, who had one of the most obstreperous two-year-olds I'd ever seen, came to see the boat and went over it with a fine tooth comb while Stan and I tried to keep Chris, their two-year-old, from turning off the bilge pump, fridge, and battery charger and from trying to wreck the delicate switches on the searchlight and auto pilot! They wanted the boat, but had to sell their house on Hilton Head first. Probably a good thing, as Chris would have had them crazy.

On the 20th of September, 1979 we sold *Steelaway*! We had been aboard for almost three years. We were happy it finally sold, but sad that this era of our life had ended. It helped that the couple who bought it were so nice and so in love with it.

We got the price we wanted and now had to get all our stuff packed and off the boat. We rented a small U-Haul truck and as we loaded it, we couldn't believe all the things we had aboard!

After we cleaned the boat, the new owners came aboard and we cruised to midway on the C&D Canal, where a wonderful restaurant was, docked, had dinner and stayed overnight. The next morning, one of them drove us back to Oxford where we'd left the truck.

We headed to Cleveland, where we were going to live with Barbie and Tom until we found a house there. Despite all of the gorgeous places we'd looked at on our trip up north, we decided to live in Cleveland to be near family.

As we were pulling out of the parking lot, I thought, "Oh, what have we done!" But as we came to Cleveland, I found myself looking forward to a new life there. It had been a wonderful experience meeting so many terrific people, seeing so many beautiful places and having such adventures. I'll miss *Steelaway*, but the land lures me!

The End

ABOUT THE AUTHOR

After her husband Stan's retirement, JoAnn Orr agreed to live out her husband's dream of living aboard a boat. After selling most of their worldly, they embarked on a nearly three-year journey as "liveaboards," traveling around the East Coast of the United States and the Bahamas. JoAnn lives with her husband Stan near Cleveland, Ohio.